YOU AND
THE GIFTED CHILD

YOU AND
THE GIFTED CHILD

By

CREGG F. INGRAM, Ed.D.

SALLY M. TODD, Ph.D.

Department of Educational Psychology
Brigham Young University
Provo, Utah

CHARLES C THOMAS • **PUBLISHER**
Springfield • *Illinois* • *U.S.A.*

Published and Distributed Throughout the World by

CHARLES C THOMAS • PUBLISHER

2600 South First Street

Springfield, Illinois 62717

© *1983 by* CHARLES C THOMAS • PUBLISHER

ISBN 0-398-04836-3

Library of Congress Catalog Card Number: 83-637

With THOMAS BOOKS *careful attention is given to all details of manufacturing and
design. It is the Publisher's desire to present books that are satisfactory as to their physical
qualities and artistic possibilities and appropriate for their particular use.* THOMAS
BOOKS *will be true to those laws of quality that assure a good name and good will.*

Printed in the United States of America
Q-R-3

Library of Congress Cataloging in Publication Data

Ingram, Cregg F.
   You and the gifted child.

   Bibliography: p.
   Includes index.
   1. Gifted children — Education. I. Todd,
Sally M. II. Title.
LC3993.I58 1983   371.95   83-637
ISBN 0-398-04836-3

To JoAnne and Henry

PREFACE

THE purpose of designing and writing this particular text was twofold. First, we wanted to provide teachers and parents of gifted and talented children with an up-to-date view of the state of the art in education of the gifted through a review of current and classic studies. This information should acquaint the reader with vocabulary, concepts of identification, and characteristics presently utilized within this field. Second, we wanted to provide teachers and parents with some "how-to-do" or "how-to-work-with" activities and strategies for planning programs for gifted and talented youth. It appears important to us that teachers and parents go beyond mere recognition of the child's gifts and talents to educate, stimulate, and evaluate the balanced and well-rounded growth of those gifts and talents.

The book is divided into three sections. The first two sections are informational and theoretical in scope. That is, they contain an overview of the history, characteristics, diagnosis, and general treatment strategies related to the education of gifted and talented children. They include a theoretical stance emphasizing the importance of stewardship and balance as requisite to good instructional planning for the gifted child.

The contents of the third section are more directly applicable to teaching gifted and talented children. Research through existing literature as well as through interviews with teachers and parents has brought to light activities or materials that have been found or reported to be successful in working with these children. The third section of the book is very much a "how-to-do" collection of activities for developing a well-balanced instructional program for gifted and talented children.

One unique feature of the book, found in Chapter 2, is our emphasis on the precepts of stewardship and balance. We feel that these principles are critically important in education. Stewardship, in our emerging microcomputerized world, is vital to education in general and to gifted and talented children in particular. The precept developed is basic to the question of who (teacher, parents, or child) has stewardship or responsibility for the life and education of the child. We attempt to point out, both to the teacher and to the parent, the importance of proper stewardship roles in the designing, planning, and evaluating of programs for a given child and the importance of enhancing feelings of stewardship within a child for management of his or her own gifts and talents. This teaches a child self-discipline and the importance of cooperative effort in education.

The precept of balance is also explored and encouraged. The child who is gifted in a given area, say, mathematics, should be placed in a structured environment that fosters development in other areas of his/her life, i.e. physical, social, and emotional. These other areas of balance should be directly incorporated into the child's educational plan to ensure a well-developed, well-rounded individual.

Within the "how-to-do" chapters, we have attempted to provide examples of how to plan instructional programs and activities that can be used to stimulate growth in a particular area, e.g. math, art, language, and creative thinking. These suggestions should provide teachers with ideas that can be directly implemented in the classroom and should offer suggestions for utilization by parents in the home.

The book has been designed as a self-contained, self-instructional text. At the beginning of each chapter, questions are posed to serve as an advance organizer informing the reader of the content and direction of material therein and also to allow the reader who can answer the questions to bypass that chapter or section. Answers to all the questions are provided at the end of the book to facilitate study and review.

We extend our appreciation to many people who have contributed to our efforts in writing this book: to our students and friends who have willingly shared their research information and their personal experiences regarding programs and activities for the gifted; to Lana Hakari and Roger Trunk who put in hours of research time and effort in the final stages of the book; and to Sherry Southworth, Jill Hibbert, and others faithful and efficient secretaries who helped with the typing and preparation of the manuscript.

It is our sincere desire that the text may be useful and helpful to teachers, parents, and teachers-in-training as they prepare and seek wise programs for the gifted and talented and that the text may serve the wonderful young people who have such potential and capacity to excel and contribute to the benefit of others as they themselves are enriched and magnified.

CONTENTS

YOU AND
THE GIFTED CHILD

PART I

PART I is composed of chapters that provide the reader with an overview of gifted and talented education. The information contained within these chapters is a summary-synopsis and not intended to be an in-depth review of the current state of the art in gifted and talented education. A brief look is taken at the historical development, and some of the more pertinent literature is identified and presented within these chapters. This initial section is simply an introduction, a means of acquainting the reader with gifted and talented education, a way of helping the reader understand learning characteristics, diagnostic measures, and other general information that can be used to identify gifted and talented children.

CHAPTER ONE

GIFTED AND TALENTED — AN INTRODUCTION

Can you answer the following questions?

1. Who proposed the first special provision for gifted children in America?
2. What are the most widely implemented curriculum provisions for gifted and talented children in the public school?
3. What has been the contribution of Terman to the development of programs for gifted children?
4. The Intelligence Quotient (IQ) has historically been used as one of the determiners of gifted students. What are some other criteria that are presently being considered in defining this population?
5. Can you outline characteristics of gifted children in the following areas: physical, cognitive, academic, social, and performing arts?
6. How useful are teacher nominations in the identification of giftedness? Parent nominations? Peer nominations?
7. If you were going to develop a program for the identification of gifted children, what would it include?
8. How valuable do you feel the reservoir model would be in the identification of giftedness?
9. What standardized tests are available to assess a child's intellectual, social/emotional, and academic potential?
10. What standardized tests are available to assess a child's aptitude in the performing arts area?

THE purpose of this chapter is to provide an overview of the nature of gifted and talented persons. As a part of that overview, some historical information should be helpful in formulating a better perspective of present-day programs for the gifted and talented. A variety of approaches and attitudes have confronted gifted and talented children in this country, from "elitism," misidentification, and lack of proper programming to some very valiant attempts at proper or accurate identification and adequate instructional program development. Even though today we see an increased emphasis on gifted and talented education, there still exist many inconsistencies in the identification of, programming for, and general public awareness of these children. There are people today who still feel that these "bright" children can make it on their own and therefore do not need special programming. Of course, special programming requires special funding, and special funding usually seems to be the crux of all the inconsistencies that have existed in planning programs for gifted and talented children.

HISTORICAL PREVIEW

Historically, programs have evolved that have been both good and bad for the gifted child. Early educational thought in America was dominated by European thinking, including the belief that all children's minds were exactly the same, to be instructed in the same way. In fact, a popular thought was that a thin line separated genius and insanity. Thomas Jefferson proposed the first special provisions for gifted students in 1779. The first systematic approach to providing for the gifted began in St. Louis in 1868. This involved a system of flexible promotions, with selected members of the school being promoted, when appropriate, at five-week intervals. Soon to follow were several other programs for the gifted in major cities throughout the United States. In 1898, ability grouping for bright students was begun. The emphasis was placed on broadening the students' experiences rather than encouraging them to progress more rapidly through the curriculum. Since these meager beginnings in programming for the gifted, much has changed and improved.

In the United States today, programs for the gifted exist in almost every state. However, there are still children who are not being served, and a need exists for upgrading existing programs. Discussions concerning curriculum provisions for the gifted have been in most part limited to three possibilities: special classes, acceleration, and enrichment (Anderson, 1960; Fleigler, 1961; Torrance, 1960; Gallagher, 1960, 1975).

Special classes or ability groupings have not been uniformly successful. Results show that ability grouping does not solve automatically the problems of individualizing instruction (Passow, 1958; Shane, 1960). Also, as Marland (1972) points out, the gifted students themselves prefer not to be totally separated from their regular program. *Acceleration* has taken the form of early entrance to kindergarten or first grade, middle and junior high school acceleration, and advanced placement or acceleration into college. The research on acceleration is generally more favorable than that on special classes, as evidenced by the number of positive surveys completed (Anderson, 1960; Gowan, 1958; Reynolds, 1960). Most generally approved among the curriculum alternatives has been *enrichment*; this approval comes in spite of the lack of good research results to support it (Torrance, 1960).

Greater emphasis is being placed on enrichment and differentiated teaching patterns within regular education classrooms (National School Public Relations Association [NSPRA], 1979). Some programs such as the Cleveland Major Work program (NSPRA, 1979) are glowing examples of what can be done in the development of programs for gifted and talented children. In essence, the Cleveland Major Work program began as a segregated classroom for elementary students who had measured IQs above 125. The program is marked by enrichment activities in areas of need and interest to the children. Other schools and programs have also been designed to specifically deal with or work with gifted children. Hollingsworth (1926) started special elementary school classes in New York in the early 1920s. These were followed by other schools in the New York City area that focused directly on advanced or accelerated learners both in elementary and high school.

Other states have also attempted to provide educational programming for advanced students. In the late 1960s and early 1970s, monies from federal sources began to be specifically earmarked for gifted and talented program development. Title III and Title IV monies have been used by states to develop programs in the gifted and talented area. These government-subsidized movements toward programs for gifted and talented children are some of the more positive steps in the historical development of programs.

Gifted and talented youth have not always been viewed in a positive manner. Prior to the turn of the century and into the early 1920s, some of these children were considered to be bizarre and out of place, even out of "sync" with the real world. This misconception existed until the classical work of Lewis Terman in the 1920s.

Terman (1925) selected approximately 1,500 children with an average IQ score of 150 on the Stanford-Binet Intelligence Test for an extensive study. These children came essentially from middle-class America and certainly did not represent the full range of ethnic and economic strata of American life. Terman's findings in studying these children became quite revealing and helped change the attitude of the general public toward these types of children. He found that these children were not bizarre in their behavior but were in fact "appreciably superior" in almost all areas of life from physical development to social adjustment, including of course their overall academic performance.

Terman's study initially generated a great deal of interest in gifted children, and at that time a renewed emphasis was placed on programming or making special adaptations in existing educational programs for these children. Over succeeding years, this interest has both increased and decreased in accordance with the developing events of the world. For example, renewed interest in accelerated learners emerged in the late 1950s with the advent of the Russian Sputnik, yet by the end of the 1960s gifted and talented programs had very little effort or money focused on them by either federal, state, or local educational agencies. It was not until the late 1960s or early 1970s that interest was renewed when a study was completed by the Office of Education, which concluded that programs for the gifted and talented were being grossly neglected. By the end of the 1970s, stimulated by the passage of Public Laws 95-561 and 94-142, more and more states were applying for federal funds to support gifted and talented programs. The Special Projects Act of 1974, in fact, made or set aside funds specifically under the category of gifted and talented education. As we move into the 1980s, it appears that the interest in gifted and talented education still exists, an interest that is greatly stimulated by parents and other groups who wish to see their children more appropriately dealt with in the public school system. It is, in fact, a major boost to gifted and talented children when parents can group together and demand that the public education system provide appropriate and equitable amounts of time and energy to their gifted and talented children.

DEFINITIONS OF GIFTEDNESS

Over the years many definitions of giftedness have been proposed. Prior to 1950 most attempts at identification of the gifted had their roots in intelligence, with many of the basic facts about intelligence coming as a result of the longitudinal studies of Lewis Terman and his associates on 1,500 children (Terman and Ogden, 1959). During the 1950s a broader, more inclusive definition of the gifted was developed, with emphasis being placed on creativity, the idea that the intellect is multifaceted, and the thought that giftedness could be manifest in highly specialized areas of achievement other than academics. Paul Witty (1951), using criteria other than IQ, defines giftedness as "outstanding ability in some dimension of constructive talent." Participants in a symposium on the gifted (Stram, 1954) define the gifted person as "a person whose performance in any line of socially useful endeavor is consistently superior."

Creativity began to find a prominent place in the definition of the gifted child when Getzels and Jackson (1962) decided to test earlier predictions (e.g. Stephenson, 1949; Guilford, 1950; Thurstone, 1952) that creativity and intelligence were not closely related. Their studies revealed a low correlation between intelligence scores and scores on tests designed to measure creativity. They saw the heavy reliance on the IQ score as the sole measure of giftedness as a hindrance to a true understanding of giftedness in its many facets. IQ tests seemed to measure "convergent thinking," the ability to recall and recognize facts, but neglected to measure "divergent thinking," the ability to invent and innovate (Jackson, 1962). These findings have had obvious impact on the thinking of educators about the processes through which the gifted are identified.

Guilford (1956, 1967, 1968, 1970) brought creativity into the realm of intelligence with his expanded concept of intelligence and the Structure of the Intellect Model, which focused not only on the many ways a person could be intelligent but also on the qualitative differences in intellectual functioning, which included divergent thinking. Guilford (1975) later stated that creative abilities are a vital part of intelligence and not something apart from it. In line with Guilford's thinking, Gowan (1971) defines a gifted child as "one who has the potential to develop creatively." Despite these inclusions of creativity as part of intelligence, studies continue to show low correlations between IQ test scores and scores on tests that attempt to measure aspects of creativity (Torrance, 1962; Guilford and Christensen, 1973; Guilford, 1975).

All of this has stimulated an abundance of research into the measurement and identification of creativity and the ways in which it might be nurtured, and it has also had a tremendous effect on the present definitions of a gifted child, which in most cases now include both creativity and intelligence. The continued disagreement as to which talents and abilities really constitute giftedness is evident by the numerous definitions one can find today. A White House task force (Talent Development, 1968) defines giftedness as "a complex, multifaceted quality of human functioning that takes many different forms depending on the circumstances in which an individual grows up and the multiplicity of tasks and rewards that exist for him in a rapidly changing and imperfectly predictable world." The report outlines three essential aspects of giftedness.

1. Fields of attainment in which excellence may be manifest, such as scholarly inquiry, artistic activity, professional service, and spiritual leadership.
2. Personal attributes underlying high attainment in the physical, intellectual, motivational, attitudinal, and personal-social areas.
3. The stages of individual development in which these attributes take form and nature.

Taylor (1968, 1972) sees possible exceptional talent in the areas of academics, creativity, planning, communications, forecasting, and decision making. Mary Meeker (1976) also sees giftedness manifested in three areas: academics, intelligence, and language/linguistics; emotional and social adjustment skills and environmental and motivational factors; and physiological, psychomotor, and perceptual motor development.

Renzulli (1977) provides a simple and interesting definition of a gifted child as a combination of three essential components: above average intelligence, creativity, and high task-commitment. He finds justification for the ideas of motivation and task-commitment in the need to design defensible educational programs as well as in research (Renzulli, 1976).

A widely accepted definition of a gifted and talented child that is used in the schools today is the definition offered by Martinson and others in a 1971 report to the Congress (*Education of the Gifted and Talented*, 1972).

> Gifted and talented children are those identified by professionally qualified persons who, by virtue of outstanding abilities, are capable of high performance. These are children who require differentiated educational programs and/or services beyond those normally provided by the regular school program in order to realize their contribution to self and society.

Children capable of high performance include these which demonstrate achievement and/or potential ability in any of the following areas, single or in combination:

1. General intellectual ability.
2. Specific academic aptitude.
3. Creative or productive thinking.
4. Leadership ability.
5. Visual and performing arts.
6. Psychomotor ability.

CHARACTERISTICS OF THE GIFTED

Prior to the work of Guilford (1956), Torrance (1962), Taylor (1972), Meeker (1976), Renzulli (1977) and others, the characteristics of the gifted had primarily been isolated to include intelligence test scores and accelerated performance in academic areas. When Guilford (1956) proposed that there were at least 120 different facets of intellect, the focus on IQ alone began to diminish. It has been said that within a group of persons it would be difficult *not* to find many of the characteristics used to describe and identify gifted and talented children. Feldman and Bratton (1972) indicate that if all the acceptable criteria being used in schools today were applied to one group of students, all but a few of those students would be selected for gifted programs. However, despite the thrust to include multiple criteria in selecting children, the bias in schools clearly remains in favor of the use of intellectual ability as measured by a test of intelligence.

It appears that the characteristics of gifted and talented children should include multifaceted criteria. It now seems quite obvious that gifted and talented children will show themselves in almost every area of society, every ethnic group, and almost every conceivable socioeconomic condition. The characteristics of gifted and talented children, therefore, are very broad and varied. However, some characteristics seem to set apart the gifted child from his or her peers. Sisk (1977) points out that some of the characteristics include

1. Early use of advanced vocabulary
2. Retention of a variety of information
3. Periods of intense concentration
4. Ability to understand complex concepts, perceive relationships, and think abstractly
5. Broad and changing spectrum of interests
6. Strong critical thinking skills and self-criticism
7. Special creative abilities, which include a reputation for having wild, seemingly bizarre ideas that seem somewhat out of sync with reality
8. Sense of playfulness and relaxation with an emphasis on being a nonconformist, thinking independently, and demonstrating considerable sensitivity to both emotions and problems

There has been much information to support Terman's (1947) conclusions that gifted children are superior in social, moral, emotional, and physical traits when compared to the general population. Terman concludes that great contrasts between the gifted and control groups within the study appear in the drive to achieve by the gifted person and in the all-around social and mental adjustment more easily made by the gifted person.

Pendarvis (1981) specifies three categories in which gifted and talented children could be categorized; these include *intellectual abilities*, which show up either through a test of intellectual ability or in the child's superior academic performance in the classroom. These children seem to memorize and retain what they have learned more readily and at an earlier age than their peers. Intellectually, they seem to be more curious about a variety of school subjects. Even though they are sometimes neglected and abused socially because of their accelerated performance in the classroom, they seem to make better or appropriate adjustments within the social milieu. Again, creativity is seen distinctly apart from a child's memory, comprehension, and reasoning abilities.

TALENT AREA	ABILITIES	CHARACTERISTICS
Mathematics	Ability to manipulate symbolic material more effectively and more rapidly than classmates	Highly independent Enjoy theoretical & investigative pursuits Effective in social interactions Less conforming than general population (girls)
Science	Ability to see relationships among ideas, events, and objects Elegance in explanation, the ability to formulate the simplest hypothesis that can account for the observed facts	Highly independent Loners Prefer intellectually rather than socially challenging situations Reject group pressures Methodical, precise, exact Avid readers
Language Arts	Capability of manipulating abstract concepts, but sometimes inferior to the high general achiever in working with mathematical material Imagination and originality	Highly independent Social and aesthetic (girls) Theoretical and political (boys) Greatly enjoy reading
Leadership	Ability to effect positive and productive change Good decision-making ability Proficiency in some area, such as athletics or academics Ability to communicate	Empathetic Sensitive Charismatic — can transform the group through their enthusiasm and energy
Psychomotor Ability	Gross motor strength, agility, flexibility, coordination, and speed Excellence in athletics, gymnastics, or dance Fine motor control, deftness, precision, flexibility, and speed Excellence in crafts — jewelry making,	Enjoy and seem to need considerable exercise Competitive Like outdoor activity Interested in mechanics, crafts or electronics Have hobbies such as model building,

	model building, mechanics, working with electronic equipment	origami, pottery
	Ability to use complicated equipment with little or no training	
Performing Arts	Ability to disregard traditional methods in favor of their own original ones	Self-confident
	Resourcefulness in use of materials	Competitive
		Ambitious
	Ability to express their feelings through an art form	Prefer working alone
		Sensitive to their environment
	Attention to detail in their own and others' artwork	Gain satisfaction through expressing their feelings artistically

Sources: Ellison, Abe, Fox, Coray, and Taylor, 1976; Kough and Dehaan, 1958; Kranz, n.d.; Lindsay, 1977; Passcow and Goldberg, 1962; Renzulli and Hartman, 1971; Roe, 1953; Stanley, George, and Solano, 1977.

Figure 1-1. Pendarvis's summary of the characteristics of children with special talents. Adapted from Blackhurst and Berdine, *An Introduction to Special Education*, 1981.

Creative ability is often measured by a test of divergent thinking that measures the child's ability to produce a great number of solutions to a single problem. Creative children do not necessarily score high on intellectual tests but do score high in their divergent thinking skills. Children who are creative manifest unusual and clever ways of solving problems. They appear to be independent and nonconformist in their attitudes, and they prefer to attend loosely structured, open-ended learning activities that stimulate development and expression of their own ideas.

The final area in Pendarvis's list is *special talents*. Talent should be considered a specialized ability, and talents can range from the performing arts and physical ability to language arts and the sciences. There is also the child who is especially talented in leading and directing other people. A summary of the characteristics of children with special talents as outlined by Pendarvis (1981) is included in Figure 1-1.

To outline further the characteristics of gifted and talented children the following checklist of behaviors is provided.

Giftedness Checklist

Physical Characteristics

1. Started to walk and talk before the so-called average child does. While still very young, demonstrated the ability to put words and phrases together meaningfully.
2. May be somewhat above average for his or her chronological age in height, weight, physique, physical endurance, and specific measurements like breadth of shoulders, muscular strength, and lung development.
3. Shows a high degree of originality in play, work, planning, and adjust-

ment to situations. (This may even extend to a method for cutting the grass and washing the car.)

Cognitive Characteristics

1. Demonstrated an early interest in time. Talked about yesterday-today-tomorrow, days of the week, then and now, and calendars and clocks at an early age. Showed an awareness of time and relationships.
2. Often shows an understanding of meanings that seems premature for his or her age. Interpretation of current events and of international and political developments demonstrates an ability for abstract, critical, and creative thinking.
3. Has interests that are varied and spontaneous, accompanied by an intellectual curiosity that is broad and expansive.
4. Is able to adapt what has been learned to other situations; transfer of ideas comes rather easily.
5. Has an attention span longer than might be expected.

Academic Characteristics

1. Often learned to read before entering school and almost always had an early desire to read.
2. Possesses reading capabilities higher than the so-called average child of the same age.
3. Learns easily, requiring fewer explanations and less repetition by the teacher than most students. May be less patient than others with meaningless drill or "busy work" assignments, often feeling that the time could be used more profitably.
4. Usually shows his or her greater capacity through a higher achievement and mastery of school subjects, but achievement might be much lower than expected because of boredom with the slow pace and perhaps an uninspired, unaccepting, or even threatened teacher.
5. Has a vocabulary beyond other children of the same age or grade and uses and understands the words in reading, writing, and speaking.
6. Asks questions because he or she really "wants to know" and demonstrates that fact by the later use of information acquired through verbal curiosity.
7. Usually likes school and shows a desire to learn without prodding. Participates in and seems to have time for numerous extracurricular activities without letting them interfere with academic achievement.
8. Frequently chooses the more difficult school subjects for the simple reason that he or she likes them.

Social/Emotional Characteristics

1. Reacts to comments in a way that indicates a real meeting of minds. Responds quickly.

2. May be impatient with and rebellious toward the more passive attitudes of others, including adults at home and in school. May prove to be a little "difficult" in this society that is too often adjusted to the average.
3. Prefers the companionship of older children, even though they may tend to reject "a little runt among us big kids."
4. Creates jokes and laughs at the humor of others on a level more mature than his or her age indicates, often on an abstract or imaginary basis.
5. May look much as other children do and frequently act as they do — and therein lies a problem since it is so easy to overlook the gifted youngster.
6. Is shown in some studies to be more trustworthy when under temptation to cheat, higher in honesty, higher in emotional stability, and more adaptable in social situations.
7. Is less inclined to have nervous disorders, to be poorly adjusted emotionally, or to boast despite his or her superiority.

Talent Characteristics

1. By performing, can win "rave notices" from parents though not necessarily from a captive audience of visitors. Unusual poise may be one of the first indications of giftedness in some children.
2. Shows a mature ability to express himself or herself through creative writing, oral expression, and picturesque ways of getting an idea across; both the vocabulary and the content may be unusual.
3. May show unusual skill or creativity in art or music, carry a tune well at an early age, have a persistent desire to learn music, possess an unusual sense of rhythm, or show a vibrant sense of color.

Personal Characteristics

1. Has hobbies which seem numerous and involved in comparison with those of other children the same age. May have as many as three to six different hobbies.
2. Collects things in an orderly manner (not always — may be among the sloppy, disorderly children too). Collections may include birds, stamps, chemicals, or pictures of current motion picture favorites. Often these collections are of a complicated or scientific nature.
3. Seems to be adept in analyzing his or her own strengths and limitations objectively. An awareness of himself or herself may create unpopularity with students who are not as bright. Not recognizing the cause of this antagonism, may feel a need to withdraw or to associate chiefly with adults.

IDENTIFICATION PROCEDURES

It is not uncommon to find many stories of misidentified or, more appropriately, unidentified gifted and talented children. Many times their unusual and bizarre behavior leads to classification as something other than what their real gifts and talents indicate. Thomas Edison is one example of misidentification. His teachers identified him as "mentally addled," and it was mostly through the efforts of his mother, who worked with him individually at home, that his true gifts were developed and brought to fruition. Several outstanding individuals and scholars in recent history, e.g. Albert Einstein, Franklin Roosevelt, John F. Kennedy, and Sir Winston Churchill, were men who at times were not motivated to learn what their schools offered and performed well below their capabilities. Werner Von Braun failed his high school courses in math and physics, but after becoming enthusiastic about rocketry he excelled in these areas (Torrance, 1965).

Identifying giftedness is not always easy. Perhaps the most important thing involved in the identification is that it happen early in the child's life. The earlier the better, obviously. Without early identification, the possibility exists that children may lose some of their potential and not realize all that they could have had if their gifts and talents had been identified early in their lives. Early identification is not easy for a number of reasons, one of which is that the child under five years of age shows a great deal of unstable development and therefore may manifest growth and development spurts that could disguise accelerated potential. Academic and intellectual giftedness appear to be the areas most easily identified at an early age. These areas, composed of the child's use of numbers, language, and word concepts, relate directly to academic performance and are most easily stimulated at an early age. In the physical and emotional areas, children may not demonstrate unusual gifts until they have matured enough.

There appear to be few totally accepted procedures for identifying all gifted and talented children. There are many suggested procedures that include everything from observation of the child's behavior to the administration of norm-referenced tests of intelligence. Prior to the 1950s, identification of gifted children was based almost entirely on IQ or intelligence test scores. Today the trend is toward broader definitions of giftedness based on multidimensional traits and a more comprehensive, in-depth look at a child's abilities. It has been distinctly shown that gifted children are located in virtually every type of home and living condition imaginable. Giftedness is no respecter of color, race, or creed. Giftedness is found in every class and culture. Even though some groups have higher proportions of gifted individuals than other, it behooves all those involved in the education of children to search out and identify every gifted child.

Gifted and talented abilities may be determined by a multiplicity of procedures, many of which include objective measures and professional evaluation. Professionally qualified persons include such individuals as teachers, administrators, school psychologists, counselors, curricula specialists, and others with special training that qualifies them to appraise a child's gifts and talents. Renzulli and Smith (1977) suggest that the identification process should be based on a variety of information that reflects several indicators of a youngster's superior performance or potential. In essence, they suggested that traditional approaches such as the use of standardized intelligence tests, as well as case study techniques, would be desirable in a comprehensive identification system. A case study approach appears more sensitive to identifying academically able students in schools that serve minority group populations, and this method overall is a good subjective approach to identifying large numbers of potentially gifted children in any school setting.

Today it is not uncommon to have gifted children identified through *teacher nominations; parent identification;* administration of *achievement tests, personality tests*, and individual *intelligence tests;* review of a child's *school records*; or *interviews* with the potential candidate. Ward (1962) found attention being given to the following seven types of data as indicators of giftedness; group intelligence tests, teacher judgement, school records including achievement test grades, individual intelligence tests administered by a qualified person, appraisal of school and emotional maturity adjustment, and parent interview.

Torrance (1965) outlines many ideas that appear useful in developing procedures for identifying gifted children.

1. Intelligence tests should be utilized; however, such tests should be supplemented by observation of behavior and/or other types of tests such as those dealing with creative thinking — both divergent and convergent.
2. Creative ability should be evaluated on a separate but almost equal basis to intelligence. For example, there is much evidence to indicate that the relationship between measures of intelligence and creative ability is so low that identification of gifted children based on measures of intelligence alone misses large portions of creatively gifted children.
3. In identifying gifted or even creative children, other types of talent may be overlooked in a classroom situation. Therefore, the assessment or the identification procedure should be broad enough and comprehensive enough to select all potentially gifted children.
4. It appears that gifted children can be identified most effectively when children are placed in situations that require gifted behavior.

Taylor (1962) offers a number of very exciting illustrations of how teachers can create situations to identify gifted children.

1. At times, let students do most of the planning on their own and make their own decisions. Observe which ones are most dependent and which ones have the least need for training experience in self-guidance.
2. Develop exercises through which children report their inner feelings and impulses and then have them see how well they can intuitively anticipate a correct course or action.
3. Pose complex issues and see which children take a hopeful attitude rather than a position that things are in an impossible state of affairs and

nothing can be done. Creative children stick with difficult and frustrating learning tasks.

4. Have idea-generating sessions to see who comes up with the most ideas, whose ideas bring out the strongest negative reactions from their classmates, and who tends to lead in expressing strong negative reactions. Observe who has the most courage to hold his/her ground or move ahead instead of retreating or giving up in the face of negative reactions.

5. Ask students to do a task that they have done before but take away most of the facilities previously available, to see how they will utilize resourcefulness in accomplishing the task.

6. Structure some classroom tasks for those who tolerate uncertainty or ambiguity and those who are unable to do so; in other words, create a situation in which the rewards go to those who keep the problem open and keep working on it with their own resources until they eventually obtain a solution.

In a publication of the NSPRA (1979) several procedures are outlined for identifying gifted and talented children. They include

Tests. Group tests of intelligence used to screen children and individual tests for more intensive analysis of the child's intellect should be considered, e.g. individual tests such as the Wechsler Intelligence Scales, the Stanford-Binet, and other accepted standardized individual and group intelligence tests. Other tests to be considered would be individual, group-administered achievement tests that assess a child's academic and achievement capabilities. Aptitude and interest tests are available in standardized forms for use in identifying gifted and talented children. Tests that have been specifically designed as "culturally free" should be identified and considered for use.

Parent Nominations. It appears that parents are a fairly reliable source from which children's gifts and talents can be accurately identified. This is especially true in the child's early years.

Teacher Nominations. Even though teachers are not always the best source of identification, teachers can, with the assistance of rating scales and behavioral checklists, be a good source of screening gifted and talented children.

Peer Nominations. These are usually based on charts that indicate preferences of friendships such as would be found in a sociogram. Children who are continually selected above everyone else are possible candidates.

Auditions. Psychomotor and performing arts auditions, as well as examination of portfolios that show students' original work in the individual and communication arts, can help distinguish giftedness.

Self-Nomination. The child's autobiographical data and interest inventories should be possible considerations in identifying these children.

There is no agreed-upon procedural format to be followed in identifying gifted children; however, a suggested one is as follows:

Nomination. Parents, teachers, and peers should be heeded in identifying or considering further testing of gifted and talented children. If a parent, teacher, or other child from the child's peer group is consulted for more information concerning a child's accelerated or unusual performance, then that child should be further assessed on an individual basis.

General screening. In the classroom it may be necessary to utilize individual and group achievement test scores or checklists similar to the one presented previously in initially identifying potential candidates for further individual assessment.

After the screening or a more thorough review of already existing achievement test information, student performance through anecdotal records should lead to *in-depth individual assessment.* Assessment should be planned in at least five areas.

1. *Cognitive/intellectual/academic area.* Formal achievement and intellectual tests are used to determine cognitive capabilities. Tests such as the Wechsler scales, Stanford-Binet, Woodcock-Johnson Psychoeducational Battery, Iowa Test of Basic Skills, Peabody Individual Achievement Test, and Stanford Achievement Test should be administered to determine overall cognitive and academic performance.
2. *Creative abilities.* Tests such as the Torrance Test of Creative Thinking or the Guilford Creative Test for Children should be utilized.
3. *Physical and/or psychomotor abilities.* Assessment is made of the child's motor performance. Specified motor and psychomotor tasks are closely observed to determine unusual ability.
4. *Social/emotional abilities.* Here the child is looked at in terms of leadership ability and overall success in adapting and controlling social situations. This would include children who are consistently identified as leaders of the class for positive as well as negative reasons. They may be the school or class president or the leader of a gang.
5. *Visual and performing arts.* Usually observations of and nominations by parents, teachers, and peers would be the most commonly used and accepted means of identifying children in this area.

A model called the Reservoir Model (Gowan, 1970) for gifted and talented has been proposed, which would help to ensure identification in all the above areas. The model is essentially a checklist of procedures to be followed in identifying these children.

RESERVOIR MODEL FOR IDENTIFICATION OF GIFTED AND TALENTED

1. Determine the percentage of students to be included in the program (not less than 1 percent or more than 10 percent).
2. Employ a group test in which teachers and peers are asked to nominate students for each of the following categories. All names are placed in the reservoir.
   Best student
   Child with the biggest vocabulary
   Most original and creative child

Child with the most leadership ability
Most scientifically orientated child
Child who does the best critical thinking
Able child who is the biggest nuisance
Best motivated child
Child the other children like best
Child who is most ahead on grade placement
Brightest minority group child in the class
Child whose parents are most concerned about increasing the enrichment of his educational progress

3. Use an achievement battery and cut at a point which will yield 3 percent. Make a list of all students who are in the top 10 percent in numerical skills. Add both of these lists to the reservoir.

4. Together with principal, curriculum staff and guidance staff plus a few teachers go over and make a list of children who
   Have leadership positions
   Achieved outstandingly in any special skills
   Are the best representative of minority groups
   Are examples of reading difficulties but appear bright
   Are believed bright but may be emotionally disturbed
   Any single individual feels might be in the program

5. All children having three or more mentions should be automatically included in the program. All children having two citations should be sent for individual intelligence testing. If possible, children mentioned once should receive testing. (Pp. 307-8)

The above Reservoir Model is only one of several methods of identification, but it nicely illustrates the involvement of many persons (professionals and peers) in the identification process. The model lends itself to application in almost any cultural or academic setting and can be inclusive of all areas considered in identifying gifted and talented youngsters.

IDENTIFICATION PRACTICES

Previous information in this chapter has outlined the characteristics of gifted and talented children. To identify one of these children, a thorough understanding of these characteristics is necessary. Further, gifts and talents in children usually occur in one or more areas of development. In considering what others have said (Renzulli, 1973; Guilford, 1962; Taylor, 1973; and others) concerning the complexity of giftedness, it is our feeling that identification must take place in at least five measurable areas. These include *cognitive abilities, social/emotional behaviors, academic performance*, and talents in the *performing arts*, as well as how the child *processes information* in solving problems. Educational practices should also be developed in these five areas.

Following is formal source information on the most common procedures and instruments used in identifying gifted and talented children. This information plus what has been previously presented in the chapter should provide a firm foundation from which to better decide who could be classified as gifted.

Cognitive Abilities

This area is usually characterized by the child's performance in an IQ test. In fact, the IQ test score is perhaps one of the most widely used criterion for classifying gifted persons. The higher the IQ, the greater the giftedness. A usual criterion is that an individual score one or more standard deviations above the mean to be considered for classification as gifted. However, cognitive abilities are more complex than standard IQ tests are capable of measuring. Most IQ tests measure a person's verbal understanding of concepts with some abstract reasoning assessed through the manipulating, physical or mental, of prescribed test items. If Guilford's (1962) model of the intellect is considered inclusive of many facets of cognitive ability, then IQ tests as presently constituted do not begin to assess all the possible abilities of the individual. An IQ test score, especially when programming for the gifted individual, should be used in conjunction with many other demonstrated characteristics.

Since the tests are used extensively, the following descriptions (Ingram, 1980) of different tests are presented to acquaint the reader with those most commonly administered in identifying gifted individuals.

Cognitive Assessment Instruments

AUTHOR ADAPTATION OF THE LEITER INTERNATIONAL PERFORMANCE SCALE. Grace Author, C. H. Stoeltig, Chicago, Illinois, 1950. This measure is a nonverbal measure designed to assess the intelligence of children two to twelve years of age. The test is not appropriate for children who have difficulty with verbal constructs, are deaf, hard of hearing, or bilingual, lack an English language base, or have different speech patterns. During the test the child is required to categorize objects, match colors and shapes, and duplicate patterns.

COLUMBIA MENTAL MATURITY SCALE (CMMS). B. Burgemeister, L. Blum, and I. Lorge, Harcourt Brace Jovanovich, New York, 1972. The CMMS assesses the general reasoning ability of children three years six months to nine years eleven months of age. It is administered individually and requires that the child discriminate between pictures on a card. The child looks at all the pictures on a card, then identifies the picture that is different from the others.

McCARTHY SCALES OF CHILDREN'S ABILITIES. P. McCarthy, Psychological Corporation, New York, 1972. The McCarthy Scales are easily administered and interpreted tests for the classroom teacher. The Scales were designed to assess the general intelligence of children from two years six months to eight years six months. There are eighteen subtests within the Subscales (verbal, perceptual, motor, cognitive memory, and quantitative). The test results are a mental age score as well as an index of cognitive ability.

SRA PRIMARY MENTAL ABILITIES (PMA). L. L. Thurstone and Thelma

Gwinn Thurstone, Science Research Associates, Inc., 1962. The PMA is designed to measure aptitude in five areas: verbal meaning, number facility, reasoning, spatial relations, and perceptual speed. The test batteries are constructed for six grade levels (k-1, 2-4, 4-6, 6-9, 9-12, and adult); however, only one of the batteries (grades 4-6) includes all of the five mentioned areas of aptitude.

SLOSSON INTELLIGENCE TEST FOR CHILDREN AND ADULTS (SIT). Richard L. Slosson, Slosson Educational Publications, Inc., East Aurora, New York, 1981. The SIT can be a useful individual screening instrument for both children and adults. The ease and brevity of the test lend it to use by teachers, counselors, and many others who might not otherwise be qualified.

STANFORD-BINET INTELLIGENCE SCALES — 1972 NORMS EDITION. Lewis M. Terman and Maud A. Merrill, Houghton Mifflin Company, Boston, 1973. This edition of the Stanford-Binet is a revision of the 1937 edition. It is a single scale intelligence test. The Stanford-Binet is an age scale test that uses age standards for performance.

WECHSLER ADULT INTELLIGENCE SCALE — REVISED (WAIS-R). David Wechsler, Psychological Corporation, New York, 1980. The WAIS-R is another IQ test developed by David Wechsler. The first edition was called the Wechsler Bellevue Intelligence Scale. The WAIS-R consists of eleven tests; six are grouped into the verbal scale while five comprise the performance scale.

WECHSLER INTELLIGENCE SCALE FOR CHILDREN — REVISED (WISC-R). David Wechsler, Psychological Corporation, New York, 1974. The WISC-R was designed and organized to test general intelligence. Recently, however, the WISC-R has established itself as a useful clinical and diagnostic tool in the areas of educational assessment and appraising learning. The WISC-R consists of twelve subtests, six of which constitute the verbal scale and six the performance scale.

WECHSLER PRESCHOOL AND PRIMARY SCALE OF INTELLIGENCE (WPPSI). David Wechsler, Psychological Corporation, New York, 1967. The WPPSI is an individual intelligence test designed for subjects between the ages of four and six and one-half years. The WPPSI has eleven subtests divided into verbal and performance scales.

WOODCOCK-JOHNSON PSYCHOEDUCATIONAL BATTERY — PART I, COGNITIVE. Richard Woodcock and M. Bonner Johnson, Teaching Resources, New York, 1977. The Woodcock-Johnson Test of Cognitive Ability is one of the most recent tests of intellectual potential. It has relatively good concurrent validity with the WISC-R (1979). The test is composed of twelve subtests covering the areas of picture vocabulary, spatial relations, memory for sentences, visual-auditory learning, blending, quantitative concepts, visual matching autonomy (synonyms, analysis synthesis, numbers reversal, concept formation, and analogies).

Academic Achievement

A gifted and talented child usually excels in one or more of the academic areas. To identify accelerated performance in the academic subjects, a teacher or parent should be aquainted with a number of formal testing instruments. The accelerated performance category for the gifted is somewhere two grade levels above a child's chronological grade placement. The following instruments are used quite extensively in assessing academic performance.

Achievement Instruments

CALIFORNIA ACHIEVEMENT TESTS (CAT). Ernest W. Tiegs and Willis W. Clark, CTA/McGraw-Hill, Monterey, California, 1970. The CAT generally measures ability to understand and use the content of the Stanford school curriculum. The child's performance in applying rules, facts, concepts, conventions, and principles of problem solving in the basic curricular materials is measured. The student's level of performance in using the tools of reading, mathematics, and language in progressively more difficult situations is also provided through this device.

METROPOLITAN ACHIEVEMENT TEST (MAT). Walter N. Durst, Harold H. Bixler, J. W. Wrightstone, G. A. Prescott, and I. A. Barlow, Harcourt Brace Jovanovich, New York, 1971. The MAT comprises a coordinated series of measures of achievement in the important skill and content areas of the elementary and junior high school curriculum. The MAT is organized in five levels or batteries, primary I through advanced, covering kindergarten through ninth grade. It is a group-administered test yielding information about a child's understanding and skill in reading, math computations, math concepts, math problem solving, science, social studies, and world analysis.

PEABODY INDIVIDUAL ACHIEVEMENT TEST (PIAT). Lloyd M. Dunn and Frederick C. Markwardt, Jr., American Guidance Service, Circle Pines, Minnesota, 1969. The PIAT is used to measure general academic achievement. It is a wide-range screening instrument for achievement in the areas of mathematics, reading, spelling, and general information. The test may be given individually to persons from ages five to adult and can be used with the handicapped as well. It gives grade and age equivalents, a percentile rank, and a standardized score that when profiled aids in comparing each subtest and the total test scores with other data.

STANFORD DIAGNOSTIC MATHEMATICS TEST. L. S. Beatty, R. Madden, E. F. Gardner, and J. Karlsen, Harcourt Brace Jovanovich, New York, 1966. This diagnostic test is best used with children from second through eighth grade. Throughout the test, the child is expected to work with numbers to demonstate how well they are understood and used in computations. The manual that accompanies the test provides very good information for interpreting and using test results.

KEYMATH. Austin Connolly, American Guidance Service, Circle Pines, Minnesota. The Keymath is an individual test intended for children from kindergarten through eighth grade. Keymath assesses skills possessed by children in fourteen areas of mathematics (numeration, fractions, geometry and symbols, addition, subtraction, multiplication, division, mental computation, numerical reasoning, word problems, missing elements, money, measurement, and time). It is primarily a diagnostic test, giving dependable information that aids in interpreting the subject's performance on subtests and individual items. It provides raw score grade placement and grade equivalent performance. Scores can be profiled to illustrate graphically a child's strengths and weaknesses in math. The manual that accompanies the test is especially good for interpreting test results, since each test item is referenced to a behavioral description that provides a distinct guide for program planning.

STANFORD ACHIEVEMENT TEST (SAT). R. Madden, E. R. Gardner, H. C. Rudman, B. Karlsen, and J. C. Merwin, Harcourt Brace Jovanovich, New York, 1973. The SAT was designed to assess skill development in different areas such as vocabulary, reading comprehension, word study skills, mathematics concepts, spelling, language, social science, science, etc. There are three forms of the test — A, B, and C — and these three forms are available from grades 1.5 to 9.5. The eleven subtests of the SAT occur at some levels but not at others, and the skills assessed by these subtests are different at the different levels. Two manuals are also available: one groups the items by their major instructional objectives, and the other provides an item analysis; instructional objectives and ways to teach these objectives.

WIDE RANGE ACHIEVEMENT TEST (WRAT). J. F. Justak and S. R. Justak, Guidance Associates, Wilmington, Delaware, 1965. The WRAT is used as a screening device for academic performance in reading, spelling, and arithmetic. It detects general skill in spelling, ability to read words in isolation, and ability to compute a variety of math problems. The test has two levels to assess children in kindergarten through sixth grade (Level I) and sixth grade through adult (Level II). This test is quickly administered and scored.

IOWA TEST OF BASIC SKILLS. A. N. Hieronymus and E. F. Lindquist, and Houghton Mifflin, Boston, 1956. The Iowa test includes subtests measuring vocabulary, reading comprehension, language skills (spelling, capitalization, punctuation, usage), work-study skills, and math skills from third to ninth grade level.

WOODCOCK-JOHNSON PSYCHOEDUCATIONAL BATTERY — PART II, ACHIEVEMENT. Richard Woodcock and M. Bonner Johnson, Teaching Resources, New York, 1977. This test assesses a student's academic abilities in the areas of reading functions, math (applied and calculation), language function, general science, and social studies. It has extensive norms and tables for use in comparing a child's performance in one or more of the above areas with others of the same age and grade.

Social/Emotional Behavior

Social/emotional behavior is one area that is sometimes overlooked in the identification of gifted children. In this category a child may manifest tremendous capacity for leadership, for directing others, for solving social conflicts between other class members, or for world problems in general. Another important reason for assessing this area is not only to identify the child gifted in this category, but also to insure that a well-balanced educational program is developed for the individual. It is not uncommon for the academically gifted child to be placed into programs that are strictly designed to stimulate development in that one area, without considering the child's social and emotional needs. Techniques for not only identifying the gifted child but also planning a well-balanced educational program would include the following:

VINELAND SOCIAL MATURITY SCALE (VSMS). Edgar Doll, American Guidance Services, Circle Pines, Minnesota. An individual assessment test of social maturity for persons from birth through thirty years of age. This device is *not* directly administered to the individual, but a confidant who knows the individual quite well is questioned. The VSMS assesses eight aspects of social ability, including self-help skills, locomotion, occupation, communication, self-direction, and socialization. This device, while providing some good information, is somewhat out of date and in need of revision.

WALKER PROBLEM BEHAVIOR IDENTIFICATION CHECKLIST (WPBIC). Hill M. Walker, M.D., Western Psychological Services, Los Angeles, 1970. The WPBIC Checklist is a tool for identifying children with behavior problems who should be referred for further psychological evaluation and treatment.

SENTENCE COMPLETION. Sentence completion is a device that is at the control and manipulation of a parent or teacher. A number of different kinds of information can be generated informally by asking the child to respond to the sentence stem of the sentence completion device. A child's attitude toward family, friends, school, and self can be revealed through the child's response on the sentence completion.

MAGIC CIRCLE. In a series of daily, twenty-minute sharing sessions the class members are gathered together in Magic Circle (Bessell and Palomares, 1971) groups of approximately ten and respond to questions such as "What did you do that someone liked?" These questions are designed to explore both positive and negative feelings, thoughts, and actions. Pictures and physical activities are presented to stimulate these responses. The aim of the Magic Circle program is to develop greater self-confidence, self-awareness, and understanding of social interaction (Biehler, 1974).

SOCIOGRAM. An example of an effective peer rating technique is the sociogram. This device is used to reveal the child's social position within the class. Biehler (1974) has presented an effective model for using the sociogram. Each child was asked to write down the names of the most liked classmates — the most fun to be with, the nicest to sit next to. The selected choices were plotted on the diagram with the "stars" in the center and the "isolates" outside the circle.

THE PRESCHOOL ATTAINMENT RECORD (PAR). Edgar Doll, American Guidance Services, Circle Pines, Minnesota, 1967. This record is an extension of the

Vineland Social Maturity Scale, directed to the first seven years of life. Its eight categories (ambulation, manipulation, rapport, communication, responsibility, information, ideation, and creativity) are designed to measure physical and intellectual development, as well as social development. Each item is norm-referenced for the average age at which a child can perform it; thus the PAR provides a quick assessment of a child's general strengths and weaknesses.

"SHARING" OR "SHOW AND TELL" PERIODS. Short time blocks are devoted to the class members sharing important events in their lives. These periods would provide an opportunity to express oneself and to demonstrate social skills.

ROLE PLAYING, CREATIVE PLAY, STORIES, DISCUSSION. These activities can be used to identify consequences of social acts and provide opportunities to experience peer interactions. Puppetry, play therapy, and modeling are also effective techniques to draw out a child's peer relationships potential.

Information Processing Skill

Another important consideration in planning well-balanced educational programs for gifted and talented individuals is to consider how best they learn and to understand what conditions will better stimulate that learning. In other words, knowing how the child processes information through the learning modalities of auditory, visual, motor, and other senses is very critical to selecting or developing the most appropriate learning environment for the individual.

Modality is usually broken down into two parts, *acuity* and *perception*. Acuity relates primarily to determining if the mechanisms for providing a pathway to learning exist. That is, is the child able to see appropriately? Does the child possess all the necessary parts of the hearing mechanism to allow sufficient auditory stimuli to be heard? Are the child's motor capabilities adequate enough to allow for performance in those areas involving motor skills?

The following tests and procedures are suggested for determining a child's best or preferred method of processing information.

Assessment of Information Processing Abilities

AUDITORY DISCRIMINATION TEST. Joseph M. Wepman, Ph.D., Language Research Assoc., Inc., Palm Springs, California, 1973. The Wepman Auditory Discrimination Tests measure the child's ability to recognize differences between phonemes in English speech. The child is asked to listen as the examiner reads pairs of words and then to indicate whether the words read were the same (a single word repeated) or different (two different words).

BENDER VISUAL-MOTOR GESTALT TEST FOR CHILDREN (BVMGT). Lauretta Bender, American Orthopsychiatric Association, 1938. The (BVMGT) is composed of nine geometric figures that the subject is required to draw from memory or reproduce while the stimulus is present. This test primarily measures visual-perception abilities but has been used to evaluate social and emotional adjustment, intelligence, and brain damage. A trained clinical psychologist should administer and interpret the BVMGT.

BRUININKS-OSERETZKY TEST OF MOTOR PROFICIENCY. R. H. Bruininks, American Guidance Service, Circle Pines, Minnesota, 1977. The Bruininks-Osteretzky Test for Motor Proficiency gives a general estimate of gross and fine motor abilities. The specific subtests include running speed and agility, balance, bilateral coordination, strength, upper-limb coordination, response speed, visual-motor control, and upper-limb speed and dexterity. Test results are reported as age equivalents and percentile ranks. It is a very thorough test of a child's motor skills.

DEVELOPMENTAL TEST OF VISUAL-MOTOR INTEGRATION. Keith E. Beery and Norman A. Buktenica, Follett Educational Corporation, Chicago, 1967. This is a technique popular with teachers for assessing visual-motor functioning in children and adolescents. It is appropriate for children from two to fifteen years of age. The test is also useful for preschool and early primary grade children. When used for screening purposes it may be administered in group settings.

GOLDMAN-FRISTOE-WOODCOCK AUDITORY SKILLS TEST OF AUDITORY DISCRIMINATION. Goldman, Fristoe, Woodcock, American Guidance Service, Circle Pines, Minnesota, 1970. This test assesses speech sound discrimination under quiet and noisy conditions.

GOLDMAN-FRISTOE-WOODCOCK AUDITORY SKILLS TEST BATTERY. Goldman, Fristoe, Woodcock, American Guidance Service, Circle Pines, Minnesota, 1976. This test battery provides a comprehensive diagnosis of auditory-perception for individuals from three years of age to adulthood. It measures auditory selective attention, the ability to listen in the presence of noise that varies in type and intensity. This test also measures auditory discrimination, auditory memory, and sound symbol.

ILLINOIS TEST OF PSYCHOLINGUISTIC ABILITIES (ITPA). Samuel A. Kirk, James J. McCarthy, and Winifred D. Kirk, University of Illinois, Urbana, 1969. The object of the ITPA is to delineate childrens' abilities and disabilities in processing information through auditory and visual channels. The ITPA has a total of twelve subtests, and each subtest is included under either the receptive process (decoding), the organizing process (association), or the expressive process (encoding) covering auditory and visual functions.

PURDUE PERCEPTUAL-MOTOR SURVEY. Eugene G. Roach and Newell C. Kephart, Charles E. Merrill Publishing Co., Columbia, Ohio, 1966. the Purdue Perceptual-Motor Survey (PPMS) is an informal survey evaluating motor performance and its relation to perceptual awareness. Skills in the areas of balance and posture, body image and differentiation of body parts, perceptual-motor matching, ocular control, and form perception are surveyed. Eleven subtests consisting of twenty-two items are presented.

Performing Arts

Observation of the child's performing behavior will usually act as the primary determining factor of the child's gifts in a particular performing arts area. However, identifying performing art talent is not an easy task. Children vary considerably in their abilities to perform as well as in the age at which their talent (even interest) may emerge. Sometimes a child is mistakenly identified as being extremely talented in an area such as music or writing when in reality the child is only manifesting acquired or learned skills (Khatena, 1982).

Testing in the performing arts area is also a difficult activity. There are few performing arts tests that would allow a person to conclude that a child's performance on the test would make that child a candidate for a gifted and talented program. Tests available do provide a relatively good idea of the child's aptitude in a performing arts area, yet nominations by parents, teachers, and peers may be the best means that presently exist for identifying the talented performing arts child. There is a great need for better identification of these children. Three performing arts areas and the corresponding tests for use in determining aptitude will be highlighted in the following discussion.

Motor Skills

To identify children with good motor abilities and aptitude the YOUTH FITNESS TEST (Hunsicker and Reiff, 1976) provides a means of comparing a child's physical capabilities on selected gross motor skills against national norms. Some subtests of the WECHSLER INTELLIGENCE SCALES (children and adults) provide normative data for visual motor coordination skills (Block Design, Coding, Mazes, and Object Assembly), while some idea of a person's visual perceptual skills can be determined through the subtests Block Design, Digit Symbols, Picture Completion, and Object Assembly. The BRININKS-OSERETSKY (American Guidance, 1981) and PURDUE PERCEPTUAL MOTOR SURVEY (Roach & Kephart, 1976) (mentioned above), while used primarily for determining deficient motor skills, can also be good measures of gross and fine motor development. For older children, the MULTIPLE APTITUDE TESTS (Segal and Raskin, 1959) will provide some indication of a person's *perceptual speed* in locating grammatical errors and differences in a series of number sequences and *spatial visualization*, which assesses two- and three-dimensional visualization capabilities. Perhaps the best test of motor aptitude is observation of the youngster. If the child is exceptionally well coordinated, agile, and strong, these abilities will manifest themselves as he or she plays with other children. The child can then be directed to a program or person that will bring those talents to even greater light. The unfortunate situation, however, is the one in which the child with exceptional motor talent does not have the opportunity to manifest those skills; this is when a test of motor proficiency is needed at least to screen children to locate those with potential.

Art Aptitude

Again, observation of an individual's manifest talent may be the best method of determining talent in the art areas. Even some of this expressed talent may be a function of learned skill and not real talent; therefore caution should be taken in making a decision as to a child's art ability. There are several instruments that can be used in assessing an individual's aptitude for art. These include Guilford's (1973) CREATIVITY TEST FOR CHILDREN. In Guilford's test an attempt is made to determine a child's (use of the test is suggested for children four years and older) use of figural concepts. Another test that could be used as an indicator of art aptitude is the TORRANCE TEST OF CREATIVE THINKING (Torrance, 1966). This test provides information about how a child can produce pictures or shapes from a variety of lines, resulting in a measure of that child's figural fluency, originality, and elaboration. Specific tests of art aptitude as discussed by Khatena (1982) include the HORN APTITUDE INVENTORY, KNAUBER ART ABILITY TEST and the ADVANCED PLACEMENT PROGRAM IN STUDIO ART (Horn, 1976).

Music Aptitude

Like art, music talent may best be assessed through observation of the expressed talent. However, there are several tests of music ability and aptitude. Gordon's (1965) MUSICAL APTITUDE PROFILE is one objective measure designed to assess the individual's aptitude in melody, harmony, rhythm, imagery, musical sensitivity, and tonal imagery. Other tests include the MEASURES OF MUSICAL ABILITY (Bentley, 1966), DRAKE MUSICAL APTITUDE TESTS (Drake, 1954), SEASHORE MEASURES OF MUSICAL TALENTS (Seashore, Lewis, and Sactveit, 1960), STANDARDIZED TESTS OF MUSICAL INTELLIGENCE (Wing, 1961), and MUSIC ACHIEVEMENT TEST (Aliferis, 1969).

In summary, it is at best difficult to assess a child's performing arts abilities with present technology. Caution should always be the watchword, for the child's expressed talent may be more a reflection of learned behavior than real talent. However, of even greater concern is not attempting to uncover the performing arts talents that may go unrecognized and undeveloped through the lack of applying technology (tests, observation, and nominations) presently available.

CHAPTER TWO

STEWARDSHIP AND BALANCE — KEY PRINCIPLES IN STRENGTHENING THE GIFTED AND TALENTED

Can you answer the following questions?

1. What is the meaning of stewardship?
2. Can you explain the Five Principles of Supervision?
   How do these principles teach personal stewardship?
3. Why is balance a crucial factor in the happiness and well-being of the gifted or talented? How can balance be emphasized in the programs developed by and for the gifted child?
4. What should be the main goals in managing behaviors of the gifted or talented?
5. What are the Five *R*s of Remediation?
6. What is an Individualized Education Plan (IEP)? How does this relate to goal setting? To stewardship? To the gifted or talented child?

WITHIN this chapter some key principles are presented, which are essential in effective relationships and supportive work with the gifted child.

After the advanced skills and special needs of a given child are identified, a plan of action is needed. In establishing such a plan or learning program, the wise teacher will consider the stewardship principles, the importance of balance and a well-adjusted child, behavior management, and the effective use of an Individualized Education Plan (IEP).

STEWARDSHIP DEFINED

Each individual needs to learn to administer and manage his or her own life, time, energy, responsibilities, and materials if he or she is to become a self-

29

sufficient, independent, and productive member of a family and a community. This, in essence, is stewardship, defined in *Webster's New Collegiate Dictionary* as "the process of being an administrator or manager." Stewardship is the administration or management of those things in one's life for which one is legitimately responsible.

Many parents, teachers, and leaders* ask the same questions regarding a gifted or talented child. "What can I do with him or her?" "How can I wisely lead this bright child? In other words, a person may ask, "What is *my* stewardship role and how can I wisely teach stewardship and self-discipline to this child?" Many methods of supervision have been introduced in education, business, and other organizations. These methods are generally designed to replace the widespread traditional approach to supervision in which the person "in charge" supervises the child or student in an authoritarian way, telling the child what should be done, watching, as the child carries out the instructions, and being quick to correct mistakes that the child may make. Treating gifted or talented children this way often gives them negative feelings about their teachers, because it not only does little to help them become more effective, it often makes them nervous or irritated and robs them of opportunities to take initiative and to grow. The traditional approach has its time and place but rarely with the gifted.

A wise leader once suggested that whenever one has supervision or direction over another person's life, a good plan to follow is

> *Teach them correct principles, and then —*
> *They govern themselves.*
>
> *Joseph Smith (1851)*

The Five Principles of Supervision were developed from the plan stated by Joseph Smith. These principles are a practical and excellent means of teaching effective stewardship.

FIVE PRINCIPLES OF SUPERVISION

1. Teachers teach correct principles (rules, expectations).
2. Students set goals in harmony with the correct principles taught.
3. Teachers prepare themselves to be thought of as a source of help and to be available to give help.
4. Students ask for help when needed, and teachers give the help.
5. Students give an accounting of their stewardship.

The Five Principles of Supervision constitute a stewardship plan applica-

---

*People in many different roles take part in supervising activities in the lives of others. Rather than mention these many roles again and again, parents, leaders, teachers, employers, etc. will within this text fall under the heading of *teacher*.

ble to all levels of authority, for teachers must also set goals, curriculum, and plans in harmony with the rules and expectations of their administrators and give an accounting of their stewardship in terms of student grades, progress reports, and the accounting of materials and supplies utilized. This is such a pragmatic and effective program that it deserves closer consideration.

1. Teachers Teach Correct Principles.

Teachers have a responsibility to maintain professional and personal integrity and to teach truth and wisdom to the best of their understanding and ability. When this is not adhered to, the result is chaos and confusion for the student. Teachers are respected, honored, and trusted when they are consistent in teaching true principles and when they themselves consistently live them and practice them, thus serving as models. The teacher can be especially significant to a child's life and growth when this respect and trust has been earned. Anyone in a supervisory or teaching capacity has responsibility to see that the individuals within his or her stewardship understand the basic rules, principles, and expectations under which they are living.

All too often it is assumed that a child or student has knowledge or understanding that he or she does not in fact possess. Preassessment is helpful here. The child may be asked what the rules or expectations are for a given situation. Then the child should be courteously taught what he or she does not know or understand. A very young child is constantly being taught and instructed as to the rules and expectations of the family or culture, but when the child gets older, false assumptions may be made regarding his or her understanding. Children come to school from many different family backgrounds and situations. Their early training can differ drastically. Review and reinforcement of key principles is important. Students need to know the expectations of the teacher and the rules they are expected to follow. A gifted child can relax and function better when helped to understand the key principles and rules involved in his or her environment. Sometimes the child's attention is so absorbed in a task or interest of his or her own that he or she is hard to reach in terms of basic rules or principles. A wise teacher will take the time to get the child's attention and then gently help the child to understand some of the subtleties and realities of the environment.

2. Students Set Goals in Harmony with Correct Principles.

A gifted or talented person may appreciate freedom to grow and learn, but it is a simple truth that there is not enough time in life for one person to experience everything for himself or to learn it all by personal discovery through trial and error. In the interest of time and personal progress, the gifted or talented need to benefit from the knowledge, wisdom, mistakes, and experiences of others. By thus learning true principles from others, they save valuable time, avoid a lot of pain and anguish, and do not have to undo a myriad of mistakes and consequent problems. They can proceed much more rapidly and success-fully and experience far more personal progress.

Please note the order of the Five Principles of Supervision: *First* the teacher teaches correct principles, and *then* students can set their own goals in harmony with correct principles. There is order and reason to this plan. When true prin-ciples have been clearly taught to the child and understood by him or her, the child should then be encouraged to establish his or her own goals in harmony with the principles taught. In other words, when the rules and expectations are understood it should be easier for the child to use freedom wisely, map out his or her plan of action, and accept stewardship and responsibility for the deci-sions made. Age and maturity must be taken into consideration, but even a very young child can enjoy and progress when given trust and responsibility based on wise teachings.

All too often a teacher can feel intimidated by the advanced knowledge or abilities of a gifted or talented child. Feeling inadequate, the teacher may make one of two mistakes. First, the child may be forced into conforming to the ex-pected mold for his or her own age-mates. Many gifted children will either rebel against such restricting forces or slip into mediocrity, not even trying any-more — a terrible waste. Some will do well in spite of the restricting system and come along on their own power. Second, the teacher may just turn the child loose and leave him or her to do as he or she may. Some gifted individuals func-tion well with unguided freedom, but for most the consequences can be frus-trating and painful.

Stewardship should be taught and practiced. Biehler (1978) introduced the situation of the obnoxious genius.

How should you handle an obnoxi-ous "genius?"

Imagine that you are teaching in a third grade. It is the end of the first month of school. A new boy is assigned to your room. During his first week in class he manages to antago-nize just about everyone. He gets perfect scores on all his work and makes sure the entire school is well aware of this. He shouts out answers to questions when you call on other children. (He gives the impression that he can't help doing this — he is just bursting with information.) He makes re-marks about the stupidity of children who can't answer as rapidly or as accurately as he does. When he recites, he somehow works in all kinds of slightly relevant information he has memorized. He even corrects you on particular points (you spoke of "crocodiles" when you should have said "alligators"); and upon looking the matter up, you dis-cover that he is right. How could you encourage him to be humble without squelching his undeniable gifts?*

---

*From Robert F. Biehler: *Psychology Applied to Teaching*, 3rd ed., p. 749. Copyright© 1978 by Houghton Mif-flin Company. Used by permission.

This child needs to be taught stewardship. He needs to understand that all people have gifts and talents, that these talents differ from person to person, and that with a special talent comes extra responsibility to use it wisely and productively. Each person needs to work cooperatively and respectfully with others so that all may learn and progress. To develop personal stewardship, this child (or any person) needs a plan. A very effective plan to utilize in redirecting the "obnoxious genius" into more productive behaviors and wiser goals was advanced by Glasser (1980) with his Reality Therapy, in which he proposes eight steps.

1. Make friends and then ask, "What do you want? What are you seeking?"
2. "What are you doing now?"
3. "Is it helping you in your progress? Is it against the rules?"
4. "What can you do instead? What might be a better plan?"
5. Get a commitment. (When, where, how will you do it?)
6. Don't accept excuses. (Refer to 3.)
7. Don't punish but don't interfere with reasonable consequences. Don't criticize.
8. Never give up. Be consistently caring and involved (within reason).

When the child is thus taught to consider wiser alternatives, i.e. the principles are reestablished, he once again needs to be encouraged to establish his own plans and goals.

3. Teachers Prepare Themselves To Be Thought of as a Source of Help and To Be Available To Give Help.

It is important that the teacher be perceived as a source of help and support by the gifted or talented child, or that child may not trust the teacher for guidance and assistance. Sometimes, teachers themselves need to take enrichment classes in order to be better prepared to help their students. It is comforting to know that a teacher is not expected to know everything about everything, but it is a wise teacher who has learned about sources of information and the resources available so that the student can be referred to appropriate research materials and people. Teachers need to recognize their limitations honestly and not be afraid to bring in outside resources. There are usually specialists and resource materials available if one will but look. There are many resource people among the students' families, their neighbors, and others in the community.

It is helpful to a gifted and/or talented child to see the teacher as a learner also and to watch the teacher solve problems and correct personal errors. When the teacher is seen as "human" and still supportive and understanding, the child can see in him or her a partner in learning and can share and exchange ideas and information productively. This partnership can enrich and strengthen the life of the teacher — a bonus for working with a gifted/talented child.

Teachers need to be physically and mentally available as sources of help. This means that a teacher needs to set aside specific time when service or counsel may be offered to students. The students also need to understand clearly that the teacher will often be busy with other tasks and other people. Communication and time planning are essential.

A constructive, supportive attitude on the part of the teacher is part of being considered a source of help. Teachers need to be flexible, and they need to avoid criticism and snap judgements. A listening, caring attitude is important. Appreciating another person's point of view, needs, and interests is another part of being a source of help; it also is part of being a growing, developing leader.

4. Students Ask for Help when Needed, and Teachers Give the Help.

Teachers can smother a child with their abundant help and direction, and the child can lose the opportunity to think and feel and do for himself or herself. In essence, teachers release children from personal stewardship by doing too much for them and holding on too tightly. To learn and develop properly, children need to be trusted to decide for themselves and to accept the responsibility and consequences of their own decisions and actions. Freedom to do this should increase with age and maturity. To protect a child's agency a teacher, who is thought of as a source of supportive help, should encourage a child to seek out this help when it is needed and trust the child to work alone when the help is *not* needed. The child should be allowed and encouraged to ask and pursue ideas with natural curiosity. A child will naturally seek help from those whom he or she trusts, and the child will feel better about being the initiator of the interaction. This will affect the child's self-concept positively and add strength to his or her feelings of capability and personal responsibility.

5. Students Give an Accounting of their Stewardship.

Accountability is essential. Reporting their progress does several things for the children.

1. It is a way of sharing their achievements and knowledge with those who care (form of personal validation).
2. It is a way of receiving feedback about their progress and mastery of the tasks undertaken.
3. It is a way of showing what was done with their time and materials (rationale of the experience).
4. It is a form of evaluation that helps them to evaluate externally (with feedback from teachers and others) and internally (considering consequences and results of their labors in relationship to their goals and objectives).
5. It is a way for them to deal responsibly with their inadequacies that otherwise might be rationalized, ignored, or unwittingly neglected.
6. It is a way of reestablishing new goals and moving forward.

Teachers should help those under their care to gain an appreciation and understanding of the accountability principle. It is a part of our culture and way of life. It is important to growth and should be truthful, helpful, and reassuring. It teaches about justice and natural consequences. Teachers should take a good look at the methods of student accountability, asking what the objectives and purposes of the activity are and how accountability can best be demonstrated by the gifted or talented child. Teachers can get locked into thinking about written exams as the only means of assessment; more appropriate means of assessment might be products, productions, journals, mastery of skills, demonstrations, oral reports, or creative endeavors.

The Five Principles of Supervision are powerful tools for directing and assisting an individual in the assuming of stewardship or responsibility for his or her own life and growth. This plan is especially helpful to the gifted and talented because it does not insult the intelligence. It can serve as a reality check, and it fosters team effort and a healthy learning partnership between parents or teachers and the child. This plan does not foster rebellious or frustrated feelings when it is implemented wisely. It is a reassuring and helpful guide for development.

BALANCE DEFINED

In planning or developing programs for gifted or talented children, it is important to consider balance and the development of a well-adjusted child. In setting up programs, establishing stewardship, and guiding the gifted, balance should be an underlying concern. A gifted or talented student needs to be taught or reminded to keep his or her priorities realistic and to maintain a balance of activities and growth in his or her life. Four areas of development should be considered:

1. *Intellectual* — gaining of knowledge and learning skills
2. *Social/Service* — learning to interact constructively, kindly, and supportively with others
3. *Physical* — maintaining good health through proper rest, nutrition, exercise and personal hygiene
4. *Spiritual* — gaining a sense of purpose in life and a serenity and inner peace through proper understanding and relationship with Diety. Or, acquiring a comfortable feeling within one's personal psyche

A fifth category, emotional well-being, is often included but it is the opinion of these authors that if good balance in the other four areas of life is maintained, the result is good mental and emotional health.

Unless the gifted or talented student is naturally interested and active in all four areas of development he may neglect one or more, and this will affect his overall progress and well-being. A gifted or talented child may place his attention and energies in the arts or creative areas and neglect some important intellectual development. No matter how musically talented a child may be, he or she still needs to learn to spell, to read, to do simple math, to understand history, and to learn from knowledgeable forebears. We must not let a gifted or talented student be cheated out of learning the basics. To neglect the social/ service part of development is to miss out on learning important social skills and proper relationships with others. Social relationships are so crucial to learning and to basic happiness and adjustment that wise teachers will assist the gifted or talented to develop effectively in this area. To neglect the physical aspect of development can affect health, thought processes and ability to cope with stress and fatigue. It can also affect social acceptance and abilities. Finally, as man is always interested in his origin, destiny, and relationship with the infinite, he needs to have time to come to terms with his spiritual needs.

A well-balanced individual is usually happier, stronger, and far more prepared to cope with and conquer the trials and challenges of life. He or she is far more interested and interesting, healthier, and more at peace.

MANAGING BEHAVIORS

The goal in managing behaviors of the gifted or talented child should be the child's wise management of his or her own behavior. Once again, we are speaking of stewardship. The gifted or talented child should be taught principles of stewardship over self. With this objective in mind, the teacher will alter methods of reproach or correction of the gifted/talented child. It may, simply stated, be a time to review or reteach important principles or rules to the child. A child who is mentally and emotionally capable and physically able to govern his or her own behavior should be encouraged to do so within the framework of the principles taught and treated respectfully and courteously in the process.

Modeling of good self-discipline and personal management is an essential teaching responsibility. The gifted child will be watching and learning from the management practices of others. When a teacher can exercise good self-control and wisely prioritize, manage time, act and not react, and maintain good life balance, this good example can be the most effective teaching method. The teacher is not expected to be perfect, but it is helpful to the gifted and talented child if the teacher is learning self-mastery and dealing wisely with the challenges of life.

Glasser's (1965) eight steps of Reality Therapy are helpful behavior management tools. Another good approach is the Win-Win plan, in which both teacher and child sit down and work out a plan to a mutually beneficial solution, one in which both teacher and student "win" and one does not "win out" over the other, leaving the other feeling resentful, bitter, or rebellious.

FIVE RS OF REMEDIATION

When a child is feeling bad because of negative consequences, when a law or rule has been seriously violated or a friend alienated, then the Five *R*s of Remediation can be helpful.

1. *Recognition* — What happened? What did you do? What were the results?
2. *Remorse* — How does this leave you feeling? Do you regret the action? How do you feel about the results of the action?
3. *Restitution* — What can you now do about it? Can you make it right again? To whom must you go and what must you do? (The student should be helped to commit and to follow through.)
4. *Resolve* — What have you learned from this situation? What will you do or not do in the future? How can you avoid having this problem again?
5. *Refrain* — How can you demonstrate that you've mastered this problem? How can you know that you really mean to improve your behavior regarding this problem?

In leading the child through this remediation process, it is very important that the teacher do so when not personally angry or upset over the situation. The child needs to feel a helpful and supportive attitude behind the questioning, not condemnation and judgement. If the child feels that he or she is expected to behave more nobly or wisely and that the teacher is merely trying to help him or her to master self and situation, the child will be far more willing to follow through and make the commitments necessary to right the wrong.

INDIVIDUALIZED EDUCATION PLAN

An effective tool for teaching stewardship in the management of behavior is the increasingly more familiar Individualized Education Plan (IEP). The IEP and other processes for the special child have been emphasized in Public Law 94-142.

Public Law 94-142

Helpful direction has been brought to the gifted and talented child because of Public Law 94-142, the Education for All Handicapped Children Act. The gifted or talented at one time came under this law because they, too, needed a change in curriculum to meet their special needs. They are often handicapped in regular classroom situations because of some of their advanced skills. While the gifted no longer come under this law, much can be gained from the tools recommended therein. Turnbull (1979) clarifies Public Law 94-142. He states that the law sets forth regulations and requires action by teachers and school systems. The major principles and requirements of the law are as follows:

FREE APPROPRIATE PUBLIC EDUCATION. An appropriate public education must be available free to all handicapped students between the ages of three and twenty-one. This must be consistent with or adapted within the state law or practice regarding public education for these age-groups. The educational implication of this legal requirement is that school systems may no longer refuse to admit handicapped students into educational programs. For the gifted child, this can be translated to mean that they, too, have a right to an appropriate education that meets their individual needs.

PROTECTION IN EVALUATION PROCEDURES. Procedures must be established and practiced in each school system to ensure that testing procedures are conducted prior to placing or denying placement of a special student from a special education class in a regular class and that these evaluations are administered to assure racial and cultural fairness. Evaluation requirements include the following:

1. Having licensed personnel to administer the test
2. Using tests that are appropriately validated
3. Testing the child in his native language or mode of communication
4. Ensuring that the sensory and or physical handicaps of students do not jeopardize their capability to demonstrate their aptitude and achievement level on the test
5. Taking into consideration specific areas of educational need rather than on general intelligence
6. Using minimum of two tests or types of tests in making decisions for educational placement
7. Considering physical development, sociocultural background, and adaptive behavior, along with test scores
8. Assembling a "team" of persons in the school who possess knowledge about the child and the placement alternatives and who can interpret evaluation data in order to provide an appropriate education plan for the child
9. Placing the child in a regular class unless, according to the evaluation data, he does require a special setting for his education

Teachers are encouraged to ask for a copy of their school system's written policies in this area of evaluation. In situations where classroom teachers refer students for evaluation, the teacher automatically is placed in a position of responsibility for seeing to it that these legal requirements are followed.

INDIVIDUALIZED EDUCATION PROGRAM (IEP). In accordance with the specifications of P.L. 94-142, each school system must establish a procedure for developing and implementing an individualized education program for each of their handicapped students. The IEP is such a helpful and powerful tool for implementing stewardship plans and for the education and progress of the gifted or talented child that it will be discussed in greater detail later in this chapter.

LEAST RESTRICTIVE ENVIRONMENT. The law requires that policies be set up by state and local education agencies to assure that handicapped students are educated to the maximum extent appropriate in programs with nonhandicapped students and that they be placed in special classes or special schools only when the handicap is so severe that education cannot be satisfactorily accomplished within the regular education program with the use of supplementary aids and services. School systems are required to include a continuum of educational alternatives. Schools should review the placement of handicapped students on at least an annual basis. Placement decisions should be based on the student's IEP, and unless the IEP requires some other arrangement the handicapped child should be educated in the same school that he would attend if he were not handicapped. P.L. 94-142 provides that steps must be taken to insure that the least restrictive placement does not result in a harmful effect on the student or reduce the quality of his educational program.

PROCEDURAL SAFEGUARDS. By law, parents of handicapped students are entitled to examine all their child's educational records for identification, evaluation, and placement information. They also have the right to obtain an independent evaluation of their child by a professional examiner outside of the school system and to have this evaluation considered when decisions are made by the school about educational placement.

Another procedural safeguard states that prior notice must be provided to parents of handicapped students whenever a change is proposed or refused regarding the identification, evaluation, or placement of the handicapped child. Prior parental consent is also necessary when a student is initially evaluated for special education placement with psychological or educational tests that are over and above those routinely given to nonhandicapped students.

Parental notices should include the following, all in language understandable to the parent: a complete explanation of all procedural safeguards; a description of the proposed or refused action with respect to placement or the obtaining of special services for the student; the rationale for the action; a description of other options considered with a justification of why those options were not chosen; a description of the evaluation procedures, reports, and records upon which the proposed action is based; and a statement documenting the right to challenge the proposed action.

Parents must be afforded the opportunity to present to the school system complaints on any issue related to identification, evaluation, or educational placement. They are entitled to an impartial due process hearing, which must be conducted by the local educational agency according to state policies and regulations. At this hearing they must be permitted to be represented by counsel or by persons having expertise in the area of handicapping conditions, to present evidence and cross-examine the school witnesses, and to have a written record of the hearing. Either the parents or the school system may appeal the hearing decision from the local education agency to the appropriate state or federal court. While the proceedings of the hearing are pending, the handicapped student should remain in his current educational placement.

P.L. 94-142 may no longer include the gifted, and the law may not be perfect in all facets, but it has been beneficial in emphasizing the need for all students to be placed in their most comfortable and supportive educational setting. Also, if an IEP is implemented properly, the gifted student may be afforded the opportunity to assume stewardship for his or her own learning program and the right to establish personal goals in harmony with wise principles. The IEP in the school is often facilitated with the help of a team of resource specialists who can test and guide the child to his or her maximum opportunity for growth. In a school setting, the team may consist of the teacher, the school psychologist, the school counselor, and any other specialists who logically could render insight (the coach, computer specialist, or music teacher). The parents should be a definite part of this team, too, for they have the ultimate stewardship of the child, and no change of curriculum or grade level should be made for a given child without the approval of his or her parents. The gifted or talented child should also be an important member of the IEP team. The child should be receiving counsel and help to set his or her own learning experience goals, short-term and long-term. A teacher should sit down one-on-one with the gifted or talented child. When the child feels good about the program and feels that he or she has been personally involved in setting the goals with counsel and help from appropriate leaders, it greatly strengthens the child's positive attitude, sense of commitment, and potential for progress.

An IEP is, simply stated, a contract between the child and the teacher, in which the child agrees to accomplish certain tasks or master certain skills in a specific way, by a specific time, and with a predetermined reporting or accountability system. A simple IEP, useful in the home, based on the four areas of balance, may be seen in Figure 2-1. Figure 2-2 denotes an IEP that might be used in a school setting to aid the gifted or talented student. This IEP is formulated on the principles of balance. First, basic information is collected, such as name, age, address, school, etc. As an example, data has been collected on a hypothetical gifted and talented student named Gregory A. Thompson. The present levels of Greg's performance are considered in the areas cognitive/academic, social/service, physical modality, emotional/spiritual, and the performing arts. This inquiry serves as an evaluative check as well as a motivator for considering the different areas of Greg's activity and development as a well-rounded person. Space is given on the IEP for recording the evaluative instruments used and the findings for each area of Greg's performance. The IEP consultants are also listed. Consultants should be involved because of their stewardship with Greg or their ability to give supportive and helpful recommendations regarding this student's learning program. In the event of a gifted or talented child being of another culture or language than that predominating in the school setting, a logical consultant to the IEP team would be a specialist or interpreter from the child's own culture. This person could give insight as

Four of my personal goals for progress are as follows:

1. *Intellectual*

   What I want to accomplish:
   How I plan to achieve this goal:
   Person with whom I am setting this goal:
   Target date of completion:
   How I plan to account for my achievement:

2. *Social/Service*

   What I want to accomplish:
   How I plan to achieve this goal:
   Person with whom I am setting this goal:
   Target date of completion:
   How I plan to account for my achievement:

3. *Physical*

   What I want to accomplish:
   How I plan to achieve this goal:
   Person with whom I am setting this goal:
   Target date of completion:
   How I plan to account for my achievement:

4. *Spiritual/Character*

   What I want to accomplish:
   How I plan to achieve this goal:
   Person with whom I am setting this goal:
   Target date of completion:
   How I plan to account for my achievement:

_____
(Signature)

_____
(Date)

Figure 2-1. A sample IEP useful in the home, showing personal goals based on the four areas of balance.

to the expectations and norms of the child's family and background and could serve as an advocate for the child and as an interpreter if needed. In keeping with the principles of stewardship, the child and his or her parents or guardian should be key members of the IEP team. A gifted student should welcome the evaluation, input, and support from consultants when the student can see this as a means of helping him or her to establish goals that are realistic and wise for personal learning and achievement. If the student can catch the spirit of team effort in his or her behalf (wherein the student, teacher, and parents are seen as team members, along with others as needed), healthy interaction can ensue. With the team members pulling together, greater progress can be achieved. Therefore, one of the most important parts of the IEP form is the space in which parents and student sign their agreement and endorsement of the program.

INDIVIDUALIZED EDUCATION PLAN

Name Gregory A. Thompson	Birthdate (Age) 8 years 6 months
Address 237 Elm Street	Telephone 374-8320
School Eastmont Elementary School	IEP Beginning Month 9 Day 6 Year ___
Present Placement Third Grade	Evaluation Date Month 8 Day 20 Year ___

Present Levels of Performance Cognitive/Academic I.Q. 147 Reading 8.3 Math 6.2 Social/Service Appears to get along well with peers and adults. Physical Modality Motor skills appropriate for age level. Emotional/Spiritual Appears to be well adjusted in relationship to self, peers, and adults. Performing Arts Exceptional skills in piano.	Tests: Woodcock Johnson Psychological Battery, pt.II Achievement. Wisc-R, Sentence Completion - Vineland Soc. Mat. Scale, Informal Behavior Rating Scale, Oseretzky Test of Motor Proficiency Observation, Observation of interaction with peers and personal behaviors.

IEP Consultants:
 	
     Parents, Psychologists, Teacher, District Specialist,
     Others Parents, School Psychologist, Present teacher,
         District Music Specialist, and home music
         instructor.
	We have participated in the development of this program and agree to implement it.
	
	Participant (Sig) _____ Date _____
	
	Parent/Guardian (Sig) _____ Date _____
	     (s) (s)
	                  _____ Date _____

Accountability/Stewardship Review   Date _____   Persons Conducting _____
Results & Recommendations   Greg indicated that he would like to work on social development goals with his
peers and others.

BALANCED GOALS - LONG TERM

AREA	Projected Placement Regular	Projected Placement Special	DURATION
Cognitive/Academic		Accelerated math & reading programs with gifted & talented specialist.	Academic year.
Social/Service	Seems best with age level peers in most developmental situations.		Academic year.
Physical Modalities	Appears that present 3rd grade P.E. program is adequate for his present level of performance		Academic year.
Emotional/Spiritual	Appears adjusted for 3rd grade placement Some interaction w/ adults is encouraging for stimulating progress.		Academic year.
Performing arts		Has demonstrated such exceptional talent in this area that he could benefit from other instruction.	Academic year.
Other			

Figure 2-2a. A sample IEP of the type that might be found in a school setting.

| SHORT TERM INSTRUCTIONAL GOALS | | | | Gregory A. Thompson |

Balanced Goals 1. Cognitive/Academic 2. Social/Service 3. Physical Modality   Teachers _____
4. Emotional/Spiritual 5. Performing Arts

Short Term Goals	Date Initiated	Instructional Strategies	Resources Methods & Person	Evaluation	Date Mastered
Academic: Math	9/15	Present academic achievement goals should be challenged at his level. 1. Should demonstrate competence in general math. 2. Begin introductory to Algebra. Not held back or pushed forward unrealistically	District G&T Program	State Ach. Tests	
Social/Service:	9/15	Tends to give undue time and effort to music. Increase positive interaction with peers and adults in normal settings to decrease isolationist behavior.	Provide situations where he interacts with others as a member of small & large groups.	Observation of behavior	
Emotional/Spiritual:	9/15	Interaction with Character Models needed.	5th grade honor student with well balanced outlook. Resource Adults	Observation	

Balanced Goals 1. Cognitive/Academic   2. Social/Service 3. Physical Modality   Teachers_____
2. Emotional/Spiritual 5. Performing Arts

Short Term Goals	Date Initiated	Instructional Strategies	Resources Methods & Person	Evaluation	Date
Physical:	9/15	Continue placement in normal P.E. program.	P.E. teachers DUSO program	Observation	
Performing Arts:	9/15	Needs instruction beyond that offered by home or district teachers, however, not at the expense of social and emotional being.	University or College specialist close by may be considered.	To be tested at each new level.	

Figure 2-2b. A sample school IEP, continued.

The first page of the IEP can serve as an accountability form in itself in that it shows at a glance who the child is, where the child is in terms of performance and a balanced program, who is helping the child, and how the child is achieving — results and recommendations. Other parts of the IEP should include long-term goals and short-term goals. The long-term goals might reflect proposed placement of the child in regards to the regular classroom or special classes, special schools, or with special resource people, and the estimated duration of the project or goal. The next part of the IEP is concerned with short-term learning goals. Short-term goals should be identified with each area of balance in mind. The student should help in selecting and establishing the specific plans of action within each area of the IEP. With the help of the IEP consultants, the child can propose or agree to some instructional strategies such as the resources, methods, or persons to be involved, the means of accountability, and the dates and duration of each plan. If all goes well, the student should feel that this is his/her own plan and a good one. With a positive attitude and commitment on the part of the student, the program should be successful.

Periodic preplanned stewardship interviews should occur between the student and teacher or other partner, in which goals are reviewed, progress evaluated, adjustments made, and the next plan of action established. Figures 2-1 and 2-2 are merely examples of IEP forms that could be effectively utilized. It is important to remember that in regard to the Five Principles of Supervision and the implementing of personal stewardship, the most ideal plan is that all significant parties eventually have the right to develop their own IEP detailing their own perceived stewardship and expressed in their own style. For someone not accustomed to personal stewardship plans and to goal setting, it helps to have sample models and consultants.

While looking at Figures 2-1 and 2-2, the questions to ask regarding the gifted child are who is setting the goals; with whom are they establishing the goals, or to whom are they reporting; do the goals encourage a well-balanced development; are the long-range and short-range goals realistic and appropriate for meeting the needs of this child; how and when are the goals to be completed; and what will be the means of accountability? The teacher can use the examples in Figures 2-1 and 2-2 and P.L. 94 — 142 IEP goals as a basis for understanding and for guiding students in establishing their own learning goals. Once again, the teacher should always start by teaching correct principles and then encouraging the child to establish his or her own IEP or set of goals in harmony with the correct principles taught.

The student who is in on the planning of his or her own IEP feels better about the plan, will more readily make personal commitment, and will more likely follow through with the goals set. When the goals are reasonable and realistic, the student can feel enthusiastic and comfortable with them. The IEP is a means of protecting the student's agency and stewardship, too. No child likes to be told every little thing to do, it is an insult to the the child's intelligence and capabilities. Instead, most children like to be given a task with the expectations clearly understood and then be given the freedom and trust to accomplish the task. Sometimes the student is obviously functioning in violation of the principles taught. Therefore, the teacher needs to take time to kindly and respectfully reteach the principles, rules, and/or expectations and to clarify the roles and stewardships involved. This should be done on a Win-Win basis, where the teacher does not exercise unrighteous dominion over the student but tries to establish rapport and then works out the problem to mutually beneficial and satisfactory results. Good feelings can foster good results.

SUMMARY

When a person grasps the meaning and significance of stewardship, he has found a fundamental principle of growth and of personal development. The Five Principles of Supervision

1. The teacher teaches correct principles.
2. The student sets goals in harmony with the correct principles.
3. The teacher prepares to be thought of as a source of help.
4. The student asks for help and the teacher gives help.
5. The student gives an accounting of his stewardship.

help teachers to develop a nice balance between guiding the learning of a child (the mastery of objectives and skills) and respecting and supporting that child's free agency. It is no longer a matter of pushing and forcing but of establishing workable goals in partnership with the student, helping him or her to meet his or her own stated needs and goals. It fosters good feelings and is encouraging to both teacher and student. Understanding stewardship roles will also support cooperation in education.

Balance is essential to mental health and to a well-rounded child who has a comfortable self-concept and sense of purpose in life. Each child should be encouraged to maintain balance in the areas of cognitive/intellectual development, social/service needs, physical health, and spiritual/character development. Balanced programs should be individual and purposeful.

Behavioral management is a matter of helping the child to manage his or her own behavior. Reality Therapy, the Win-Win plan, and the Five Steps to Remediation (Recognition, Remorse, Restitution, Resolve, Refrain) are tools to help teachers and students to find workable solutions to problems.

Much can be learned from current laws such as P.L. 94-142 that have emphasized the need for special help for the exceptional child. He has the right

1. To be admitted appropriately into a public school program
2. To be shown fairness in testing
3. To attend a program in the least restrictive environment
4. To have an Individualized Educational Plan (IEP) designed for his needs
5. To be protected by procedural safeguards and parent involvement with certain specified rights

These legislative safeguards for the handicapped support individualization and personal progress, also strong needs of the gifted.

An IEP is a valuable means for helping the gifted/talented student to develop personal stewardship, self-discipline, and effective learning goals. When used properly, it is an excellent tool and a comfortable way for the student to progress and to develop. The secret of implementing wise and workable goals is to base them on the principles of balance and to aid the student in considering each area of balance in setting his or her own developmental goals.

PART II

PART Two is composed of three chapters: "Thought Processes," "Intervention Considerations," and "Exceptional Populations of Gifted Children." Each of these chapters is designed to give foundation considerations and a perceptual base from which programs for the gifted may be more appropriately developed.

Chapter Three, "Thought Processes," reviews the perceptual system in a concise manner. Volumes have been written on perception, and much can be learned about this sensory and cognitive domain. For the purposes of this text in aiding teachers of the gifted child, an overview of perception is important, for each child will receive information individually and often uniquely in terms of past experience and present knowledge, needs, and feelings. Thought processes are the foundation of interpersonal relationships; therefore, Chapter Three covers some interesting teacher-child relationships that are founded on cognitive processes. Memory is introduced as another important part of thinking processes, for teachers can greatly facilitate learning in the child if good memory devices are utilized. The self-concept is a crucial factor in the healthy functioning of a gifted child, and this thought process is also explored. In this chapter, consideration is also given to language, thinking styles, and creative thought processes. An understanding of thought processes is essential for the teacher of the gifted and talented child. Such understanding places the teacher in a position to more wisely guide stewardship and more effectively establish learning programs founded on sound principles.

Chapter Four, which explores "Intervention Considerations," is a key chapter in providing many alternatives and options to teachers and administrators as they develop educational programs for the gifted and talented child. Conventional strategies such as acceleration approaches, ability grouping, enrichment, independent study programs, mainstreaming cluster grouping, mentorships, and pull-out programs are discussed. The ecosystem of program development is explored, and many suggestions regarding the child, the environment, and the evaluation of achievement are considered. Teacher traits, scheduling the curriculum, and parent support are also taken into consideration. Excellent suggestions are given to teachers in encouraging greater productivity in their gifted students, and some interesting dos and don'ts are proposed. The very important precepts of parent stewardship and responsibility for their own children and the helpful approaches that may be taken at home are the concluding emphases within this chapter.

Chapter Five focuses on "Exceptional Populations of Gifted Children" such as preschool, handicapped, culturally different, and underachievers. Many people incorrectly assume that a disability is total or that in essence if a child has a disability in one area then it affects all others. Many believe that physically handicapped individuals are mentally handicapped as well. This is a false assumption, for the handicapped can run the range of intelligence and abilities. In fact, while many of the handicapped may have physical disabilities, they can also have great gifts and talents. Throughout Chapter Five, abilities and disabilities of exceptional populations are considered. Suggestions are offered for helping those exceptional populations of gifted rise to their potential and be recognized for the capable contributors that they may become.

CHAPTER THREE

THOUGHT PROCESSES

Can you answer the following questions?

1. What is the perceptual system?
2. What are six of the human sensory receptors?
3. Can you give an example of selective perception?
4. Why is comprehending figure-ground relationships important in learn-ing?
5. How can understanding Piaget's stages of intellectual development be helpful to a teacher of gifted children?
6. How do thought processes and attitudes affect interpersonal relation-ships and vice versa?
7. What are some key principles facilitating memory?
8. How does Erikson's Eight Stages of Social Development relate to thought processes?
9. What is the difference between spontaneous and reflective thinking? What is the difference between convergent and divergent thinking?
10. How does language relate to thought processes?

TO understand a gifted child's thought processes many factors must be considered, such as perception and the various facets of perceptual thought, and the child's intellectual development, interpersonal relationships, memory functions, self-concept, thinking styles, and language patterns. From birth each individual child functions with a unique set of traits, needs, and feel-ings. All children have commonalities, but all children also differ from one another. What motivates one may or may not motivate another. How one per-ceives life and circumstances may be very different from how another does. The life tempo, thought processes, and growth patterns can differ remarkably from child to child. To expect the same of all children is faulty reasoning.

PERCEPTION

Perception is a complex thinking process that has been defined as the process of organizing raw data obtained through the senses in the vestibular proprioceptive area of the brain, which then interprets its meaning (Kephart, 1960). Figure 3-1 should help clarify the component parts of the perceptual system and their functions within the perceptual system.

Perceptual System

System	Physical Action	Sense Receptor	Available Stimuli	Information Obtained
(Basic Orientation)	(Posture Movement)	(Optical Organs, Kinesthetic Receptors, Vestibular Organs)	(Gravity, Acceleration, Movement)	(Forces of Gravity Push and Pull)
Homeostasis:	Internal Equilibrium	Receptors in the Tracheobronchial Area, Thermal-Sensitive Neurons in the Hypothalamus, Carotid Sinus Receptors, Pressor Sensory Cells in the Vestibular Nuclei, Depressor Sensory Endings in Walls of the Intrapericardial Vessels and Pulmonary Veins	Temperature, Pressure, Oxygen, Carbon Dioxide, etc.	Comfort, Body Adjustment to Heat and Cold, Physical Well-being
Visual:	Looking	Eyes and the Ocular System	Light, the Portion of the Electro-Magnetic Spectrum to Which the Retina is Sensitive	Information About Objects, Size, Shape, Location, Distance, Color Texture
Auditory:	Listening	Auditory Canal, Middle Ear, Cochlea	Acoustic Pressure Waves	Nature and Location of Acoustics, Sources
Olfactory:	Smelling	Chemo-Receptors, Nose	Chemical Composition of Inspired Air	Nature of Odors
Savor:	Tasting	Mouth	Chemical Composition and Thermal State of Ingested Matter	Nutritive and Palatable Attributes of Ingested Materials
Haptic:	Touching	Skin, Joints, Muscles, Tendons, Ligaments	Stretching of Muscle Fibers, Configuration of Joints, Deformation of Tissue, Thermal and Structural Qualities of Matter	Contact with the Ground Material and Object States Identified, Mechanical Encounters

Figure 3-1. The perceptual system's component parts and their functions.

Even those who study perception are not in complete agreement as to its function. It is not an overt event subject to direct observation. Perception is selective.

Selective Perception

Baller and Charles (1968) stated that ·

An individual's expectations control his attention and determine what he will notice and respond to and the sort of response he will make. Out of his living and learning he develops his system of expectations. The more learning he has acquired — that is to say, the more he has been forced by his experiences to modify his responses — the more expanded and refined his system of expectations becomes. (P. 103)

In other words, a gifted child may see, hear, feel, and notice those things which are relevant to his/her needs, feelings, and associations of the moment. For example, when a child is very hungry, objects, language, and circumstances are readily perceived in relationship to food.

Volumes have been written on such perceptual properties as figure-ground

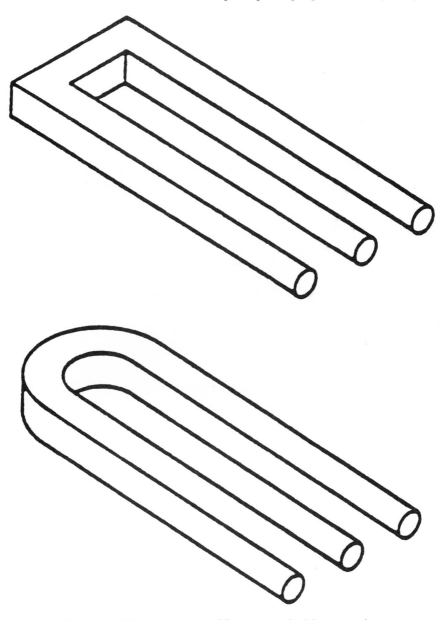

Figure 3-2. Classic examples of figure-ground misinterpretations.

relationships, proximity, similarity, symmetry, continuity, and closure. A brief review of these perceptual occurrences may provide helpful insight into the thought processes of the gifted child.

Figure-ground Relationships

Comprehending *figure-ground relationships* is important to perceiving reality and to learning. This is a unifying principle that gives sense and purpose to that which is seen. Uncertainty of figure identity is a frequent problem in everyday life. Perception is so affected by past experience and present needs and feelings that important visual cues can easily be missed, as can be noted in the variety of eyewitness reports that may be given at the time of an accident. Classic examples of figure-ground misinterpretation can be seen in Figure 3-2 and Figure 3-3, in which it is possible to see either the light or the dark region as the object pictured.

Figure 3-3. Another classic figure-ground problem. It is possible to see two different images in this figure.

Another example of figure-ground comprehension is seen in Figure 3-4, which shows one of the "Street" figures (Street, 1931). If one looks long enough one will see a familiar figure in what initially appears as a meaningless collection of black and white patches; when one does see the figure one will have little trouble seeing it again.

One way to facilitate perception is to provide the viewer with an appropriate mental set or advance organizer. For example, Figure 3-4 might be more easily perceived if the viewer is told that it is a scene familiar at a race track.

Figure 3-4. One of the "Street" figures. A familiar figure may appear in what initially seems a meaningless collection of black and white patches.

Proximity

Perception is affected by the proximity of objects. Items are often perceived as in horizontal, vertical, or curved planes in·terms of proximity (*see* Figures 3-5 and 3-6).

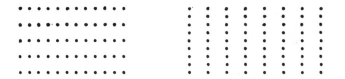

Figure 3-5. The relative proximity of objects to each other alters perception of them.

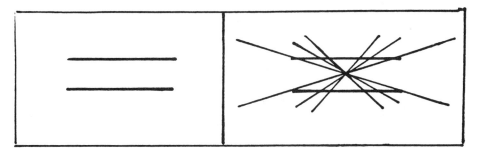

Figure 3-6. The Herling Illusion. The two horizontal lines in each panel are straight and parallel, but in the panel on the right they appear bowed in opposite directions.

Symmetry

Other things being equal, similar items tend to be grouped together perceptually. In other words, in a random pattern of objects or among objects spaced with equal distance, there is a tendency to perceive similar items in relationship to one another and as family groups. This may be noted in Figure 3-7.

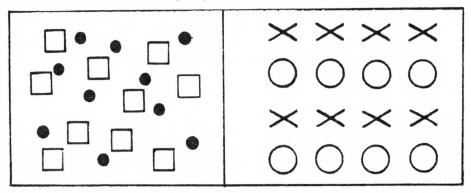

Figure 3-7. In a random or an evenly spaced pattern of objects there is a tendency to group together similar objects.

Continuity

Our visual system seems to prefer good continuity, lines and contours that continue smoothly along their original courses. This is a powerful organizational principle that may function even when up against prior experience. An example of this is the camouflage used by some insects, which are seen as part of the twig rather than as separate entities. This principle has been applied to military camouflage, also.

Closure

Another perceptual principle, which is actually part of good continuity, is closure. One tends to complete visually the contour of an item even if parts are missing (*see* Figure 3-8).

Figure 3-8. Examples of the principle of closure, the visual completion of the contours of an object even though parts of it are missing.

Interpretation or misinterpretation of facts based on proximity, symmetry, continuity, or closure can affect one's understanding or perception of objects, relationships, or events. Some examples of such perceptual problems are trying to find a needle mixed in with straight pins, seeking to locate a small news item within a printed page, or assuming similar characteristics for all deaf or blind people (or gifted).

Depth perception, motion, stability, adaptation, and many other factors could be considered in a review of perception. The important point to remem-

SPOT THE 10 DIFFERENCES

Can you spot 10 differences between the two pictures?

Figure 3-9. One popular game based on the complexity of perception. Courtesy of Let's Play Games, Globe International Inc.

ber is that each individual perceives so differently because of past experience and learning styles that it is at times amazing that class members can learn the same topic when taught as a group.

MATCH THE SHADOW

**Study the bowlers numbered 1-7 very carefully
One of them matches the shadow bowler lettered A exactly.**

Figure 3-10. Another perception game. Only one of the bowlers numbered 1 through 7 exactly matches the shadow bowler lettered A. Courtesy of Let's Play Games, Globe International Inc.

Many puzzles and games are based on the complexity of perception, as demonstrated in Figures 3-9, 3-10, and 3-11. In each of these puzzles one needs to be highly discerning perceptually and also needs to become more discriminating in terms of figure-ground relationships, proximity, symmetry, continuity, and closure.

Figure 3-11. Another perception game. Coloring all the sections with dots in them reveals a hidden picture. Courtesy of Let's Play Games, Globe International Inc.

INTELLECTUAL DEVELOPMENT

Another important component in thought process is that of intellectual development. Piaget (1950) defines broad classifications of children's intellectual processes at different levels of development from infancy to adulthood. Piaget's four main periods are as follows:

1. *Sensory-Motor Intelligence (0-2 Years)* — Children conceptualize the world through sensory impressions and motor manipulations. This is a time of permanence, schemas, and imitation.
2. *Preoperational Stage (2-7 Years)* — The child can think of objects and events in their absence, but does not as yet possess a system of rules by which the ideas can be manipulated. Key issues: Conservation, egocentrism, moral reality.
3. *Concrete Operations (7-11 Years)* — A system of rules is now established but overly bound to concrete reality. Children are now moral relativists capable of convergent thought.
4. *Formal Operations (11 Years and older)* — Genuine symbolic and abstract modes of thought are attained. Reasoning and conceptual judgement are active. Abstractions, divergent thinking, and creative efforts are more natural and prevalent.

While gifted children may for the most part be ahead of schedule chronologically in view of Piaget's intellectual stage theory, the teacher is wise to consider the developmental stage in which a child is in fact functioning, so that the teacher's expectations may be realistic and fair in terms of individual student thought processes and abilities. This should also be considered in terms of the areas of balance. For example, a six-year-old child may be accelerated in problem-solving skills and may be functioning on a level of concrete or formal operation in terms of abstract modes of thought, but the same child may be on a preoperational and egocentric level socially. Developmental levels will differ from child to child and particularly within a given child. A wise teacher will get to know each child and will be flexible in terms of expectations and assumptions of abilities until all areas of the child's development have been tested or evaluated. A challenge for teachers is how to teach the whole child as development progresses at different speeds depending on the talents and capabilities or inadequacies of a given student.

INTERPERSONAL RELATIONSHIPS

Thought processes are influenced by interpersonal relationships and vice versa; therefore, the teacher of the gifted child has some special challenges regarding that child's perception of him or her. It is important that a child perceive the teacher as a source of help. The child's perception of the teacher can be based on several factors. Rogers (1961) poses some interesting questions that can apply to these personal relationships between the teacher and the gifted child.

Can the teacher be perceived as trustworthy, dependable, or consistent in some deep sense?

According to Rogers (1961), teachers might feel that if they keep appointments, respect confidentiality, and act consistently they should be thought of as trustworthy, but he found that it involves more than these qualities. To act accepting and in fact to feel annoyed, skeptical, or some other nonaccepting feeling is sure to be perceived by the student as inconsistent or untrustworthy. The teacher need not be rigidly consistent but should be dependably real. To be congruent is the important principle. It is important that the teacher be aware of his or her own feelings and attitudes and be honest with them. This is a reality that children perceive as dependable.

Can the teacher be expressive enough that what he or she is will be communicated unambiguously to the child?

When the teacher is striving to be accepting but actually feeling annoyance toward the child, this can be communicated as a contradictory message, creating ambivalence. The words are giving one message, but in subtle ways the annoyance felt by the teacher is communicated. The child thus feels confusion and distrust, though he or she may be unaware of what is causing the difficulty. As Rogers (1961) stated, "If I can form a helping relationship to myself — if I can be sensitively aware of and acceptant toward my own feelings — then the likelihood is great that I can form a helping relationship toward another" (P. 51).

Can the teacher experience positive attitudes towards this child — attitudes of warmth, caring, liking, interest, respect?

It is not easy. Rogers (1961) indicates that a teacher may be afraid that if he or she freely experiences positive feelings toward the child he or she may be trapped by the feelings. They may lead to demands, or the teacher may become disappointed in his or her trust and the outcomes he or she fears. As a reaction, many teachers may tend to build up distance between themselves and others — aloofness, a "professional attitude," or an impersonal relationship. The teacher needs to come to terms with these feelings and to learn that it is safe to care and to relate to the gifted child with positive feelings.

Can the teacher be strong enough as a person to be separate from the child? Can he or she be a sturdy respector of his or her own personal feelings and needs as well as the child's?

The teacher needs to acknowledge his or her own feelings and if need be express them as separate from the child's. It is important not to be downcast by the child's depression, frightened by the child's fears, or engulfed by the child's dependency. A teacher needs to be personally strong enough not to be destroyed by the child's anger, taken over by the child's needs or dependence, or enslaved by the child's love. Teachers need to exist separately with feelings and rights of their own. When teachers can freely feel this strength of being separate and capable persons, then they can let themselves go much more deeply into understanding and accepting the child.

Is the teacher secure enough within himself or herself to permit the child his separateness?
Can the teacher permit the child to be what he is — honest or deceitful, infantile or adult,
despairing or overconfident? Can the child be given the freedom to be?

Some teachers feel that children should always follow their teacher's advice,
or remain somewhat dependent, or mold themselves after the teacher. Less well
adjusted teachers may demand more conformity and modeling after themselves. The converse is also true. The better adjusted the teacher, the better interaction with the child and the more freedom for the child to develop
according to his or her own individual life-style and personality.

Can the teacher enter fully into the world of the gifted child's feelings and personal meanings
and see these as the child does?

According to Rogers (1961), it is difficult to step into the child's private
world so completely as to lose all desire to evaluate or judge it. Can the teacher
enter so sensitively that he or she does not trample on meanings that are precious to the child? Can the teacher sense the child's world so accurately that he
or she catches not only the meanings of the child's experience but also those
meanings which are only implicit, which the child sees only dimly or as confused? Many children seek fervently for understanding and empathy. Although
there is a strong temptation for the teacher to "set the student straight" or to
point out the error in thinking, much can be gained if the child can see the
teacher as an understanding partner and an empathetic guide and facilitator.

Can the teacher be acceptant of each characteristic of this child that is presented?

Can a teacher accept a child as he or she is? Can this attitude of acceptance
be communicated? Or is the child received conditionally? When a teacher's attitude is conditional, then the child has difficulty changing or growing in those
areas in which he or she is not fully received. A teacher may find that he or she
has been frightened or threatened in some aspect by the feelings of the child. A
teacher is more helpful if he or she can come to terms with personal feelings
and rejections.

Can the teacher act with sufficient sensitivity in the relationship that teacher behavior will
not be perceived by the child as a threat?

Rogers (1961) has stated that if a child can be freed as completely as possible from external threat, then the child can begin to experience and to deal with
the internal feelings and conflicts that he or she may find threatening within
the psychological and physical atmosphere that surrounds him or her. Obviously this freedom from threat will make a great difference in the child's
learning and development.

Can a teacher free a child from the threat of external evaluation?

In almost every phase of life can be found the rewards and punishments of
external judgements. "That's good," "that's naughty," "that's worth an A," and
"that's a failure" are phrases used to correct these judgements, a part of life from
infancy to old age. They do have a certain usefulness, but according to Rogers
(1961) they do not make for personal growth, and hence they are not a part of a

helping relationship. Curiously enough, a positive evaluation can be as threatening as a negative one, since to inform a child that he or she is good implies the right also to tell the child he or she is bad. The more a relationship can be free of judgement and evaluation, the more this will permit the child to reach the point where he/she recognizes that the locus of evaluation, the center of responsibility, lies within the self. Remember that the first step in teaching stewardship is to teach correct principles, and the next step is to trust and leave children free to do things their own way within the framework of wise principles (rules, goals, etc.).

Can the teacher meet the child as a person who is in the process of becoming, or is the teacher bound by the child's past and his or her own past?

Many times labels and prejudgements can limit the child's development in the relationship between teacher and child. According to Rogers (1961), if the teacher can see that the relationship is an opportunity to reinforce all that the child is and that the child exists with potentialities worth pursuing, then the child tends to act in ways that support this hypothesis. This becomes a "self-fulfilling prophecy." Teachers need to work on their preconceived attitudes and ideas of the child (based on past history) and to recognize the qualities and potentialities of the child at any given age, time, situation, or relationship.

In conclusion, it is the teacher who *lives* the principles of balance and stewardship, who has his or her own life and feelings in order and can perceive proper roles and stewardship responsibilities, who is in the best position to teach a child to develop these same qualities. If the child can feel safe and comfortable in the presence of the teacher and if the child can feel that it is all right to be himself or herself to be accepted as an individual, and to be given the trust and belief necessary to perform and pursue goals in his or her own unique and creative way, then the school environment can be perceived as a place of freedom and productivity.

MEMORY

Our individual perceptual world is not chaotic but is an organized, coherent whole. It makes sense to the individual and has been "programmed" by him or her for meaningful relationship to other bits of information. This leads to *memory*, the individual's information storage system. Attention needs to be given to short- and long-term memory systems. For example, when looking up a telephone number a person might remember the number long enough to complete the call, and then the memory fades; it is no longer part of conscious experience. If the information is meaningful to the individual and perceived as of relative value for future use, it may be incorporated into long-term memory through rehearsal, association with other knowns, and direct and indirect application. All elements of communication are dependent upon memory. A person could not speak, write, listen, or comprehend effectively without memory.

Two key principles that facilitate memory are *recognition* and *attention* (Baller and Charles, 1968). The process of *recognition* is said to be interactive. The ability to recognize an item depends on associating its features with prior learning. As discussed earlier, perception is selective, and for something to enter memory for short-term or long-term storage, *attention* must be given to it. A teacher can do several things to draw attention to an item. For example, a new or unusual teaching approach may be used to introduce a new topic; the teacher may utilize sense perception by introducing the topic with music, a fragrance, bright colors, or new textures, to draw attention to it.

Rehearsal also helps in retention. To repeat information can help a person to keep that information for short-term or long-term periods. *Imagery* is another useful retention device. If the individual can picture the item, especially in association with a concrete situation, it can be retained longer. *Encoding* and *decoding* are important processes in memory, too. When material is taken in and encoded verbally or visually, it is organized into meaningful *associations*. Later, decoding is facilitated through associating familiar items and easily remembered relationships.

There is a great value in *organizing* what is to be learned. Placing topics in categories, in order of priority, or in alphabetical relationship can aid retention.

Mnemonic Devices are rule-oriented systems designed to improve recall. They can be easy or complex. Most students learn mnemonic devices in the process of their schooling. Some examples are as follows:

Rhyme Mnemonics — "Thirty days hath September, April, June, and November. . . ."

Acronym — First letter mnemonic. The first letter from each set of items to be learned is used to make up a new word. For example, the Great Lakes — Huron, Ontario, Michigan, Erie and Superior — form the word *HOMES*.

Acrostics — A sentence mnemonic. A sentence is made up using a word with the first letter of the item to be learned; SPWBOT becomes "Some People Write Better On Tables." Another variation of the acrostic is to place the information to be learned in a meaningful sentence. For example, people confused about daylight savings time have quoted the thought, "Spring forward and fall backward."

Pegwords — The process in using pegwords is to attach a list item with a memory peg. The pegs, previously learned associations based on rhyme, are one-bun, two-shoe, three-tree, four-door, five-hive, six-sticks, seven-heaven, eight-gate, nine-line, ten-hen. If the first item on a list is toothpaste, picture toothpaste coming out of a bun. If the next is shampoo, picture a head of hair and shampoo flowing out of a shoe, etc. The pegs serve as retrieval clues or cues. When retrieval of the list is needed, let imagery take over and go forward or backward with the rhymes.

Loci Method — Locations or places serve as memory pegs. Most common is the use of the individual's own house, or a local store, or even the neighborhood — whatever is a natural and close series of locations. These can be numbered or ordered for a logical starting and finishing place. Images of the items to be remembered are placed in each location as one walks through mentally. Items should be placed specifically in each location — on or under furniture or in a silly situation within the room.

Teaching gifted children mnemonic skills can be very beneficial to them. First, it teaches the student that the ability to learn and remember large amounts of information can be an acquired skill. Second, mnemonics are fun and interesting to use. While some gifted students are fast learners and can retain material very well on their own, all students can benefit from the fun and comfortable use of mnemonics.

There are many other retention methods available, and gifted students can profit from learning and using these good study and research skills. Listed below are a few examples.

Flow charts — This tool is derived from computer programming, in which the programmer maps out a pictorial view of the flow of logic. Flow charts can help a student in productive thinking as well as recall.

Learning trees — While a student is listening to a lesson or gathering material, the facts can be organized into a learning tree, which can help him or her to identify the main points and learn the key principles involved.

Time management practices — By prioritizing daily objectives and time allotments, giving them their rightful value and allocation in the day, the student can accomplish more, feel more in control of his or her life, and remember tasks and duties more readily.

Teachers of the gifted can also help their students attend to and retain information by making that information meaningful and relevant to the students, by helping them to organize and group associative information; by using advance organizers wisely, by allowing practice and rehearsal, and by helping the students to apply the principles that they have learned.

Figure 3-12. A sample flow chart for a decision about what to have for lunch. A = a peanut butter sandwich, B = a tuna sandwich, and C = the available options.

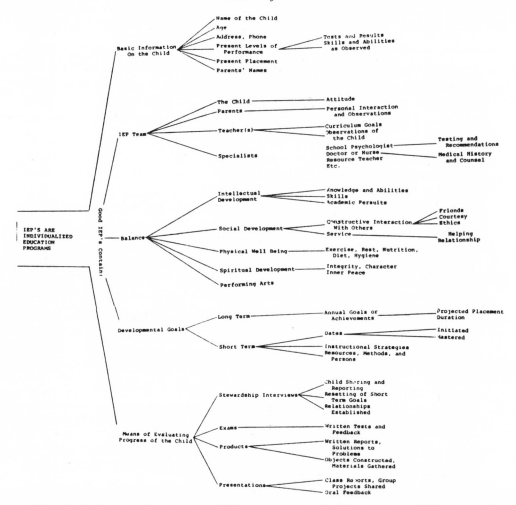

Figure 3-13. A sample learning tree. This one organizes the information on IEP's presented earlier in the text.

The teaching technique *show, discuss, apply*, and *evaluate* is another tool for learning and retention and is a sound plan that works well in most teaching situations. A wise teacher may also use *discovery learning* — encouraging the child to discover principles for himself or herself. In this process a teacher will bring in motivating materials or topics and then encourage students to seek out the facts or processes through personal research and exploration. Or a teacher may use *inquiry learning*, in which students are invited and motivated to ask questions. One of the more effective methods of inquiry learning is experienced when a teacher brings in an object, word, or story, and students are instructed to ask questions that can be answered yes or no by the teacher. The teacher will then indicate when they are getting "warm" (close to the answer) or when they are indeed on the right mental track. Such involvement exercises will greatly facilitate learning and retention.

SELF-CONCEPT

A child's thought processes are greatly influenced by his or her self-concept. This self-evaluation and attitude of one's abilities and disabilities sets the limits on behavior. An individual's self-concept is developed from birth. A baby learns that the world is a friendly or hostile place by how his or her needs are met or not met by parents and family. Development of self-concept can be viewed from different stages in a child's life. Erikson (1950) describes these growth and identity stages in his Eight Stages of Social Development, as follows:

1. *Trust vs. Mistrust.* Trust is developed through the infant's experience of having basic needs met. Adequate care and genuine affection can lead to the child's perceiving his/her world as safe and dependable. Inadequate care and inconsistent attention to needs lead the child to feel rejection, fear, and suspicion.

2. *Autonomy vs. Doubt.* Two to Three Years. As children begin to develop in terms of bones and muscles, they begin to reach out and experiment. If children are permitted and encouraged by parents and family members to try to do what they are able to at their own pace and in their own way, they will develop a sense of autonomy. If parents or teachers are impatient and do too many things for the child he/she will doubt his ability to deal with the environment.

3. *Initiative vs. Guilt.* Four to Five Years. At this time the child is beginning to use language, to move about, and to try new things. If children are given freedom to initiate activities, if teachers take time to answer questions, their tendencies toward exploration will be expanded, and they will reach out and try things on their own. If children are held back or restricted and made to feel that their activities and questions are of little value or a nuisance, they will feel guilty about doing things on their own.

4. *Industry vs. Inferiority.* Six to Eleven Years. At this time children leave childhood dreams and hopes behind and move into the school years. As children enter school there are new demands and a new way of life imposed upon them. If they are allowed to try new things, if they are encouraged to finish what they start, if their efforts are acknowledged and found to be worthy, the children will feel industrious and will feel that they are of worth. If what the children try to do is treated as bothersome, inadequate, or inferior, if they are derided, inferiority will be the result.

5. *Identity vs. Role Confusion.* Twelve to Eighteen Years. This is the time when growing and developing adolescents face physiological and emotional upheavals and changes within themselves. It is also a time when academically they are getting into a lot of abstractions, there is a lot of depth in their thinking processes, and in the things that are happening at school they find themselves confused about their roles. They take a look at the adult tasks

ahead, and the expectations are a bit different. They find that as they separate from parents and families and become independent individuals they become confused as to who and what they are. Young adolescents need a lot of love and support, so that they might feel that they are accepted and so that they can come to terms with who and what they are and where they're going. They need to feel good solid values as a foundation of their lives. If they're unable to establish a sense of stability, personal worth, and personal identity, role confusion results.

6. *Intimacy vs. Isolation.* Young Adulthood. Emerging from this resolution of self-identity, the young person is now ready to reach out and establish close and intimate relationships with others. Those who are able to do this find that they have deep, enduring friendships and are able to build a foundation for marriage where they are willing to give and receive, to trust and interact, with another individual. Those who are unable to establish this experience isolation. These individuals isolate themselves from others and dare not trust, dare not establish a close, intimate relationship.

7. *Generativity vs. Self-Absorption.* Middle Age. At this time individuals have moved to the point of guiding the next generation and passing on the strengths and insights that they have. Those who are able to accomplish this feel a fulfillment and self-satisfaction in strengthening others, in reaching out and helping to train those coming up. Those who are unable to do this become self-absorbed. They turn in and only focus on their own lives and their own needs.

8. *Integrity vs. Despair.* Old Age. At this time of development, persons reaching into the later years of life may experience an integrity, a serenity, a feeling of accomplishment. They have come to terms and are at peace with their own lives and with that which has gone before, recognizing strengths and weaknesses but still accepting this and still growing and reaching out to others. Or, having turned in during that earlier period, they may feel remorse or regret at having a wasted or unhappy life, and they may go into despair. An older person can experience either of these, a personal integrity and an inner serenity or a feeling of despair and frustrated discouragement.

As a person goes through these stages experiencing the many trials and challenges of life, his or her actions and perceptions in relationship to others begin to make up that person's self-concept. It is important for the teacher of the gifted child to be able to understand social development in order to help children to progress comfortably and gain good feelings about themselves. Much of self-concept emanates from the home and earlier experiences within the family, but later, as the child enters the school system, significant relationships occur with classmates and with the teacher. Each stage seems of importance to thought processes, for if children can feel good about themselves and can feel that theirs is a comfortable and trustworthy environment, then they can reach out and progress stage by stage. If children can feel autonomy in the situation — that their efforts are worthwhile and acceptable by the teacher — much growth in self-worth can be experienced. Thought processes, perception, motivation, and application of problem-solving skills are all dependent on self-concept. Teachers and other leaders must be aware of this very sensitive area, for if children can feel comfortable and secure within themselves they will reach out and try new things and experience tremendous self-actualization and success in their efforts. The study of the self-fulfilling prophecy, *Pygmalion in the Classroom* (Rosenthal and Jacobson, 1968), illustrated how important it is for teachers to have proper and effective expectations of each of their students. Teacher expectations will be reflected in how students both perform and perceive themselves. Of course, this Pygmalion effect can be for good or for ill, and consequently it is a great challenge to teachers to keep realistic and positive expectations in order to strengthen and uplift the children under their care.

LANGUAGE

A treatise on thought processes should not exclude the role of language. Many psychologists (MacDougal, 1913; Hymes, 1964; Greenfield and Bruner, 1971) maintain that symbolic thought is impossible without language; others believe that language is merely the means by which thought is conveyed. It is the opinion of these authors that language plays an essential role in thought processes and that the greater the facility of the gifted child with vocabulary, spoken and written language, and the ability to construct new words or thoughts, the more progressive and abstract can be the learning and expression of the child.

Language is creative and rule governed. It is amazing that a person can speak and understand an unlimited number of sentences never heard before. This is because rules of grammar and meaning are learned, permitting an infinite quantity and arrangement of sentences to be spoken and understood. The skills for language — rules, structure, syntax, and meaning — are generally learned in the first few years of life.

Some gifted children learn language far more rapidly than others, and with language as an essential tool of thought they progress faster in learning and understanding. It is not surprising that language arts are given such emphasis in school. All children need language skills not only for their thinking and expressive processes but also in order to develop essential reading skills and have access to literature and written materials.

THINKING STYLES

Tied in with language and thought processes are thinking styles of the individual. Some children are *spontaneous thinkers* who think and process information rapidly. These are students who quickly raise their hands in response to a question and who have a thoughtful answer readily available. Other students are *reflective thinkers* and require more time to ponder and consider the alternatives or meanings of a question. Teachers need to be aware that students with both types of thinking processes will be in the classroom. Consideration and courtesy need to be rendered to each. It is also true that nearly every child will incorporate both thinking styles to some degree, depending on the circumstances, the comfort of the student in the social situation, and the complexity and familiarity of the material.

Two other types of thought processes are found in *convergent thinkers* and *divergent thinkers*. The *convergent thinkers* tend to bring things into order and to seek relationships. Their questions will be on-task, relevant, and usually very supportive of and insightful to the topic at hand. The *divergent thinkers* are the brainstormers. These individuals find that a question will cue associations that can run into very creative and innovative directions. Often their questions appear to be off-task and alien to the topic at hand.

A student can be both a convergent and a divergent thinker, depending on his or her situation, knowledge, and comfort at a given time. When in a comfortable setting with friends and trusted others, the student may be free to think more divergently, creatively, and spontaneously, while in a more formal or less comfortable setting a student may find it more expedient to think convergently and reflectively. Some of the gifted tend to fall more into one category than the other, and they should be guided to practice both thinking processes so that skills are developed for appropriate use of either.

CREATIVE THOUGHT

Torrance (1965) and Khatena (1982) recommend the following for aiding gifted children in creative efforts:

1. Give children opportunity to use what they learn as tools in their thinking and problem solving.
2. Provide them with a chance to share what they learn.
3. Show an interest in what they have learned.
4. Give them learning tasks of appropriate difficulty.
5. Accord them a chance to use their best abilities. Offer them the freedom to learn in their own preferred style.
6. Recognize and acknowledge many different kinds of excellence.
7. Provide genuine purpose and meaning to learning experiences.

Creative thinking and problem solving are essential to learning and living. (Processes of creative thinking are discussed in detail in Chapter Ten.) Daily a person faces a series of problems necessitating decisions and creative thoughts; examples range from such mundane things as what to wear, what to eat, and how to use one's time to more pressing matters such as how to deal with the requirements of one's stewardship and one's associates. The more experience children can have in making their own decisions and being responsible for the consequences thereof, the more independent and capable they can become.

Wise teachers will strive to remember the purpose of a problem-solving task or learning exercise for the child and not be confused by misplaced goals for perfect results or products. To illustrate this point there is the account of the teacher who introduced a project for making Easter baskets. Each child was given the necessary strips of paper for a basket with a handle. Careful instructions were given and each child was expected to follow the plan exactly. One creative thinker decided to cut up the "handle" strip of paper and glue it on the side for decoration. The teacher became upset and scolded the child for "ruining the basket." It is regrettable when teachers become rigid in their thinking and cannot allow for individual creative innovations. It is learning and growing that should be the goal in most teaching situations. Perfection and excellence come with practice, personal motivation, and experience.

To assist a gifted child in developing creative and problem-solving skills, the teacher should consider each of the topics within this chapter. Perception plays an important role in creative thought. How the child perceives events and objects around him or her will greatly affect his or her definition of the problem and consideration of alternative solutions. Intellectual development is essential to problem solving, for until a child is ready and has an intellectual base or foundation of information and learning skills the child cannot deal with abstract problems and their solutions. Interpersonal relationships have an impact on problem solving in that the child needs to know that others care and will be supportive and accepting of his or her contributions and ideas. Without this support the child will either turn in or give up. Recall and memory capacities help in problem solving and creative thinking, for they provide the intellectual matter with which and from which solutions are derived. The child's self-concept describes the limitations and abilities within which he or she lives, and it is very important that a gifted child have a healthy and realistic understanding of his or her strengths and inadequacies. A positive and enthusiastic attitude and concept of his or her abilities also strengthens the child's creative capacity and can facilitate problem solving. Language as a thinking tool and describer of situations, events, objects, and people is essential for problem solving.

In conclusion, each of the elements of thought processes discussed in this chapter serves as an important facet of learning and development and is woven into the warp and woof of cognition, thus forming the basis of the child's behavior.

To the teacher of the child with complex cognitive processes (which applies to all children), motivating or guiding the learning or growth of such a child may look like an overwhelming or even an impossible task. The solution to this challenge for the teacher lies in understanding development and thought processes and then applying this information within the framework of the Five Principles of Supervision, e.g. teaching correct principles, trusting the child to govern himself or herself by setting goals in harmony with the principles and rules perceived, being thought of as a teacher who is a source of help, knowledgeable, and willing to provide time and attention to the child, encouraging the child to seek help when it is needed, and establishing a means of feedback or reporting of the child's stewardship and accomplishments. If the teacher will pay the price of knowing each child as well as possible and becoming aware of the child's thought processes, and if he or she will remember the important principles of stewardship, then individual differences in children's thinking and learning styles can be maintained and treated with dignity and courtesy. Thus teachers may teach and students may learn.

CHAPTER FOUR

INTERVENTION CONSIDERATIONS — DEVELOPING EDUCATIONAL PROGRAMS FOR THE GIFTED AND TALENTED

Can you answer the following questions?

1. What is meant by acceleration?
2. Can you outline an acceleration program?
3. What are four different educational programs used for gifted and talented children?
4. What is the Enrichment Triad Model?
5. How practical is a mentorship program in the public school?
6. How effective are pull-out programs?
7. Can you outline the ecosystem of program development?
8. What are the planning steps to follow in developing an educational program for the gifted and talented?
9. What are some "dos" and "don'ts" for working with gifted children?
10. Can you outline the role of the parents in the development of educational programs?

EARLIER, in Chapter One, a brief review of educational programs for the gifted and talented was presented to illustrate how varied the programs are and how they have been met with mixed reviews as to their effectiveness. It appears that not only do programs vary in their approach but so do learners in their interests and abilities to grasp concepts, teachers in their types of presentation, and administrators in their methods of administering the programs to best serve a particular population. Over the years, educational programs have focused on prescribed content and age-level grouping. Recently, however, that focus has shifted toward assisting individual children in better utilizing their inherent abilities. This new approach has been stimulated by functional application of Guilford's Structure of the Intellect and emphasis on how the child learns and processes information (Meeker, 1969; Guilford, 1977). The challenge now is identifying the learning strengths and weaknesses of the individual child, locating interests and abilities, and then providing an appropriate environment in which to stimulate further those strengths and capitalize on those interests. Certainly adapting the curriculum to meet the child's needs is a shift from the more traditional approach and, the authors feel, more functional and easily applied by educational program planners.

The purpose of this chapter is to provide an overview of traditional and current approaches to educational program development for gifted and talented children. The chapter provides a discussion of existing programs, suggestions for how to begin a program and considerations for how teachers should be trained to work with these children and to interact with parents.

CONVENTIONAL INTERVENTION STRATEGIES

There have been many programs proposed for how best to serve the educational needs of gifted and talented children. Following is a discussion of several of the most commonly implemented programs. It is not the authors' intent to pass judgement as to the effectiveness of these programs, only to provide the reader with an introduction to and an overview of the literature related to each of these approaches. The programs include *acceleration, ability grouping, enrichment, independent study, mainstreaming or cluster grouping, mentorships,* and *pull-out time.*

Acceleration Strategies

Acceleration can take many forms. Most commonly acceleration is thought of in terms of having a child skip a grade or a sequence of curriculum. One positive aspect of acceleration is that research seems to support its utilization (Clark, 1979). The end result of acceleration is that the student completes the formal portion of his or her education in a reduced amount of time. It has been suggested that acceleration allows capable students to enter their careers sooner, resulting in more productivity while spending less time in school (Clark, 1979). Suggestions for acceleration are outlined by Stanley (1977) in his Study of Mathematically Precocious Youth (SMPY) project and should be considered when prescribing acceleration for gifted and talented children. These suggestions include

1. Entering school early, preferably at the kindergarten level.
2. Exiting from school early by skipping senior year to attend college courses.
3. Skipping grades, preferably the last one prior to moving from one school level to the next. For example, as the child moves from elementary to junior high, instead of moving from the sixth grade to the seventh, moving

from the sixth to the eighth or ninth grade.

4. Accelerating the course content or taking courses required in the senior year during grades 10 and 11.
5. Obtaining college credit upon entering college through board examinations or college departmental examinations to validate acquired learning.
6. Completing correspondence courses while in high school or college in coursework that is accelerated.
7. Attending private schools that may have a distinct academic, social, or athletic standing.

While there is much evidence to support the use of acceleration, two great stumbling blocks to its effective implementation are the school's administrative approach to gifted and talented programs and parental opposition to these types of programs. Therefore, it may take a great deal of education of school administrators and parents as to the positive benefits of an accelerated program before it can be implemented effectively.

Ability Grouping

Ability grouping separates an individual from other students or coursework on the basis of some selected or predetermined criteria. Learners are simply placed in classes with other students of comparable ability to study similar content. There are a variety of ability options that are outlined by several authors; however, Clark (1979) provides a continuous model for ability grouping that includes the following: regular class, regular class with cluster, regular class with pull out, regular class with cluster and pull out, individualized class, individualized class with cluster, individualized class with pull out, individualized class with cluster and pull out, special class with some integrated classes, special class, and special school. She suggests that not all children, especially gifted and talented children, can be placed equally across this continuum. In fact, *regular class placement* and *regular class placement with cluster* appear not to be adequate for gifted and talented education, simply because these approaches do not accommodate the accelerated learning performance of most gifted children. Beginning with *regular class with pull out* and moving on through the continuum to *special schools*, Clark feels accommodations can be made for better serving the gifted and talented child. Within each of these areas two aspects of educational programming are apparent. First, the child is given an opportunity to work at his or her interest and ability level, and second, each of these grouping methods provides an environment in which flexible planning can be implemented to meet the needs of the gifted individual. Pehaps the key to any good educational program for gifted and talented children lies quite simply in the ability of parents, administrators, program designers, and so on to be flexible in their attempts to educate this population.

Enrichment

Enrichment is an attempt to provide the learner with stimulation for acquiring new ideas or reinforcing individual interests that go beyond the normal school curriculum. Enrichment includes such things as field trips and extracurricular or cultural experiences. Enrichment, like acceleration, can have some very positive effects upon the learning curve of the gifted and talented child. However, Stanley (1977) feels that enrichment without acceleration may have some detrimental effects upon the advanced learner. Much of what appears to be enrichment activities could simply be busywork or irrelevant academic activities. Gallagher (1975) suggests that when enrichment activities are used they should have as a major focus the development of productive behavior. To do this the enriching activity should attempt to associate and interrelate concepts, assist the child to evaluate facts and arguments, provide opportunities in which new ideas can be created and new concepts originated, provide an opportunity in which complex problems can be reasoned, and place the child within situations or times or with other people to better understand his or her own environmental surroundings.

Renzulli (1979) proposes a model from which enrichment activities can be developed more efficaciously. His *Enrichment Triad Model* provides for three types of enrichment activity: general exploratory activities, group training activities, and individual investigation of real problems. Renzulli considers the first two to be appropriate for all learners while the third is primarily for gifted children. The first two types of enrichment assist the learner in expanding interests and developing his or her thinking and feeling skills. This model represents hierarchical thinking with Type 1 activities being exploratory in nature; the individual utilizes all senses in the identification and exploration of new and unusual information. Type 2 activities focus more on the application and utilization of that learned information. The purpose of these activities is to develop thinking and feeling that will later allow the learner to better integrate and utilize information learned. Type 2 activities could be classified as brainstorming, utilizing divergent or convergent thinking, analysis and synthesis of information, and so on. The activities suggested in Type 2 and Type 3 enrichment require the learner to attempt to solve real problems. Type 3 activities are built upon Types 1 and 2, and while it appears that Type 3 activities are primarily applicable in nature, they require the learner to use higher and more sophisticated levels of thought processes in identifying and solving problems — for example, applying empirical methods to investigating and solving problems.

One of the biggest drawbacks of enrichment lies in its lack of definition and focus. Functional enrichment activities must focus on the development of productive behaviors. To be productive, enrichment activities must focus on end behaviors, that is, behaviors that result in growth within a field of interest to the learner or in observable changes in behavior. Otherwise, enrichment activities can be nice ways of wasting time.

Independent Study Programs

These types of programs are, as their name implies, independent and more or less controlled by the individual learner. There are many obvious advantages to independent study programs. First, they are highly flexible, allowing the learner to focus on his or her interests and abilities, and can easily be designed around the individual's ability to perform. These programs should be based upon very sound diagnostic information that pinpoints accurately where the learner's interests lie and what his abilities are, as well as the learning style that the learner may possess. This is important because not all children can benefit from an independent study program. Some will need more direction and control, while others revel in independence (which is usually characteristic of the gifted and talented, but not all gifted and talented children can handle learning that is not controlled and directed). The teacher is more a facilitator in an independent study program than in most other types of educational environments; therefore, he or she should have a good understanding of the child's learning abilities so that the best facilitation for learning can be made.

The most common control factor in an independent study program, which is used quite effectively to control the learning performance of the individual, is a written contract. This contract is between the learner and the teacher and specifies clearly what work is to be done, when that work is to be completed, and usually how it will be evaluated.

Mainstreaming and/or Cluster Programs

Not all public schools can afford the luxury of well-developed gifted and talented programs. This may be due to either lack of funding or in some cases even disinterest on the part of the administrators, teachers, or parents. Therefore the gifted and talented child may be found within the regular classroom without any appropriate educational plan being utilized. However, every child can have a program that is based upon his or her ability to perform. Gifted and talented children can be clustered in a group within the regular classroom and can work side by side or parallel to children of average to lesser abilities. The teacher has to be careful to plan integrated or mainstreamed activities for students in this situation, as well as to insure that at specific times during the day these children meet as a group for directed learning enrichment and/or accelerated activities that provide them with the opportunity for educational advancement at their level. There are many educators in the area of gifted and talented who feel that this type of educational program would be unsatisfactory for gifted and talented children. However, within the total realm of education, programs sometimes become circumstantial; that is, the circumstances sometimes dictate how educational programs will and can be developed. In this case, cluster grouping within a mainstreamed classroom may be the only alternative available to the teacher.

Mentorships

Mentorships are characterized by having the learner paired with a highly skilled resource person who acts as a mentor within a specified area of education for that learner. Since a mentor is the teacher for that child, the teacher role that the mentor fills includes counseling, advising, and even being a companion to the learner (Boston, 1976). Even though the mentor program has not been used very extensively in gifted and talented public education, it appears to be one of the more viable models in providing education for this type of learner. The reason behind its lack of utilization perhaps lies in the administrative headaches that it incurs. On the surface it would appear to be very expensive (one teacher, one child) and time-consuming (again, one teacher, one child), and therefore the feasibility of its use within the public school system would appear to be limited. However, it is a viable intervention strategy and when used in combination with the individualized study program could overcome some of the administrative and financial hurdles that it seemingly imposes. A mentor could work with several different learners, and with the proper individualized education program with prescribed goals, objectives, and strategies to be followed by the learner and facilitated by the mentor, a great deal could be accomplished in helping gifted and talented children reach their potential.

Pull-Out Programs

Quite simply, pull-out programs are designed to release learners from their classrooms on a regular basis to spend time with a special teacher who gives direction and assistance to either an individual or a group of learners with the same interests or educational focus. The success of this type of program rests primarily with the teacher in charge of the pull-out student and how that teacher plans programs for the individual or group of gifted and talented learners. The pull-out program does provide the child with the opportunity to interact with others of similar interest and ability levels. However, if the learning experience has not been adequately planned it can be a waste of time, as not that much time can be allowed for the individual learner to participate in the activity. If pull-out time is not used productively, the learner may have been better off suffering through the regular classroom curriculum.

Within some public school districts, the pull-out program is used as an economical way of serving gifted and talented children on a cost per pupil ratio. However, its functional and productive utilization rests solely upon the capabilities, interests, and training of the teacher.

THE ECOSYSTEM OF PROGRAM DEVELOPMENT

Perhaps it is safe to conclude that no one model of intervention is best suited to every gifted and talented learner. Due to the variability of the learner as well as the curriculum, it would seem impossible or almost impossible to create the one environment in which all learners would progress to their optimum level of performance and reach their full potential. The key to any effective educational program rests upon the stability of the administering agency, e.g. school district and school principal, and the implementing agent, e.g. the teacher, parent, or mentor, as well as on the adaptability of the individual child. The learner must be taken into consideration in terms of his or her attitude and ability to adapt to the learning environment that is provided.

If there were to be one approach that could be followed in developing educational programs for the gifted and talented learner (or for that matter, for any learner), it would have to consider the entire environment in which the learner performs. There is not one aspect of the learner or the environment that can be considered separately. In essence, this view could be called an ecosystem of educational program planning that begins with an assessment of the learner from the standpoint of all the environmental influences that have an impact upon his or her life. This ecosystem is a balance between both the cognitive and the affective domains of the child's individual learning system, as well as an attempt to balance the child's interest and abilities against the environmental elements that have direct impact upon that individual system.

Ths ecosystem of learning has at its focal point the learner. The learner is seen as the center of the learning system, while the entire educational system that surrounds the child is taken into consideration when attempting to plan educational programs (*see* Figure 4-1). The child is composed of at least four or five elements that should be considered in program planning. One of these is the learner's cognitive capabilities, another is the emotional/social (affective) side of the child, while another is the child's physical capabilities to perform. These may include everything from the child's physical attributes of strength, endurance, and coordination to the visual, auditory, kinesthetic acuity, and/or perceptual abilities that he or she may possess. Finally there is the unknown element of the psychic or spiritual side of the child — that unknown force which provides direction, motivation, and reason for movement and activity to all the other elements. These are elements that comprise the individual learner and must be understood before appropriate program planning can be facilitated.

Once the different elements of the individual learner are understood, an analysis of the external environment that has an impact upon that learner must be made. What are the expectations, the goals, the circumstances, and the criteria that have external influence upon the learner? Even if the child is gifted mathematically, for example, it means nothing within an environment that will not allow stimulation in that area or perhaps lacks physical material necessary to the advancement of development in that area. If important environmental information is discovered through analysis, then more appropriate educational programming steps can be followed.

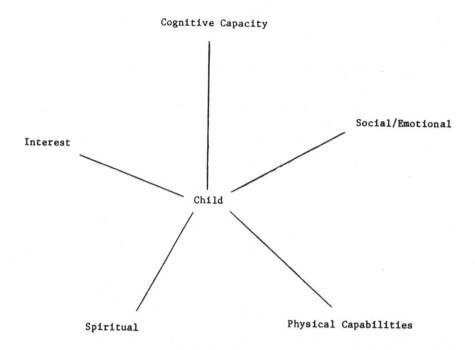

Figure 4-1. The ecosystem within which each child must learn.

In terms of program development, the ecosystem concepts proposed are not new but are emerging as viable program planning alternatives. For example, Clark (1979) proposes a very similar analysis to be followed in developing programs for gifted and talented children. In her discussion of the Cooperative Learning Environment she specifies quite succinctly that the development of the learning environment is organized around the student. The environmental model that she proposes has the inherent ability to meet learners at their present levels of cognitive, emotional/social, physical, and intuitive development. In other words, learning centers around the student, and the curriculum interacts with the student, whereas traditionally the learner has had to interact with the curriculum.

Meeker (1969) suggests that educational program planning should focus around how the learner processes information. Utilizing Guilford's Structure of the Intellect as a model, Meeker contends that learning should be seen from the perspective of the individual and not from an external education system such as a school district, a school, or even a classroom. In other words, learning comes from and is evaluated from the perspective of the individual.

Other programs similar to the ecosystem approach include the Individually Guided Education (IGE) program proposed by Bahner (1979), in which there is outlined a systematic approach to managing the learning environment of the individual child. The concept of IGE is to take into consideration all elements of the learning system when planning, implementing, and evaluating what learning does take place.

One of the most dramatic changes in program development occurred with the passage of Public Law 94-142, in which it was specified that an Individual Education Program (IEP) be developed for exceptional children (*see* Chapter Two). Inherent within this law and within the provisions for developing the IEP is an emphasis on involving several elements of the educational community, including the learner. To be appropriate, programs must be based upon the individual learner with an attempt at understanding all the other elements or parts of the educational community, e.g. teachers, resources, media, and materials, which have an impact on the individual learner. If those parts are understood in conjunction with the learner and are planned around the learner's abilities and interests, more productive behavior will result.

The Eco Assessment

A first step in the development of a learner-centered educational program is the completion of an assessment that takes into consideration both the learner and the environment. This assessment should include a *discrepancy analysis* of the learner's behaviors, an analysis that determines where he or she is actually performing and where the teacher, parent, or school system specifies that he or she ought to be performing. This discrepancy analysis is based upon looking at the individual learner in relationship to all the elements that make up and have an impact upon him or her. For example, an assessment must be made of the child's *cognitive abilities, academic interests, physical capabilities* (this includes visual, auditory, and motor processing capabilities as well as gross and fine motor skills required to perform the tasks), and *social/emotional* makeup, e.g. is the child quiet, withdrawn, overt, or intraverted.

Then an analysis must be made of the *environmental parts* that surround and have an impact upon the child. Does the teacher support and have the training to conduct appropriate educational programs for gifted and talented youngsters? Are the learner's parents interested in, capable of, or motivated to assist in the implementation and evaluation of educational programs for the child? Do the school district, school principal, and other teachers within the building support differential programming for gifted and talented children? Is the school flexible in its ability to adapt or change existing educational programs to accommodate the learner? Is there a financial base available to support development of these types of programs?

Analysis of these parts of the educational system that surround the child can be quite extensive; however, the important part of the analysis is to identify the major elements that may have an impact on the child. Once identified, the intensity of the impact is then determined before an appropriate educational program can be developed and implemented.

Balanced Programs

Upon completion of the eco assessment, a more balanced educational program can be outlined. The program is balanced in the sense that it takes into consideration all domains of the learner's world, the *cognitive/academic, physical/ social,* and *intuitive/spiritual* areas for which he or she can then be more appropriately prepared. How to develop that balanced program is illustrated in Figure 2-2 of Chapter Two in the form of the IEP.

STARTING A PROGRAM

Prior to the development of any individual education program, an atmosphere must be created within the district or the school system that will facilitate and accommodate education for gifted and talented children. This section will highlight what must be taken into consideration from a state and district level to facilitate the initial development of programs for gifted and talented children. In the next section, an illustration of how the individual classroom could be structured to accommodate gifted and talented children will be presented.

Planning

Renzulli (1976) conducted a study to determine important features of programs for the gifted considered as such by authorities in the field. He identified in his study seven features that appear to be critical in planning programs for the gifted. They are as follows:

1. Special attention should be given to the selection and training of teachers for gifted and talented students.
2. The curriculum for gifted and talented students should be recognizably different from the general educational program.
3. Special student selection procedures should be identified and implemented.
4. A statement of the program's philosophy and objectives should be made.
5. The staff should have orientation as to the philosophies, objectives, and instructional programs to be used.
6. An evaluation plan to determine the effectiveness of the program should be developed and implemented.
7. Administrative responsibility should be identified and outlined.

Clark (1979) outlines eight steps within her Cooperative Learning Environment that can be considered an important foundation for educational programs. These include

1. Identify the provisions the district has for meeting the needs of gifted learners.

2. Specify the usual needs of gifted learners and then match what the current district program is doing to meet those needs.

3. Familiarize teachers or those working within the gifted and talented program with gifted education as well as individualized education through reading, attending workshops, and taking courses.

4. Develop a plan that can be utilized and implemented by the district and that will expand and change the present gifted program to better meet the needs of gifted learners within the district.

5. Present that plan to parents, teachers, administrators, and other professionals for input, criticism, and evaluation. Modify the plan if necessary based upon the input from these individuals.

6. Modify the plan based upon the individual.

7. Inform all interested groups, i.e. parents, school administrators, other related professionals, and teachers, to solicit their cooperation and assistance in the implementation of the plan.

Del Giorno (1979) proposes seven planning steps that should be considered in establishing a gifted and talented program.

1. Planning committee. Bring people together who are interested in starting a program to improve the quality of education offered to gifted students. Include people who represent the community.

2. Type of Program. Determine a type of program that meets the community's needs and is possible to start. (For instance, a pull-out program, special class, acceleration, ability grouping, and/or other programs discussed previously would be considered here.)

3. Criteria for Identification. Find out if the state department of education and/or the district has already specified guidelines for identifying gifted and talented children.

4. Teachers. Determine if there are already teachers specifically trained in the area of gifted and talented in the district and/or school. If not, ask for volunteers among experienced teachers. It may be best simply to ask teachers if they would like to teach gifted and talented children and if they themselves are gifted and talented, would they like this opportunity.

5. Program Objectives. Develop objectives specific to the program — objectives based upon the resources, e.g. teachers, materials, funding, and support available.

6. Orientation. All persons who are to be affiliated with or affected by the program should be, if not involved in the planning, at least given an orientation as to the concepts and objectives that comprise that program.

7. Coordination. To make a good program and improve communication between schools and classes within schools, one person should be designated as the coordinator and agent responsible for implementing the program.

Finally, Bahner (1979) suggests that before starting a gifted and talented program within a district or school there are four important steps that must be followed. These summarize what Clark (1979), Renzulli (1976), Del Giorno (1976) and others have proposed. First, it is essential to investigate state and federal laws, regulations, and guidelines relative to serving gifted and talented children. Second, both the policies and the position statements related to this population must be studied and understood. Third, it will be necessary to find out the various attitudes of the community towards serving gifted and talented children. In some communities, either large or small, this may be a stumbling block to eventual development. Fourth, information from various state and federal resources relating to all aspects of gifted and talented programs should be obtained. It is suggested that funding within a district and state be identified as to the amount set aside for supporting development of gifted and talented programs.

CLASSROOM CONSIDERATIONS

While it may be easy for some to discuss the ideal organization of the gifted and talented classroom, its practical applications are quite another reality. Implementing a program in a regular mainstreamed classroom, beginning a pullout program, or attempting to develop ability grouping can be quite a challenge. At least six factors should be taken into consideration in building such programs, including desirable teacher traits, scheduling and curriculum, physical arrangements, learning activities, parental support, and available resources. These factors should be considered the foundation of any good classroom organization. Each will be discussed in detail.

Desirable Teacher Traits

In a survey conducted by Renzulli (1968), experts in the field of education for gifted and talented were asked to select the most important features of the program. These experts identified the selection and training of the teacher as the most important feature of the classroom. The results of a poll in 1977 (Instructor) identified four teacher characteristics that were ranked significantly above all others as being the most important for working with children. These characteristics included flexibility and the acceptance of difference, the ability to develop independent activities for the individual learner, originality, imagination, and curiosity, and desire to teach gifted and talented children.

It could be said that the teacher becomes a model of the skills that he or she wishes to teach the learner or hopes that the learner will develop. Teachers are to provide the education climate and environment necessary to facilitate the discovery of talent and children's potential. Obtaining the properly trained, experienced, and interested teacher is a necessity to having a good educational program within the classroom (Larkin, 1982).

Scheduling and Curriculum

Larkin (1982) provides a concept for teaching to multiple talents that can be incorporated into all subject areas. She suggests that in planning the lessons for each week, the teacher should plan thinking activities for each of the following areas: academic, creative, planning, communicating, forecasting, and decision making. These activities should be interspersed among class subjects such as language arts, social studies, humanities, art, biological sciences, physical sciences, math, and other. An *academic skill* might be developed by teaching study techniques or in thinking through a complex math problem. *Creative thinking* can be practiced in divergent, convergent, and evaluative thinking exercises. Students could brainstorm ideas for the layout of a future city, narrow down their possibilities, and decide what alternatives they would use. *Planning talents* could be used in organizing science projects or class activities. A lesson on advertizing gimmicks followed by an activity of students making their own ads would exercise the communication talents. *Forecasting talents* could be used to predict what might be the effects of current issues appearing in the newspapers. After studying a science unit on plants, *decision-making skills* could be used by each child to decide what plants he or she would plant in his or her own yard. These types of thinking skills can be applied to already existing materials, producing three advantages: each child has the opportunity to use and develop a variety of thinking skills; the subjects being studied become more alive and exciting; and retention increases because of multiple exposure and interest.

As the teacher finds such learning activities in books and magazines, from other teachers, or in his or her own imagination, it is advantageous to file them for ready access. Manila folders can be labeled and divided into content areas and then into thinking skill areas. A folder for general principles that could be applied to more than one area of thinking should also be created.

Individualized instruction is not "do what you feel like" instruction. It involves testing a child to find out the child's abilities for placement within appropriate work and then having the child contract to accomplish a certain amount of work per week. Appropriate emphasis for the gifted is described by Gallagher (1975).

1. Teach to the highest cognitive level possible.
2. Teach gifted children to use all their thinking processes.
3. Teach important ideas about all aspects of their life and times.
4. Teach methods by which gifted children can discover knowledge for themselves.
   (P. 152)

Small and large group activities are appropriate to use with individualized instruction; in fact, they are an excellent way to introduce new concepts. Activity packets need to be designed based on the different skill levels present in the class. All of this may sound overwhelming to the beginning teacher or even to one with a few years of experience. A plan such as this does take a great deal of effort to implement at first. New teachers may want to begin by first individualizing their reading and math programs and then individualizing additional subjects each year.

As students see themselves progressing through learning materials at their own optimum speeds and as they see these principles applied to the real world around them, learning will become exciting. Just imagine how a gifted child could move ahead when he or she feels the thrill of learning and discovering at his or her own rate.

In selecting or making programmed materials these guidelines by Renzulli and Stoddard (1980) should be helpful.

1. The materials should be able to be administered individually (with or without an instructor present), in small groups, or as a large group.
2. Materials should be flexible enough to be used as a total package or individual pull-out units without gaps or repetition.
3. Materials should provide challenging queries to inspire further investigation, as opposed to answering all questions and discouraging divergent ideas. (P. 90)

Learning centers provide ways to enrich the standard topics. Here again, the beginning teacher may wish to start with a few learning centers and add more as ideas and materials are collected. Individual research may be inspired by a learning center. Libraries provide information for research papers and also enrichment through reading. In one school, as students complete a specific amount of productive classwork they earn mobility within the building and access to the school library. This special privilege is retained only as long as the students use and respect the time allotted to them (Bierly, 1978).

As teachers organize their classrooms for individualized instruction, more students will be able to develop their talents. There is much work and preparation involved in reaching this worthwhile goal.

Physical Arrangement and Learning Activities

Organization of materials facilitates the functional use of the classroom. For variety and efficiency, the teacher should plan several different physical arrangements for the room. Desks can be moved to fit the needs of individual, small group, and class work. Learning centers can be set up all around the room, in the corners, or just on one side. Of course, much depends on the size of the room, but it is good to include at least one or two learning centers in addition to the reading area. These centers can use many different kinds of equipment such as tape recorders, records, books, pictures, and if possible real-life objects. The key is variety. The gifted and talented students may be involved in planning and setting up their own learning centers. Figure 4-2 shows a classroom plan involving many learning centers.

Students may keep folders with a list of progressive math skills, a list of books read, and scores of their accomplishments in other units. Also in their folders the children should keep a list of assignments that they have contracted to do for the week. In Figure 4-3 can be seen a sample activities checklist that could be found in a child's folder. These folders allow children to see what activities they are to engage in and also allows the teacher to keep track of each student's educational activities. Folders may be kept in the students' desks or in a filing cabinet made available for student use.

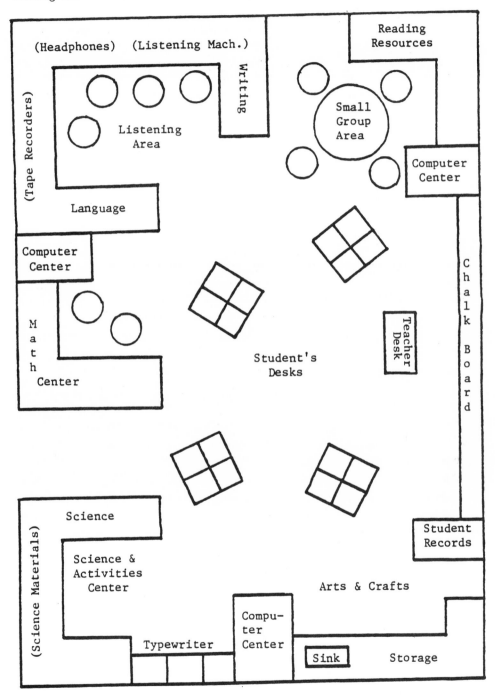

Figure 4-2. A sample classroom physical arrangement involving many individual learning centers.

Name _____   Date _____

	M	T	W	TH	F
1. Reading Center					
2. Math Center					
3. Language					
4. Science Center					
5. Creative Writing Center					
6. Spelling					
7. Art Center					
8. Library					
9. Interpersonal (Small Group)					
10. Activities Center					

Figure 4-3. A sample checklist of weekly activities.

Parental Support

Parental support of education is of prime importance, and this is especially true with the parents of gifted and talented children. These parents can offer teachers insights concerning the interests of their children. They can provide additional opportunities for the child to learn at home and also provide volunteer aid in the classrooms, allowing the teacher to work with more children.

It would be beneficial for a teacher with gifted and talented students to have a small resource center for parents or to see that such a center gets established on a school basis. Such a center would contain several comprehensive books on the gifted and talented, pamphlets, handouts, lists of games, ideas for teaching in the home, and any other information that would help parents with their gifted and talented children. A concerned and informed parent helps make gifted behavior a way of life and not just an artificial situation created in the schools.

Available Resources

Often in thinking of resources we think of money. Money is helpful, but there are other, largely untapped, resources available to teachers. There are people, places, and programs in the community that can be used to enrich classroom discussions.

One of the primary resources is the people located throughout the school:

the principal, other teachers, media specialist, secretary, custodian, cooks, and parent volunteers. It would be a good idea at the beginning of the year to send out surveys to all parents asking what talents or vocations they have that they would be willing to share with others. A file of responses can be included in a resources card file. Many members of the community will want to share their time or money if only they are asked. Local professionals, laborers, artists, naturalists, and special interest groups are possibilities. The senior citizens group may be a gold mine of talent that has only been slightly tapped. Many of these citizens may enjoy a short-time opportunity to share their talents with youth. High school and college students are available in some areas as aides. They can be very helpful if instructed well in what needs to be done.

Other inexpensive resources available to a teacher are the places within the community where classes may go on field trips. These vary somewhat from city to city, but some are similar. Examples include museums, historical society displays, government offices, local factories, newspaper offices, and parks.

Programs offered in the community make up a third resource available to the teacher. This might include visits by the Red Cross to discuss first aid, fire prevention and paramedic programs by the fire department, or energy-saving presentations by gas and light companies. Other organizations will send free or inexpensive materials to educators when requested, such as maps, travel pictures, and pamphlets. There are many resources in the community, but it is up to teachers to find and use them to benefit the students in their classrooms.

TRAINING TEACHERS

Though several teaching characteristics seem to be common to teachers of gifted and talented, it appears quite obvious from the literature that little if any well-founded research has been completed to document what those characteristics should be. Khatena (1982) provides a summary of the many lists of characteristics that have been presented in a number of different studies. His summary illustrates the relative futility of gifted teacher characteristic research over the past few years, with the "research" results identifying behaviors that would be characteristic of any good classroom teacher. In the authors' own survey of both teachers and gifted students in a localized area of Central Western America, the teacher characteristics identified were not too much different from those found by Khatena. Maker (1976) recommends several different criteria for the selection of teachers to work in gifted and talented programs. These include having *knowledge* of the areas of giftedness as defined by United States Office of Education Standards, having the ability to relate to those with whom they are going to work and having the disposition to be open to change.

In the survey conducted by the authors on a limited population (thirty teachers and administrators of gifted and talented programs in the public school system, a comparable number of gifted and talented children ranging in grade levels from junior to senior high school, and parents of gifted and talented children), essentially the same characteristics proposed by Maker (1976) were identified. Of these characteristics, one related to both the authors' and Maker's studies. The disposition to be open to change stood out — consistently, students, teachers, and administrators identified *flexibility* as the most overriding characteristic in developing programs for gifted and talented children. Learners were especially sensitive to this area and identified teachers who lacked flexibility in changing the day-to-day curriculum as being less effective than those who could make almost minute-to-minute changes. Teachers and administrators in the survey looked at flexibility as both adjusting to the identified needs of the student at the moment and being flexible within the total curricular structure of the district, that is, adjusting to the prescribed and specified needs of the district and/or school within which they work.

Another characteristic identified by teachers (which is perhaps a function of current technology) was a basic understanding of computer (microcomputer) technology and its application in the classroom. Of course, this could be easily corrected with some in-service training with the proper equipment, but it is one technical skill that will soon be required not only of teachers of gifted and talented children but of all educators.

In this same survey, parents of gifted and talented children were also questioned. Their most overriding characteristic was the *communication skill* of the teacher. In other words, parents felt that the teacher had to be able to communicate data from an educational assessment with parents, provide programming suggestions for use in the home, and utilize parents as resources within the classroom, as well as communicate directly with the student, the learner.

In summary, it appears that the literature does provide some direction in terms of teacher preparation. One such direction of teacher preparation is *knowledge*. This of course applies across all areas of teaching. The teacher must be *flexible* in directly programming for children as well as in dealing with district and school level changes. Primarily, teachers should be prepared to alter or change curriculum based upon the identified needs of children. Next, *communication skills* are essential in communicating programs, program intent, and program strategies, especially to parents. And finally, an emerging teacher preparation skill is related to *understanding and applying microcomputer technology* in the public school classroom. These are four skill areas that could be considered in the preparation of teachers.

Callahan (1978) provides fourteen considerations that teachers might use to encourage greater production by students in their classrooms.

1. Provide a nonthreatening atmosphere. The classroom environment should be structured in such a way that students' ideas and opinions are respected, ridicule of new ideas is eliminated, questioning is encouraged, and questions are asked that allow students to be open and uninhibited in response.

2. Refrain from becoming the judge of the worth of all products in the classroom. An open, nonjudgmental attitude on the part of the teacher will allow more freedom for divergent production as well as the evaluative skills necessary for the complete creative process. Encourage students to develop criteria to judge the work both of peers and of themselves.

3. Model creative thinking and/or introduce other individuals who are able to illustrate the creative thinking process to the students. The teacher should take care to model creative problem-solving procedures on as many occasions as possible, not simply during "creativity time."

4. Attempt to integrate activities and questions that encourage divergent production and evaluation into as many content areas as possible. The necessity of illustrating transfer of these skills to all areas of thinking cannot be overestimated.

5. Make a conscious effort to remind students to be creative, to be original, to try to think of new ways to solve a problem, etc.

6. Reward novel production systematically. The use of operant conditioning to reinforce specific types of novel behavior can lead to an overall increase in creative production. For example, the reinforcement of the use of a variety of sentence structures in an essay has been shown to influence overall creative writing skill. Care should be taken to choose appropriate reinforcement. Gifted children can be expected to value rewards that are unique.

7. Provide a stimuli for as many of the senses as possible. A variety of stimuli encourages the student to view the problem from a variety of perspectives and also seems to enhance the sense of openness and psychological freedom.

8. Make use of warm-up activities when moving from highly structured convergent or memory activities into activities requiring students to engage in creative production. Such brief activities should be used to reaffirm the nonthreatening environment and are most effective if they relate to the task to be accomplished.

9. Incorporate into classroom instruction activities that require students to generate a large number of correct responses. That is, provide open-ended questions that have no single right answer.

10. Instruct students in the principles of brainstorming, but incorporate strategies for self-evaluation of the quality of ideas. Furthermore, brainstorming activities will be most productive if tied to "real problems" or "meaningful production" rather than simple games.

11. Be a participant in the actions. Do not merely pose problems, but be an active problem solver.

12. Encourage students to express positive self-statements about their creativity and avoid negative self-evaluations. Provide them with guiding statements of attitudes, approaches to problems, and orientations to

the process.

13. Attempt to incorporate published material into the curriculum. This is dependent on the understanding and commitment of the teacher who is using the curriculum. No packaged materials are independent of the teacher's use of those materials, and the effectiveness of creativity training materials seems to be particularly influenced by the teacher's attitude and the environment of the classroom.

14. Evaluate whichever strategies are adopted for classroom use within the particular classroom with the particular students and teaching style. What works in one situation will not always work in others. Continual assessment of the objectives of instruction is crucial.

Lundsteen and Tarrow (1981) have nine suggestions for what the teacher can do to work with children in the classroom.

1. Encourage their curiosity, exploration, and questioning.
2. Be willing to explore and to accept their alternative solutions to problems.
3. Involve them in special projects that benefit them and can be of value to the class or school.
4. Don't feel threatened if you don't know the answers to some of their questions. Do be willing to help them search for the answers.
5. Encourage them to use a variety of resources — people, books, multimedia.
6. Encourage higher levels of thinking. Questions and assignments should draw upon their abilities to analyze, synthesize, generalize, and solve problems creatively.
7. Help them early to learn specialized reference skills that will help them throughout a lifetime of learning.
8. Keep them motivated and constructively creating, as their high energy level can often be diverted into negative behavior.
9. Don't fill their time only with errands, clerical jobs, or helping others in the class.

One last principle that seems to be inherent within the literature relative to teacher training is the view that a desire to protect the rights of the individual and to nurture the qualities that make an individual unique are characteristics that gifted and talented teachers must possess. It appears that many educators of the gifted prescribe to the humanistic philosophy of education (Stanley, George, and Solano, 1977), which implies to others that programs for the gifted should provide an open learning environment and freedom of choice within the curriculum (Renzulli, 1977). If the teacher cannot construct a student-centered program, be a facilitator of learning, and possess the qualities of flexibility, knowledge of the field, communication skills, and understanding and application of microcomputer technology in the classroom, then he or she may have a difficult time succeeding as a teacher of gifted and talented children.

PARENTAL CONSIDERATIONS

Parents are an emerging force within gifted and talented program development, and well they should be. Parents of gifted and talented children are as concerned about what is happening to their children's education as perhaps any other parent advocacy group. Nathan (1979) reports that the number of parent advocacy groups around the country is growing, which has resulted in increased funding for local and state programs and an ever-increased role for these groups as change agents in the education of their own gifted and talented children. Ginsburg and Harrison (1977) report programs designed to increase the awareness and understanding of parents relative to their gifted and talented children in terms of advocacy, techniques, and roles that parents can play in supporting or requesting support from legislatures and local school districts for increased funding for better program facilities and resources.

The parents of gifted and talented children are not only interested; often they are very frustrated by not being aware of the issues related to financing, resources available, or teacher training programs that will directly or indirectly assist their gifted and talented children in the public school system. Some parents are disillusioned by their own lack of understanding and knowledge related to their child. They sometimes have difficulty in communicating with the child. Parents want to improve their parenting skills by having more information about specific educational strategies that will help them better cope with their children (Haring, 1982).

Parents and Program Development

The following information on how parents should consider their roles in the development of programs is extracted from Van Osdol (1972) and Tuttle (1980) as an example of what parents should consider in becoming an advocate for or assisting in the development of programs for gifted and talented children.

1. Support school efforts to plan for gifted children. Help to interest the PTA in the gifted. Support study groups on gifted children. Form with other parents into cooperative endeavors and associations.
2. Investigate scholarship programs in your community for gifted children.
3. Work to provide better community understanding and appreciation of the role of the gifted child in society and the importance of community planning.
4. Support community action for gifted children, including bonds and school taxes for extra educational advantages. Advocate more guidance and special education for the gifted.
5. Establish open communication with teachers and administrators about educating the gifted and talented. Some parents are reluctant to admit that their children may be gifted and assume that the schools will automatically take care of them or that they will get along by themselves. At

the other extreme, some parents approach the school as an adversary, establishing an antagonistic relationship that inhibits productive cooperation.

6. When discussing a gifted child with teachers, provide anecdotes illustrating the child's exceptional abilities and interests outside school. Teachers may not always recognize such abilities because the child may not demonstrate them in the classroom. A discussion of interests may also help relate activities at home with those in school.

7. Seek out other parents of gifted children and share concerns and ideas. Such communication may not only help each parent feel less alone but may also provide resources for the children, including contact with other gifted children of similar interests, trips, or even programs for the gifted. As a group, parents of gifted and talented may be able to promote program development in schools for their children.

Parents and Their Children

Gowan and Letlow (1976) developed a number of excellent suggestions for parents of able children that should be used as guidelines to those parents to help them better interact with their children. Following is an adaptation of their work.

1. Gifted children are children. They need love, but controls; attention, but discipline; parental involvement, yet training in self-dependence and responsibility.

2. Consonance of parental value systems is important for the gifted child's optimum development. This means that there should not be wide disagreements over values between parents.

3. Parental involvement in early tasks demands training the children to perform tasks themselves — to count, tell time, use correct vocabulary and pronunciation, locate themselves to get around their neighborhoods, do errands, and be responsible.

4. Emphases on early verbal expression, reading, discussing ideas in the presence of children, poetry, and music are all valuable. Parents should read to children. Parents should emphasize doing well in school.

5. The lack of disruption of family life through divorce or separation and the maintenance of a happy, healthy home are important aspects in raising able children, as well as other children.

6. Gifted children may often have only vague awarenesses of adult problems such as sex, death, sickness, finances, and war because of their lack of experience; therefore, they may need reassurance in these areas.

7. Parents should help the gifted child of age six or above to have a playmate who is talented, even if the child has to be "imported" from some distance.

8. Good books, magazines, encyclopedias, charts, collections, and other

aids to home learning are important.

9. Parents should take gifted children to museums, art galleries, educational institutions, and other historical places that may enhance experiential learning.

10. Parents should be especially careful not to "shut up" gifted children who ask questions. In particular, they should not be scolded for asking, nor should it be implied that questions are improper or subjects forbidden. Parents may, however, insist that questions not be asked at inappropriate times and require the children to sharpen or rephrase a question to clarify it.

    Sometimes questions should not be answered, but the reply should be a question which sends the child searching. A parent who cannot answer a question should direct the child to a resource that can. Sometimes questions call for clarification of concepts. One young child asked, "Why aren't all those rockets liable to shoot down God?"

11. There's a difference between "pushing" and intellectual stimulation. Parents should avoid pushing children into reading, exhibiting them before others, or courting undue publicity. On the other hand, parents should seek in every way to stimulate and widen their child's mind through suitable experiences in books, recreation, travel, and the arts.

12. The gifted child usually has a wide and versatile range of interests but may be somewhat less able to concentrate on one area for a long time. Parents should encourage children who have hobbies to follow through on them, to plan and strive for credible performance and real mastery rather than to go through a lot of hobbies in a short time.

13. Parents should avoid direct, indirect, or unspoken attitudes indicating that fantasy, originality, unusual questions, imaginary playmates, or out-of-the-ordinary mental processes are bad, "different," or to be discouraged. Instead of laughing at children, parents should laugh with them and seek to develop their sense of humor.

14. Parents should avoid overstructuring children's lives. The child should have free time. Sometimes parents are concerned that gifted children spend too much time watching TV or reading comic books. They should not be expected to perform at top academic capacity at all times.

15. Parents should respect their child and his knowledge, which at times may be better than their own and which is impatient of authority. They should assume the child means to do right, and the deviations are not intentional. They should not presume on their authority as parents except in crises, but should allow liberty on unimportant issues. They should try to give general instructions that allow some liberty, rather than specific commands to be carried out their way.

16. Gifted children are sometimes impatient with conventional situations. Parents should have a frank talk with their child about the importance of conventions such as driving carefully, politeness, manners, courtesy,

and regard for others, all of which have similar bases in experience that clarify social advantages.

17. Whenever possible, parents and children should talk things out when there has been a disciplinary lapse. Gifted children are much more amenable to rational argument than are many others, and they usually will have a well-developed sense of duty.

18. Parents should give children the stimulation of private lessons in some skill in which they excel, provide social memberships in worthy groups, and foster special experiences outside the home (traveling alone, or visiting friends overnight). They should try to facilitate chances to talk alone with an adult authority about personal interests.

19. Parents should try to improve their children's sense of taste in mass media, TV, radio, cinema, newspapers, comics, reading, art, etc. They should discuss the basis for taste and provide experience with new forms of expression in the arts.

20. Parents should take time to be with their children, to listen to what they have to say, to discuss ideas.

21. Parents should be good examples and try to provide worthy male and female adult models outside the family with whom the child can interact.

Awareness of the current trends in educational programming for the gifted and talented is a must for teachers to develop, implement, and evaluate appropriate programs for these children. Having examples of different strategies for working directly with the children, for organizing, and even for integrating the children into an educational program will greatly facilitate the teachers' efforts in helping each of the children reach his or her optimum level of performance. Being able to instruct the parents of gifted and talented children on better ways of coping with their children in the home environment will be a definite plus in bridging the communication gap between home and school and thereby making both places a more challenging learning environment for the gifted and talented youngster.

CHAPTER FIVE

EXCEPTIONAL POPULATIONS
OF GIFTED CHILDREN

Can you answer these questions?

1. What are the procedures for identifying gifted children within handicapped populations?
2. What are four criteria commonly used in identifying giftedness within handicapped populations?
3. Can you list two educational programs that are specifically designed for teaching gifted handicapped children?
4. Can you differentiate between culturally different and disadvantaged gifted children?
5. What are the limitations of standardized IQ tests and achievement tests in identifying culturally different and disadvantaged gifted children?
6. What are some procedures that should be followed in developing educational programs for the culturally disadvantaged gifted child?
7. Can you identify three programs specifically designed to serve culturally disadvantaged gifted children?
8. What are the characteristics commonly associated with preschool gifted children?
9. What are the most common characteristics of gifted underachievers?
10. Can you list three program-planning strategies to help gifted underachievers perform more adequately in school?

IN this chapter, several exceptional populations will be discussed in relationship to the gifted and talented children found in each. Specifically, the populations of preschool, handicapped, culturally different, disadvantaged, and underachieving gifted will be presented with information concerning the current literature, characteristics, identification procedures, special curriculum, and programming techniques unique to these segments of the total gifted and talented population.

PRESCHOOL GIFTED

Preschool children have often been neglected in gifted education. Khatena (1982) is one of many who have pointed out the sparsity of special programs for the gifted preschooler. Yet, as Van Osdol (1982) mentions, it is important to identify and program learning experiences for gifted children at an early age in order to adequately motivate such children to achieve their potential. Too often the gifted preschooler's needs are neglected, resulting in frustration, withdrawal, and/or extreme underachievement. Thus, early identification is essential to effective educational programming.

Identification Procedures for Preschool Gifted

One of the first steps in identifying the gifted preschooler is becoming cognizant of behaviors and traits or characteristics of this group. Several authors (Colls, 1980; Karnes, 1978; Schwartz, 1980) have developed lists of characteristics that have been found to be common among the gifted preschool population. Kitano (1980) gathered information from many sources and developed a table of behaviors and traits of the young gifted child. She organizes the characteristics into five areas: intellectual and academic, creative, leadership, music, and art. The behaviors mentioned under each of these areas are similar to those presented in Chapter One.

Knowing the characteristics *of giftedness* can be helpful in the identification process. Johnson and Tusock (1980) found that day-care workers who had received instruction relative to characteristics of creatively gifted preschoolers were more effective in properly identifying this population than were a comparable group of day-care teachers who did not receive training.

Inasmuch as the preschool gifted child may show a talent in areas other than academics, it is important to be aware of traits and behaviors relative to these other areas of giftedness such as athletics, music, art, and leadership. With respect to the latter, Perez (1982) identifies three factors that contribute to leadership ability in preschool children. They are verbal ability, independence, and a sense of structure. Another study on psychosocial giftedness among preschoolers showed that giftedness may develop somewhat independently of IQ and cognitive role taking (Abroms and Gollin, 1980).

One of the reasons for identifying the young gifted child early, other than to provide educational programming, is to provide guidance in helping the precocious child understand and accept his/her giftedness. Roeper (1977) and Malone (1974) both point out the importance of such guidance. Malone suggests that some gifted preschoolers may fear being different so much that they regress to the norm, thereby burying their giftedness. He stresses the importance of helping young children accept their giftedness and offers several considerations providing educational opportunities to these children. First, identification should be opened to the "possibly" gifted as well as to the "probably"gifted. Second, the child should be trained to value his/her individual strengths. Third, the gifted child should be placed in a small group in the regular classroom. Finally, the child should be encouraged to do in-depth study in various subject areas.

Roeper points out how difficult it may be for the gifted preschooler to accept his/her giftedness. She suggests that the gifted preschooler may not be ready to deal emotionally with that which is overwhelming in terms of the world's injustices and his/her helplessness to deal with them. Roeper states that the gifted preschooler deals with more emotions than the typical child, and because of his/her keen understanding of actions and their consequences guilt is often acquired. According to Roeper, the following traits and behaviors are often demonstrated by the gifted preschooler:

1. May have an uneven balance between emotional and intellectual development resulting in a personality structure quite different from the norm
2. May experience an earlier loss of innocence
3. May show a drive to explore the world
4. May develop his/her own method of learning
5. May walk and talk early (may also prefer communicating with adults rather than with peers)
6. May be sensitive to any kind of image making, particularly by adults
7. May be perfectionistic (often resulting in anxiety)
8. May be more dependent on adults than other children
9. May develop a great fear of death, war, and other injustices
10. May have an extremely good memory
11. May have to define words
12. May not be particularly daring (understands consequences too well)

Program Considerations

Although many authors have urged the need for special educational programming for gifted preschoolers, few have gone so far as to list specific activities and methods to be used. Kitano (1982) sought to remedy this situation, however. She lists six recommendations that can be used in enriching the preschool program. These recommendations are aimed at providing activities that will promote the gifted child's thinking processes. The six recommendations are provide activities that enhance creativity, provide activities that enhance higher cognitive processes, provide activities that enhance executive operations, provide activities that promote inquiry and problem solving, provide activities that promote effective development, and incorporate process and content objectives into units.

Morgan (1982) stresses the need for teaching the basics to young gifted children. However, he emphasizes that this must be done in a way that fosters a love for learning. He lists eight suggestions for providing the basics in an interesting manner to these children and stresses that flexibility is the key. The suggestions are

1. Use commercially prepared materials
2. Use older students to serve as mentors
3. Use the library and research skills
4. Use fluency, flexibility, originality, and elaboration in conjunction with the everyday curriculum
5. Don't be afraid to use big words
6. Teach the words and concepts in Bloom's *Taxonomy*
7. Try a variety of "business" activities
8. Take advantage of media devices

Vantassel-Baska, Schuler, and Lipschutz (1982) discuss a successful experimental program developed for gifted four year olds. The program is aimed at providing academic growth, stimulating interests, and promoting a positive self-image for each child identified. The program is highly individualized and organized into four modules. The first module consists of a planned lesson in phonics, reading, language arts, or vocabulary. This module is followed by one in which free activities are utilized to provide extensions of group time experiences. The next module returns to a planned lesson format in the areas of science and art. The last module is devoted to the subject areas of math and social studies. It is pointed out that social expectations are consistently high. The authors conclude that the program is successful in fostering academic growth as well as a positive attitude toward learning.

Many authors have proposed the use of Bloom's *Taxonomy* in working with gifted preschoolers. Bailey and Leonard (1977), for example, discuss the advantages of teaching this population of the gifted based on Bloom's *Taxonomy* and the unit approach. McIntyre (1970) suggests that science be utilized as a core subject around which the entire curriculum is developed, since it integrates many subject areas such as language, mathematics, writing, and health. She lists several ways in which science teachers can motivate children, such as encouraging potential by asking divergent questions, leading children to use reference sources, allowing for self-selection of activities, providing a flexible atmosphere, encouraging hypothesizing and imagination, and stimulating investigation into a wide area of topics. Once again, Bloom's *Taxonomy* is useful.

Finally, when providing for the education of the gifted preschooler, it must be remembered that such children are not necessarily developmentally advanced in all areas. For example, a child who excels in mathematics may not have the fine motor skills to actualize his knowledge completely. Therefore, materials developed for older children may need to be adapted in order to allow for the motor ability and attention span of a preschooler (DiNunno and Callahan, 1981).

HANDICAPPED GIFTED

It is not unusual to find gifted children in almost every population of handicapped students, including the blind, deaf, physically handicapped, emotionally disturbed, and learning disabled. Even though the handicapping condition is generally easy to identify, gifted children within the handicapped areas are not. There is a tendency in our society to point out weaknesses and to ignore strengths. What this does to the handicapped gifted is to hide their gifts and talents under the handicapping condition. Once a child is identified as handicapped, the weakness or handicap may be given more attention, thereby overriding the child's strengths.

The identification of gifted children within handicapped populations is very difficult from the frame of reference of the general population because of the difficulty in accepting handicapped persons. Often the handicap itself masks the gifted potential of the child, disabling a child from really manifesting gifts or talents. For example, a child with cerebral palsy may be a gifted literary artist, but such a gift is not likely to be evident due to the inability of the child to physically express thoughts and ideas as clearly and cogently as the general population. While it is difficult to pinpoint gifted and talented children with handicaps, the task of identifying those with handicaps becomes almost insurmountable.

Yet, history tells us that an attempt must be made to uncover these exceptionally bright individuals from within the handicapped population or at least to be cognizant that they do exist and provide opportunities for them to blossom and grow. Classic examples of handicapped individuals who were truly gifted include Thomas Edison, who was considered by many to be addled until his mother recognized his exceptional gifts and provided an opportunity for him to develop them in the home. Albert Einstein displayed many of the characteristics of a learning disabled child and could have perhaps blossomed much earlier in life had this been recognized and provisions made to assist him in developing his potential. Helen Keller provides an example of a multiply handicapped (deaf-blind) individual who must have been an exceptionally bright and gifted woman to overcome the multiplicity of impairments she faced. Although the identification of the gifted and talented is much more difficult for handicapped children, the need to identify and provide educational assistance for them is extremely critical due to the potential this population may hold for their own development and gratification and for providing society with the advantages of their skills and insights.

Some types of handicapping conditions are more easily discernible than others; blind children, for example, are more easily identified than deaf children. However, there are degrees of blindness and deafness, and as parents and teachers look at the individual who is handicapped they are sometimes overwhelmed by the handicap itself. Severely handicapped children are more easily identified and include those children who are in wheelchairs, who are quadriplegic, or who have suffered the loss of a limb or limbs. There are children who have central nervous system disorders such as cerebral palsy, who are impaired physiologically, lacking motor and/or expressive skills. These children are easily identified due to the overt manifestations of the handicap, but many others may not be, especially the epileptic. The learning disabled constitute a very large population of children who are not easily identified as handicapped yet suffer through all kinds of degradations in the public school classroom due to their apparent inability to process information — information that is presented in standard methods from which most children learn to read, write, and compute. Learning disabled children, however, sometimes suffer from an inability to process material presented in this manner and are often labeled as mentally retarded or slow learners, when in reality many of these children have an extremely high intellectual capacity but simply lack the overt skills to manifest their capabilities. The emotionally handicapped are those children who are unable to cope with the everyday world of school due to emotional crises or problems that prevent them from attending well or focusing on material being presented in the public school classroom.

All the handicapping conditions mentioned have one element in common, even though there may be a physiological manifestation of a handicapping condition, i.e. loss of a limb, spasticity, or epileptic seizure. There are children from within the ranks of these handicapped populations who have exceptionally bright minds and who could be considerably gifted in any area of endeavor including the performing arts, math, science, literature. Not one handicapping condition will preclude a gifted child from being found within its ranks. Whitmore (1981) outlines the condition for identifying gifted handicapped children. She refers to the federal definitions of gifted and handicapped.

> The mentally gifted can be defined as one with exceptional potential for (A) learning, (B) achieving academic excellence in one or more subject areas and (C) manifesting superior mental abilities through language, problem-solving and creative production. Handicapped children can be defined as those whose normal learning and development are impaired by one or more specific conditions and who need special education and related services in order to develop their abilities. (P. 107)

Children who fit within both of these exceptional areas must have their educational programs geared to both sets of characteristics.

Whitmore (1981) reports that in 1976 an estimated total of 300,000 to 540,000 children were reported to have been handicapped gifted. Previous to the implementation of Public Law 94-142, little was accomplished for this group, mostly because of the independent work by the separate professional fields of the handicapped and the gifted. Now more integration of operations between both fields occurs even though PL 94-142 did not include gifted students.

Many educational programs for the handicapped have cognitive limits even if the handicap is basically physical, not taking into account the superior abilities of the handicapped gifted. Thus, there is a great need for more experimental programs in the area of the handicapped gifted. As of 1977, a survey of special education programs in the United States came up with only eight that actually have provisions for serving the handicapped gifted student. In 1981, only three comprehensive research efforts were underway, at Johns Hopkins University, the University of Illinois, and the Texas School for the Deaf. Whitmore (1981) feels there are three causes of neglect or oversight in handicapped gifted educational programs: stereotypic expectations, developmental delays, and inability or lack of opportunity to evidence superior mental abilities.

Identifying the handicapped gifted is clearly a complicated task. For example, Stefanich and Schnur (1979) found that the four most-used criteria for identifying the gifted discriminate against the handicapped student. The first criterion, *teacher nominations*, was found to be discriminatory since teachers generally have low expectations of the handicapped. Next, *group achievement scores* were pointed out to be unfair inasmuch as they often discriminate against children with impaired sensory, manual, or speaking skills. *Group intelligence scores*, too, were found to be discriminatory against this same group of children. Finally, the criterion of *previously demonstrated accomplishments* was assessed as being unfair since handicapped children typically experience limited resources — educational facilities usually not conducive to handicapped involvement. Stefanich and Schnur give some suggestions for improving identification methods for giftedness among the handicapped, which included lowering the acceptance levels in initial screening, familiarizing school personnel with the various handicapping conditions and their concomitant text limitations, and testing with instruments that provide for a broader range of abilities.

Whiting, Anderson, and Ward (1980) outline the method used in California to identify gifted deaf children. The Leiter International Intelligence Test and the performance subtests of the WISC-R are identified as appropriate instruments to use with this group. Prior to testing, however, children must be recommended by the teacher and school principal based on characteristics that the gifted deaf were found to share with their hearing peers and manifested to a greater degree than is normally seen in the deaf population. These characteristics include the following:

1. Are more apt to be working at grade level
2. Are self-starters

3. Have a sense of humor
4. Enjoy manipulating their environment
5. Appear intuitive
6. Are ingenious in solving problems
7. Enjoy the challenge of testing
8. Check their progress without prompting
9. Have language capabilities that are clearly symbolic

Whitmore (1981) points out three causes of neglect that need to be taken into account when identifying the gifted/handicapped. The first involves the *stereotyped expectation* people have of the gifted; which leads to the belief that a child who is physically handicapped probably has a mind that is impaired as well. The next cause of neglect that Whitmore points out concerns *developmental delays*. Inasmuch as the handicapping condition may result in a curtailment of interaction experiences with the environment, cognitive growth is reduced due to a lack of stimulation. The third cause of neglect involves the inability or *lack of opportunity* a handicapped child has to evidence superior mental abilities. Since a handicapped child is often placed in an educational setting aimed at the mastery of basic skills, the handicapped gifted child has fewer opportunities to reveal his/her giftedness. Whitmore concludes that the handicapped gifted should be identified by people who can see past the handicapping condition to perceive giftedness characteristics in atypical forms.

Haring (1982) states that the handicapped gifted need to be assessed in a different manner than they typically are. Haring points out that the use of direct observation, parent reports, and self-evaluation methods are possibilities for identifying this population. Maker (1977) also suggests three techniques that can be used for identifying the handicapped gifted. They are focusing on the student's potential rather than only his/her demonstrated abilities, comparing the student with other handicapped students rather than with the general population, and observing the student's skills in compensating for the disability.

The handicapped gifted pose unique problems not only in identification but also in self-concept and mental health. Meisgeier, Meisgeier, and Werblo (1978) point out that the handicapped gifted child's perceptions of his/her own inadequacies may be keener than average, resulting in secondary emotional problems and low self-concepts. Since the handicap is often focused on and the giftedness unnoticed by others, these children may withdraw from meaningful learning experiences. Thus, such children are desperately in need of individualized programming.

Programs for Handicapped Populations

Whitmore (1981) suggests peer educational programs for the handicapped gifted in which gifted peers would help their bright handicapped classmates. Maker (1977) identifies only three programs specific to the handicapped gifted. One of these programs, RAPYHT (Retrieval and Acceleration of Promising Young Handicapped and Talented) uses two approaches for educating the handicapped gifted preschooler, the SOI (based on Guilford's Structure of the Intellect Model, *see* Chapter 1) and the open classroom. The RAPYHT program stresses extending the identification process into the actual intervention period (Karnes and Bartschi, 1978). Another program designed specifically for the handicapped gifted is the Chapel Hill Training Outreach Project, which deals with preschool children (Leonard and Cansler, 1980). Both the RAPYHT and Chapel Hill programs are funded by the Bureau of Education for the Handicapped.

Mauser (1981) suggests that an ideal program for educating the handicapped gifted should include proper diagnostic and referral systems, a variety of programs and services, and appropriate opportunities for integrating this population back into the community. Haring (1982) points out the importance of focusing on the handicapped gifted student's strengths and helping him/her circumvent the disability by providing alternate methods in teaching. Making enrichment opportunities available to such children is considered by Haring to be the key to helping them educationally. Regardless of the program in which handicapped gifted children may be educated or placed, one of the overriding concerns must be helping them develop positive self-concepts and realistic expectations for their giftedness based upon their handicapping condition. Helping the handicapped gifted child overcome his or her feelings of frustration and anxiety and develop a positive self-image should be a primary goal of any individually designed educational program. If this objective can be met, handicapped gifted children stand a greater chance of reaching their gifted potential and accepting or overcoming their handicap.

CULTURALLY DIFFERENT AND DISADVANTAGED GIFTED

Clark (1979) suggests that a delineation be made between disadvantaged and culturally different gifted children. She feels that these are two distinct populations and that discussing them as one is somewhat misleading. In effect, a culturally different child is one who has been raised within a particular culture and then placed within a new culture that has a different set of values and attitudes. A disadvantaged child is a child who because of economic reasons is precluded from participating in the normal mainstream of educational development at home and in the public school. A distinction between culturally different and disadvantaged will be made where it is necessary; however, many of the characteristics of both of these groups as well as the educational strategies to assist them are similar in nature. Like the handicapped gifted, culturally different or disadvantaged children face a society, teachers, and educational systems who do not respond well to the possibility that gifted children do in fact exist among their population. Teachers more commonly see the culturally different or disadvantaged state as being a weakness, focusing on the differences and not on the capability of the child. It is difficult for the teacher to overcome cultural barriers or to develop a system of communication that will allow the child's gifts and talents to emerge and blossom.

Identification Procedures for the Culturally Different and Disadvantaged Gifted

Culturally different children are very similar to the handicapped gifted in that they too have suffered from neglect due to the focus on their differences rather than on their giftedness. Inasmuch as the culturally different may exhibit a different learning style (Torrance, 1969), they often do not fit the stereotypical characteristics of the gifted. Thus, it is equally important with the culturally disadvantaged gifted that they be identified using methods different from those used in the predominant culture.

Because this group exemplifies traits different from the predominant culture, the identification process is complicated. Bruch and Curry (1978) suggest that the culturally disadvantaged gifted child is unlikely to perform in the average range due to negative factors impinging upon him/her. They further cite seven issues that need to be considered and dealt with in the identification of this population. These include

1. Identification of talents that are highly valued in the particular culture from which the child comes
2. Determination of talents found in various cultures that are different from those found in the dominant culture
3. Use of middle-class measurements
4. Neglect of known subcultural values and abilities in current assessment
5. Motivation problems among the disadvantaged
6. Nonrepresentative norms on standardized tests
7. Consequences of environmental factors influencing test performance

Identification of gifted and talented children within the culturally disadvantaged or different category involves some perplexing problems, especially when the utilization of standardized measurement instruments is proposed. Samuda (1975) suggests that in dealing with and identifying giftedness within minority groups standardized achievement tests should not be used because of the following:

1. Present testing practices are simply unfair to the culturally different.

2. Better trained test administrators who are sensitive to the special problems of the culturally different are needed. Without an administrator who is sensitive to these problems, results from tests may be misinterpreted and therefore misleading.
3. There is a tendency to use measures of the environment to supplement scores on IQ tests.
4. A pluralistic sociocultural model to be used in testing minorities must be developed to ensure that IQ measures take into account the characteristics of individuals from within the context of their sociocultural group.
5. New measures that utilize language features particular to the culturally different group being tested need to be developed.
6. Instruments should be utilized for description and diagnosis and not for selection and prediction.

These suggestions by Samuda (1975) tend to highlight the rather precarious nature of IQ and achievement testing in general. Many authors (Bruch, 1975; Gallagher and Kinney, 1974; Samuda, 1975; Khatena, 1980), in identifying gifted children within culturally different populations, indicate that talents do not necessarily show themselves very well on a standardized achievement test (especially a test that is or could be culturally biased and a measure of the acquisition of information relative to a particular culture. These suggestions also point to the fact that there exists a paucity of devices, instruments, and procedures that can be utilized by a teacher in the public schools to identify gifted children more adequately within culturally disadvantaged or different populations.

Chinn (1978) proposes using the Torrance Tests of Creative Thinking and Taylor and Ellison's Alpha Biographical Inventory for the identification of gifted minority children. Also, Torrance's list of eighteen characteristics of the culturally disadvantaged gifted is suggested for use in the identification process. These eighteen creative characteristics by Torrance (1977) are

1. Ability to express feelings and emotions
2. Ability to improvise with commonplace materials and objects
3. Articulateness of role playing, sociodramas, and storytelling
4. Enjoyment of and ability in visual arts such as drawing, painting, and sculpturing
5. Enjoyment of and ability in creative movement, dance, and dramatics
6. Enjoyment of and ability in music and rhythm
7. Ease of expressive speech
8. Fluency and flexibility in figural media
9. Enjoyment of and skills in group activities, and problem solving
10. Responsiveness to the concrete
11. Responsiveness to the kinesthetic

12. Expression of gestures, body language, and ability to interpret body language
13. Humor
14. Richness of imagery in informal language
15. Originality of ideas and problem solving
16. Problem centeredness or persistence in problem solving
17. Emotional responsiveness
18. Quickness of warm-up

In terms of specific minority groups, Gay (1978) points out that traditional identification techniques do not adequately identify black gifted students. She outlines a six-step plan for use in identifying this group, which includes obtaining a recurring commitment from the school district that blacks should be included in gifted programs and involving the parents in the identifying process. Gay also points out that blacks may manifest gifted characteristics in ways atypical of the predominant culture. For instance, a black gifted child may manifest the concept of keen observation by picking up more quickly on racist attitudes and practices.

With respect to Mexican American gifted students, a study by Chambers, Barron, and Sprecher (1980) found that certain personality traits differentiate those who achieve in high intellectual/creative levels from their peers who do not. Characteristics that were found to be significant in discriminating between the high achievers and the others in this group included loyalty, honesty, intelligence, dependability, calmness, and self-control. Bernal (1978) found the following characteristics typical of the gifted Chicano child: acquires English skills rapidly given exposure, exhibits leadership ability, enjoys intelligent risk taking, keeps busy and entertained, accepts responsibility, and is street wise.

Studies conducted by Gay (1978) and Chen and Goon (1976) relative to handicapped gifted Asian children indicated that when using traditional methods of identifying the gifted, a greater percentage of Asians are found to be gifted than would typically be found among other groups. It was concluded that disadvantaged Asian children appear to succeed in school despite several cultural barriers, but it was hypothesized that this was due to teacher-student interaction effects and not home environment.

Swenson (1978) found that using creativity as an indicator of giftedness appears to be an appropriate alternative to intelligence tests when identifying the gifted among the culturally disadvantaged. She defines creativity in terms of twenty-five specific, observable behaviors as listed by elementary school teachers of the disadvantaged. A study by Forman (1979) on creativity among the gifted socioeconomically disadvantaged confirmed Swenson's viewpoint. Results of her study indicate that when IQ and achievement level are similar, differences between SES groups on the measure of creativity are not significant. Tidwell (1981) found that gifted minority students have higher self-concept scores and higher internal locus of control scores than their nongifted minority peers.

Programs for Culturally Different and Disadvantaged

According to Gallagher (1975), when planning an educational program for the culturally disadvantaged gifted student, the program should reflect the cultural diversity of the population. Many different approaches have been proposed in programming for the culturally different gifted child: locating occupational success models within the community to aid the minority students planning occupational goals and to stress the importance of excellence in all study areas (Stallings, 1972), utilizing flexible scheduling, ungraded classes, and independent study (Gallagher and Kinney, 1974), and stressing the importance of modeling by the parents of these children as an important part of educational programming (Marion, 1980; Stallings, 1972).

A language arts program based on the characteristics of culturally different gifted students is proposed by Patterson and Starcher (1982). They stress the importance of making all instruction relevant. An environment opened to all cultures was also considered important. Witty (1978) discusses several considerations for educating the culturally disadvantaged gifted student. She points out the need to program in terms of the child's strengths, characteristics, and learning and living styles. Also, teaching free of limiting expectations, counseling programs, and parental and community support services are deemed necessary in educating this population.

Frasier (1979) urges the development of a combined counseling and instructional approach utilizing the following four objectives: development of communication skills, development of skills that enhance the ability to distinguish between relevant and nonrelevant information, development of testing skills, and development of familiarity with information processing. She also points out five things to consider when developing curricula for the disadvantaged gifted. They are

1. The disadvantaged child does not necessarily come from a home where love and affection prevail.
2. Such children do not necessarily suffer from sensory deprivation or a lack of stimulation.
3. In many fundamental ways, a disadvantaged child's cognition is quite similar to that of middle-class children.
4. A child's language may clash with the school's values, but it is this conflict and not the language that largely accounts for poor performance in school.
5. A child will become motivated to learn if he is taught as effectively as possible regardless of his initial lack of motivation.

With regard to specific programs, a three-week summer program for a multiethnic group of children in grades two through five, called "A Model Summer Program for Gifted Children," was established in Houston, Texas. Another program, entitled PCEP (Professional Career Exploration Program for Minority and/or Low-Income Gifted and Talented 10th Grade Students) was developed, based on the following provisions (Moore, 1978):

1. Exploration opportunities in actual community settings
2. Active professional role models
3. Special time allotted for sharing and intellectualizing experience
4. Opportunity to examine one's own self-concept and values
5. In-depth views of the career ladders for each profession explored
6. Individualized guidance
7. Sensitizing time to analyze professional lifestyles, values, ethics, and goals

Culturally different children pose their own sets of unique problems and concerns. Fuchigami (1978) suggests twelve program development activities that could be considered in helping these gifted children (and all gifted children) as follows:

1. Regional schools or programs that enable gifted to transcend traditional school district boundaries. This idea could involve a variety of possibilities within and between districts, cities, counties, states, regions, and even nations.
2. Year round educational programs involving special sessions at different locations.
3. Special educational travel-study programs to locations like the Smithsonian Institute, National Aeronautics and Space Administration facilities, marine laboratories and so forth, operated by both public and private organizations, agencies, and industries.
4. Special talent and leadership camps. Depending on location some could be operated on a year round basis and others on a seasonal basis. Gifted pupils would attend for varying lengths of time.
5. Short term student exchange programs within the state, region and nation. The exchanges could mean opportunities to move from urban to suburban or rural settings and vice versa.
6. Criss-cross national "walkabout" type programs whereby students could drop off for varying lengths of time to stay at hostel type homes and sample unique educational experiences in specialized centers of learning.
7. Short term and part-time work-study internships with private industrial and business firms, public agencies, and foundation supported programs.
8. Special cultural heritage programs for minority gifted so they can learn about their roots through a variety of activities and opportunities.
9. Establishment of regional or national universities or educational learning institutes especially planned and staffed for genius or extremely high level gifted. These rare children are potential human treasures unique to humanity and should receive very special development opportunities for their talents and abilities. Such centers might also become available for children from other countries if provisions for their families could also be included.

10. Special family programs and options that include all members of the family. The minority gifted from economically poor environments need special consideration by program planners to minimize concerns related to potential conflict and alienation in family relationships. Alternatives for family programs should range from simple inclusion of specially trained family caseworker/counselors to something as radical as family relocation options involving public or private employment for all working members of the family.

11. Special schools. At a time when busing children is widely practiced, the gifted could be easily transported to special schools without the usual problems accompanying such practices.

12. Short term boarding schools whereby students return home on weekends and holidays. (Khatena, 1982, pp. 246, 250)

UNDERACHIEVING GIFTED

A survey reported by Johnson (1981) showed that students with IQs over 130 comprised 45 percent of the student population, had *C* or lower grades, and involved 14 percent of the high school dropouts within the particular area in which the study was conducted. Such a high rate of underachievement among gifted students is alarming, considering the potential of this unique population. It is often taken for granted that bright students will excel in school; however, as the Johnson report clearly illustrates, this often is not the case. The reasons for underachievement must be thoroughly investigated in the hopes of understanding and correcting this perplexing dilemma.

Identification of Underachieving Gifted

The underlying causes of underachievement and the identification procedures for the gifted underachiever are varied and mixed. The reason usually given when defining and identifying this population of gifted children is that underachievement is due to a developmental problem or to a problem caused by external factors, i.e. family, school, environment, peer pressure. Gowan (1955) attempts to define the gifted underachiever by claiming that underachievement is performance related; the child does not perform up to his or her capabilities but usually performs one or more standard deviations below his or her measured ability.

Clark (1979) indicates that there are essentially two types of underachieving gifted students. The *situational underachiever* is that child who is underachieving only on occasion, related to a disruption in the child's home or school routine. Having difficulty with teachers or peers at school or with siblings and parents at home may disrupt the routine momentarily and cause a child not to perform up to capabilities. Clark feels that this is only a momentary problem and is corrected by removing the adverse situation. In essence, situational underachievement is short-lived. The second type of underachiever is a *chronic* one, with recurring learning behaviors that prevent optimum performance. Clark (1979) feels that these behaviors are resistant in some degree to remediation. Perhaps one of the first steps in dealing with the chronic underachiever is to rule out an organic basis for the child's underachievement, then to determine if the child's learning problems are related to an inability to process information properly. If this is the case, the child's underachievement may be dealt with dramatically by treating or correcting the organic cause, i.e. visual-motor, auditory-motor, or perceptual deficiencies, for the underachievement.

Whitmore (1979) suggests that the principal contributors to gifted underachievement include the social climate, the classroom, and the academic curriculum. A study by Kanoy, Johnson, and Kanoy (1980) compared achieving and underachieving bright fourth grade students in the variables of self-concept and locus of control. They found that the underachieving group has a significantly lower self-concept on the intellectual and social status scales of the Piers-Harris Self-Concept Scale. Underachievers also have a significantly lower internal locus of control than achievers. Other investigations (Angelino, 1960; Gallagher, 1975; Whitmore, 1980) point to effects that the social milieu (including family, school, and society in general) can have upon the child. Johnson (1981) indicates that the tendency of gifted students to question conventional standards may generate friction between them and school faculty and administrators. Also, since schools generally stress the basics at the expense of high levels of learning, gifted students often become bored and disinterested with school, resulting in underachievement. Often gifted students show more sensitivity to criticism and may stop taking risks in their academic development if met with criticism instead of approval; hence, Johnson (1981) feels that it is up to schools to stop underachievement from occurring among the gifted by having teachers and others relate to these students as people.

An interesting theory about the underachieving female gifted child is proposed by Fitzpatrick (1978). She found that differences in patterns of achievement between achievers and underachievers typically began in sixth grade. She suggests that females who are more subject to the influence of others and more traditional in their views of women's roles perform less well in mathematics, which is often considered a masculine area of expertise, than those who are less susceptible to another's opinion. Historically, it is well documented that women do not participate in the mathematics and science areas as readily as do men, and this trend has only slightly shifted in the past ten or twelve years (Sucher, 1982).

1. It could be a result of poor curriculum planning on the part of the educational community or a lack of stimulation or overstimulation in the home.
2. Pressure from immediate peers and family members is sometimes sug-

gested as a reason for the child not performing up to potential.

3. In the public school setting, the child changes from being "different" because of his gifts and talents to being "normal," thereby suppressing potential and capabilities.

4. There are also possible physiological (such as the inability to process information properly), organic-based, and developmental reasons (the child in some areas of development has outgrown or grown up to his or her capabilities).

Characteristics

Perhaps the most complete list of characteristics that have been identified among gifted underachievers is that proposed by Clark (1979). She combined the work of several authors (approximately twenty-four different studies) and made a composite list of characteristics that were identified among underachievers. These can be found in Figure 5-1.

1. Low self-concept, negative evaluations of themselves, feelings of inferiority that are demonstrated by distrust, disinterest, lack of concern, and even hostility toward others.
2. They often feel rejected by their family; they feel that their parents are dissatisfied with them.
3. Due to a feeling of helplessness, they take little responsibility for their actions; externalizing conflict and problems.
4. They may show hostility and distrust toward adult authority figures.
5. They often do not like school or their teachers and choose companions who have negative attitudes toward school also.
6. They may seem rebellious.
7. Lack motivation for academic achievement.
8. Lack academic skills.
9. They tend to have poor study habits, do less homework, and frequently nap when trying to study.
10. Appear to be less intellectually adaptive, less persistent, less assertive, and show high levels of withdrawal in classroom situations.
11. They hold lower leadership status, are less popular with their peers, and are often less mature than achievers (e.g., lack self-discipline, procrastinate, show unwillingness to complete tasks deemed unpleasant, have high distractibility, act highly impulsively, and are unwilling to face unpleasant realities).
12. They often show poor personal adjustment and express feelings of being restricted in their actions.
13. They may not have any hobbies, interests, or activities that could occupy their spare time.
14. They tend to have lower aspirations than achievers and do not have a clear idea of future plans and vocational goals.
15. They tend to state their goals very late and often choose goals that are not in line with their major interests or abilities. Often the goals they adopt have been set for them.
16. In choosing a career, underachievers show preferences for manaul activities, business, sales occupations over more socially concerned or professional occupations.

Figure 5-1. Characteristics of gifted underachievers. Adapted from Clark, 1979.

Curriculum Considerations

A frequently reported consideration in a child's curriculum is that of the teacher. Bricklan and Bricklan (1967) and Fine (1967) report that poor teaching is as a major cause of underachievement in gifted students. As Johnson (1981) points out, teachers can help by being open and sensitive to the special needs of the gifted and ensuring that they are treated as people. Teachers must also be well trained in their area of expertise and willing to provide an environment that is conducive to learning and will stimulate interesting development within the subject matter.

The school environment in general must value achievement and encourage it as a healthy attitude within all of its students. This will create a milieu in which being a high achiever will not be viewed as "different" or "strange." One important aspect of the curriculum should be to develop and build a student's self-concept and esteem; this can be done by creating an open, warm, and intellectually challenging environment in which success and opportunities to achieve can be realized.

Whitmore (1980) stresses that educational programs for underachievers should involve early identification and preventative intervention before negative attitudes and counterproductive habits become established within the child. In summation, the curriculum should be a composite of comfortable, accepting environment and social milieu that is supportive, staffed with teachers who are well trained and can provide stimulating and positive experiences for the child.

PART III

IN the following five chapters can be found information on the development of programs and curriculum for the gifted and talented child. The purpose of these chapters is to provide teachers and parents with basic information and ideas relative to planning educational programs for accelerated learners. The curriculum areas of creativity, math, reading and language arts, general science, and performing and visual arts are presented from the frame of reference of the public school. The components that should be considered in developing a curriculum in each of these areas are presented along with suggestions of how teachers can go about setting up classrooms and programs. Resources that could be used and/or investigated to better help the gifted and talented program in the public schools are given in each chapter. A section focusing on the identification of gifted and talented learners in each of these areas is also a feature of these chapters.

CHAPTER SIX

CREATIVITY

Can you answer the following questions?

1. What is creativity?
2. How would you identify a creative child? What are some characteristics?
3. What is the Five-Step Creative Process? How does it function in problem solving?
4. How might you enrich the life and experiential base for a gifted or talented child?
5. What is divergent thinking and how can you facilitate this process for the gifted and talented child?
6. Can you define convergent thinking? How is this implemented for the gifted in the classroom and in the home?
7. What are some commercial resources (games) that are founded on divergent or creative thinking?

The Blind Men and The Elephant

It was six men of Indostan,
To learning much inclined,
Who went to see the elephant,
(Though all of them were blind,)
That each by observation
Might satisfy his mind.

The first aproached the elephant
And, happening to fall
Against his broad and sturdy side,
At once began to bawl:
"God bless me! But the elephant
Is very like a wall!"

The second, feeling of the tusk,
Cried: "Ho! What have we here,
So very round, and smooth, and sharp?
To me 'tis very clear,

This wonder of an elephant
Is very like a spear!"

The third approached the animal,
And, happening to take
The squirming trunk within his hands,
Thus boldly up to spake:
"I see," quoth he, "the elephant
Is very like a snake!"

The fourth reached out his eager hand,
And felt about the knee;
What most this wondrous beast is like.
"Is mighty plain," quoth he;
" 'Tis clear enough the elephant
Is very like a tree!"

The fifth, who chanced to touch the ear,
Said: "E'en the blindest man
Can tell what this resembles most:
Deny the fact who can,
This marvel of an elephant
Is very like a fan!"

The sixth no sooner had begun
About the beast to grope,
Than seizing on the swinging tail
That fell within his scope,
"I see," quoth he, "the elephant
Is very like a rope!"

And so these men of Indostan
Disputed loud and long,
Each in his own opinion
Exceeding stiff and strong.
Though each was partly in the right,
All were in the wrong!

                                              John Godfrey Saxe

DEFINITIONS

And so it is with creativity; it is many different things to many different people. A single definition of creativity that would encompass *exactly* all the facets and functions of the creative process would be nearly impossible to express. Various definitions of creativity appear to have originated from debates on the questions of giftedness and creativity and whether they exist as separate entities. Are gifted persons necessarily creative? Is artistic creativity the same as scientific creativity? What of problem solving? Can creativity be broken into specific skills that can be taught and learned? Do we measure creativity against the individual's past performances and experiences or against societal norms? Research has not given many firm answers to these questions. Just as in the story of the blind men and the elephant, where one is standing at the time greatly affects how one perceives creativity.

Teachers are wise to define creativity in terms of application to the educational setting. Torrance (1970) defines creativity as "becoming sensitive to or aware of problems, deficiencies, gaps in knowledge, missing elements, disharmonies and so on; bringing together available information defining the difficulty or identifying the missing element; searching for solutions, making guesses or formulating hypothesis and modifying and restating them; perfecting them and finally communicating the results" (p. 22). Jones (1972) offers the following definition: "Creativity is a combination of the flexibility, originality, and sensitivity to ideas which enables the learner to break away from usual sequences of thought into different and productive sequences, the result of which gives satisfaction to himself and possibly to others" (p. 7).

Flinders (1982) recommends that students be encouraged to begin thinking about the creative process less in the mystical sense of only that which is new, novel, different, and unusual — the subconscious capacity limited to a few eccentric and marginally normal characters — and more in the practical sense of anything that is organized from existing elements for some useful purpose. This means that the creation of something that is old, similar, common, usual, and familiar to others could also qualify as a new creative act for the individual. Students need to see the elements of the creative process as commonplace components in their everyday experience. Creativity is a very concrete process that can be understood, observed, and possessed by all, from the most handicapped to the most gifted.

To elucidate upon Flinder's premise, Adams (1970) quotes Michael F. Andrews as saying, "Creativity is a process of individual experience which enhances the self. It is an expression of one's self." According to Adams, when we value creativity we are actually valuing the individual. Valuing the individual encourages optimum development and helps the individual reach toward the highest level of self-expression. Each child's individuality should be accepted and appreciated. Comparing children with peers or others in the family only encourages conformity and discourages creativity. Adams outlines several concepts important in understanding and developing creativity.

1. Creativity is developmental. We all have the potential to be creative.
2. Creativity involves individuality. If we value the individual, then we will be valuing creativity.
3. Creativity is developed through sensitivity in perception. It comes from being open to experience.
4. Creativity grows through the opportunity to experiment and explore.
5. Creativity is stimulated through imaginative and original thinking.
6. Creativity is autonomy and self-confidence. A good self-concept is a necessity for creative growth.

7. Creativity increases through expression of feelings and perceptions. Communication of creative experience increases its value.
8. Creativity is curiosity, a desire to know and experience many things.
9. Creativity is awareness, the ability to absorb and enjoy all that life has to offer.
10. Creative expression must be encouraged and provided for. Children need opportunity to present creative ideas in visual forms.

Creative force is life force — full, actualizing, satisfying life force. It holds immeasurable promise and opportunity. It is a very precious way of being committed to living. It is a worthwhile venture for parents and children — for all mankind.

CHARACTERISTICS OF CREATIVE CHILDREN

Creative children manifest a variety of characteristics that have been recorded by several authors. MacKinnon's (1962) study identified creative persons as being nonconforming and generally independent. The characteristics identified by MacKinnon are

1. Creative people do not represent stereotypes.
2. Creative people are well above average in intelligence.
3. Creative people possess verbal intelligence, spatial intelligence, or sometimes both.
4. Creative people possess unusual capacity to record, retain, and have readily available the experience of their life history.
5. They are discerning and observant in a different fashion; they are alert, capable of concentrating readily and shifting if appropriate; they are fluent in scanning thoughts and producing those that serve to solve the problems they undertake; they have a wide range of information at their command.
6. Intelligence alone will not tend to produce creativity. Creativity is a relevant absence of repression and suppression as mechanisms for control of impulse and imagery. Repression operates against creativity regardless of how intelligent a person may be.
7. The creative person is given to expression rather than suppression or repression and thus has fuller access to his own experience, both conscious and unconscious.
8. Openness to experience is one of the most striking characteristics of a highly creative person.
9. A highly creative person has a closer identification of feminine traits or characteristics in himself than a noncreative person does. He is more open to feelings and emotions.

10. Everyone perceives and judges, but the creative person tends to prefer perceiving to judging. Where a judging person emphasizes the control and regulation of experience, the perceptive, more creative person is inclined to be more interested and curious, more open and receptive, seeking to experience life to the fullest.
11. Artists in general show a preference for feeling, scientists and engineers a preference for thinking. Architects are somewhere between the two groups.
12. A highly creative person is genuinely independent.
13. The creative person is relatively less interested in small detail and more concerned with meaning and implication. He is relatively uninterested in policing his own impulses and images or those of others.
14. He has preference for complexity and his delight is in the challenging and the unfinished.
15. Creative persons almost always display a good sense of humor.
16. Creative people tend to be more self-sufficient, more self-assertive, more self-accepting, and more introverted.

For comparison to MacKinnon's traits, a list of characteristics outlined by Torrance (1966) is presented below. It is interesting to note that in both lists (MacKinnon's and Torrance's) the creative person is a more independent, energetic, curious, and unconventional individual who may deviate dramatically from peers in solving problems and answering questions. Torrance's outline is as follows:

1. always baffled by something
2. desires to excel
3. has determination
4. is a fault-finder
5. is dominant (not in a power sense)
6. feels strong affection
7. is attracted to the mysterious
8. is persistent
9. is bashful outwardly
10. defies conventions of courtesy
11. is constructive in criticism
12. attempts difficult jobs (sometimes too difficult)
13. is courageous
14. defies conventions of health
15. has deep conscientious convictions
16. is discontented
17. feels whole parade is out of step
18. keeps unusual hours
19. lacks business ability
20. makes mistakes
21. is never bored
22. is receptive to the ideas of others
23. is not hostile or negativistic
24. has oddities of habits
25. regresses occasionally
26. is resolute
27. is a self-starter
28. is reserved
29. shuns power
30. has a sense of destiny
31. is sincere
32. is speculative
33. doesn't fear being thought different
34. likes solitude
35. is introversive
36. is thorough
37. is somewhat uncultured
38. is unsophisticated
39. is visionary
40. is versatile
41. is willing to take risks
42. is not interested in small details
43. is spirited in disagreement

44. is tenacious
45. is unwilling to attempt anything on mere say-so
46. has a lively mind for retention
47. excels in size and quality of vocabulary
48. is industrious, persevering
49. has self-confidence, will-power, leadership

A great amount of literature has been written concerning the relationship between creativity and intelligence. It appears that these concepts are neither naturally inclusive nor mutually exclusive of each other. A creative individual may not necessarily score very high on a conventional test of intelligence, while individuals scoring extemely high on these types of tests may demonstrate few of the characteristics of creative persons presented in the foregoing lists. Wallach and Kogan (1965) found that these two concepts are not mutually exclusive but that creative children are in the upper range of intellectual ability. Laycock (1979) concludes from reviewing the work of Getzels and Jackson (1967), Hudson (1966), Burt (1962), and others that when ". . . studying bright childlren, we may therefore expect them to be creative to varying degrees" (p. 80). Perhaps the most important thing in planning for the creative child is not to be aware of whether he or she has scored high on a test of intelligence but to be aware of those characteristics manifest in overt behavior that parents and teachers can use in understanding and helping the child.

THE CREATIVE PROCESS

Many case studies of creative thinking processes have suggested that creativity can be explained as a series of orderly stages. Each stage is important to the overall process. Wallas (1962) described these stages as preparation, incubation, illumination, and verification. Another way of looking at these stages is through the Five-Step Creative Process, as follows:

1. Define the problem.
2. Pursue alternatives (brainstorm).
3. Prioritize or narrow down the alternatives to a workable plan.
4. Experiment (try out the idea).
5. Evaluate.

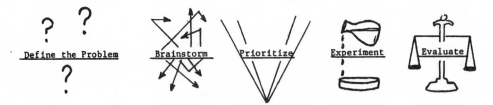

Figure 6-1. The Five-Step Process.

DEFINING THE PROBLEM. When the problem can be defined clearly and the key elements to be resolved can be identified, this provides the basis for an approach to the problem and the delimitations within which the problem solver must operate. Often in defining the problem clearly the problem solver is freed from extra, unrelated variables. The creative process is, after all, a matter of problem solving.

PURSUING ALTERNATIVES (BRAINSTORMING). Pursuing alternatives means the problem solver is opening his or her thoughts to other options. All too often the problem solver is prone to operate within the framework of the immediate and obvious solution without thinking of and taking time to consider other and perhaps more advantageous, appropriate, or beneficial alternatives. However this process may be labeled — divergent thinking, brainstorming, or exploring ideas — it is the same reaching out and looking for other possibilities before selecting or choosing a specific plan. Brainstorming is an important part of the creative process and it is wise to help students learn to brainstorm properly and productively. The rationale and procedure for conducting a brainstorming session are as follows:

Rationale: A greater fluency of ideas is believed to produce ideas of higher quality. This is a process that involves the exploring of ideas without judgement or censor. All ideas should receive acceptance and consideration. Unusual ideas or takeoffs from ideas already suggested should be encouraged.

Time Involved: Three to thirty minutes. The session may last as long as the group continues to offer ideas, but a time period encourages more rapid involvement and production of ideas and provides some reassurance of closure. Follow-up activities may take another ten to thirty minutes or could lead to a longer project.

Materials Needed: A pencil and a piece of paper or chalk and a chalkboard.

Organizational Pattern: A small group with a facilitator (teacher or group leader).

Procedures: A focus for the group should be given and the rules of brainstorming stated.

1. No criticism allowed; all ideas accepted.
2. Make your ideas as unusual as possible and give as many as you can.
3. Build on ideas you get from others.
4. No evaluation until the session is completed.

The leader or group secretary lists all ideas on the paper with no evaluative comment. Only after the brainstorming session has ceased are the ideas discussed. The teacher may now help the group to evaluate the ideas against a criteria for selection that they had agreed on at the beginning.

It is when problem solvers are thinking divergently in the brainstorming process that humor most often develops and the unusual is discovered. Humor and flexibility are key elements in brainstorming.

PRIORITIZING. Once as many of the available options as possible have been considered, it is important to move to the prioritizing stage. This involves critiquing and questioning the various ideas and narrowing down the options to one or two. This is an important part of commitment and dedication to the plan. It is not until the problem solver can prioritize and select one plan of action in which he is willing to invest his time and efforts that he will feel comfortable and motivated to follow through with the plan. Many ideas may be fun and exciting, but generally the problem solver must choose a plan and then commit to action.

EXPERIMENTING. It is sad when a person thinks creatively and constructively and then does nothing with it. The creative process can be wasted time and effort if there is not a constructive product. True, thought processes may be good exercise and productive within themselves, but it is when the problem solver can apply the process to the benefit of himself and others that gains are noted. The resulting product also provides feedback and a means of evaluation.

EVALUATING. Evaluation is often an informal process of considering the time, money, materials, energy expended, and productive results of the creative efforts. Another facet of evaluation is to consider the problem and intent. In many cases evaluation is given by the consumer or witness to the event. Time is a factor, too, in that frequently it requires time and patience to truly judge the long-term results or effects of the creative effort.

The Five-Step Creative Process is not always followed in an orderly and sequential manner. Sometimes the problem solver finds himself brainstorming or pursuing alternatives at random and discovers a different solution to a problem that can then be more clearly defined. The problem solver may be experimenting with solutions at random and find one that works; upon evaluation, it is found to be a superb solution. He can then consider the original problem involved or come through the steps and not identify satisfactory priority options, thus provoking the need to rebrainstorm. Upon evaluation, the problem solver may discover the need to return to a given step in the Five-Step Creative Process and reinitiate the efforts, as in Figure 6-2.

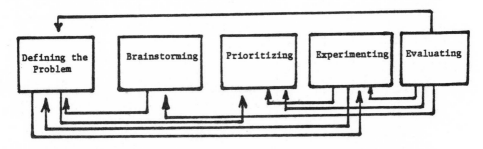

Figure 6-2. Returning to an earlier stage in the Five-Step Creative Process.

Earlier in this book, the authors stressed the need for a balanced program in the life of the gifted child. It is interesting to note that this also appears to be an important principle regarding creativity. Blake (1980), in her book *Educating Exceptional Pupils*, has stated:

> Creative production requires particular academic, intellectual, motivational, and physical characteristics.
>
> Academic: extensive knowledge and skills to apply to new problems.
>
> Intellectual: brightness, special abilities such as facility in remembering and associating diverse bits of information, sensitivity to problems, and skill in evaluation.
>
> Motivational: willingness to work long and hard, and also tolerance of ambiguity, frustration, and failure.
>
> Physical: stamina and energy level to stay with a problem over a long period.
>
> Social/emotional: willingness to face criticism or at least indifference and the ability to tolerate the aloneness and isolation required for the concentration and work needed for creative production. (P. 328)

ENRICHMENT ACTIVITIES

Dr. Merrill Bradshaw, musician and composer, once explained the need for individuals to "fill the hopper" if they are to be creative and deal with alternatives. In other words, a gifted or talented child needs a rich background of experiences and associations if he or she is to be truly effective in problem solving. These experiences should reflect a broad range of interests and activities. This experiential base can be founded on field trips, books and films, miniclasses, home experiences, and associations with interesting people of different cultures, vocations, or talents. Teachers should be resourceful in directing a child's explorations in a variety of areas. Sensitivity and awareness tasks, wherein the gifted child is exposed to hearing, smelling, tasting, touching, or visual experiences, for example, can be very helpful.

Hearing — Teachers may use tapes, music, attention to sounds in the room, or voice differences in teaching auditory awareness.

Smelling — The old parlor game of trying to identify substances from their aroma is a good olfactory experience. A clever teacher might also use a fragrance as part of a lesson (pine, fresh bread, soap, or the like).

Tasting — New and unusual foods, flavors, and textures may be introduced. Simple foods can be used to teach detection and differentiation of spices. Temperature can also add to the tasting experience.

Touching — In training the kinesthetic sense, a young child may enjoy the touch box, where children reach inside and try to identify objects from touch, texture, or weight. Textures can be brought into the lesson plan, too. Students can learn to identify and describe how things feel (sand, water, marbles, gelatin, cotton balls, and a myriad of items).

Seeing — From the time a child is a baby there should be constant visual stimulation. A child learns a lot from seeing. People, colors, toys, furniture, and miscellaneous items are part of a new world of experience. Just moving the child from room to room or to the outdoors can help in visual stimulation.

Searle (1982) proposes the following activities for creative enrichment:

Reading The Environment

A. In the Room
    1. Are there colors in the room?
    2. Are there shapes in the room?
    3. Are there textures in the room?
    4. What do people do in the room?
    5. Are there animals in the room?
    6. What sounds do we hear in the room?
    7. Encourage the children to notice the room by making small changes like pictures upside down, adding new objects, etc.
    8. Pick a spot and look at everything using a magnifying glass.
    9. Walk around the inside of the school and look for all of the above.

B. Outdoors
    1. Go for a walk and look for landmarks on the way there and see if you can find the same landmarks on the way back. Help the children find their own way next time.
    2. Volunteer committees go out and read the environment. They look for circles, squares, buildings, animals, signs, etc.
    3. Make people checklists of things outdoors and see if the children can find and mark down the objects.
    4. Make bar graphs using chips — how many of each did we see? Always discuss the graphs and read them to the children. Like 5 stop signs equal 5 chips and 4 yield signs equal 4 chips — which signs did we see the most of?

C. Look at Signs
    1. Notice numbers on street signs, house numbers, etc.
    2. Notice that words are used on signs for giving instructions, warning, labeling and information.
    3. Label things in the room, using words or just the first letter such as "t" for table.
    4. Play a getting to know you game using the child's names on cards.
    5. Read "Mr. Pine's Mixed-up Signs." Make your room into a highway using cars made out of packing cartons: road signs, traffic policeman, pedestrians. They will learn how to be better pedestrians and also learn car safety rules.

D. Looking at Geography
    1. Look for geographic features in the neighborhood and then have the children use words to describe them.
    2. Act out ocean waves, pine trees in a windstorm, etc.
    3. Have the children talk about how it would feel to be a cave, the sun, an empty playground, etc.
    4. Point out and look for attractive things in the environment. Read, "Nothing Ever Happens on My Block," by Ellen Raskins.
    5. List the things the children like about the environment.

6. List the things the children don't like in the environment and how they can change them. Read "Who Cares? I Do!" by Munro Leaf.
7. Collect things outdoors and make terrariums.
8. Adopt a block or playground. Take a picture before your clean-up campaign and after you've finished.

Mapping The Community
A. Map Thinking
   1. Take a Penny Walk. At the corners flip a coin. Heads turn right, tails turn left.
   2. Let the children tell you how to get from the room to the playground, etc.
B. Map Making
   1. Use blocks and props to make a map of the room.
   2. Make a table-top town. Make people out of pipe cleaners, cars out of clay, and boxes for buildings.
   3. Make a map with wrapping tape.
   4. Use the globe and maps in the room.
   5. Tell stories from different countries and point out where that country or area is.
   6. Draw pictures of your own homes and neighborhoods.
   7. Make a photo-map of the neighborhood.
   8. Visit a firehouse or have a fireman visit.

People in the Community
A. Role Playing
   1. Start with a housekeeping corner.
   2. Talk about animals and their homes.
   3. When you go out into the community, use poles in buckets of plaster of paris to hold signs, make doorways, store fronts or as dividers.
   4. List things people do in the community — go to school, eat, sell things, play baseball, etc.
B. Careers
   1. Who gives us food, shelter, clothing, etc?
   2. Discuss how people work to provide services.
   3. Have the children interview community workers invited as visitors to the classroom. Plan questions ahead of time.
   4. Find out what workers do, what tools they use, how their work helps us. What does a worker need to know in this job?
   5. Let the children paint a wall or fence outside using brushes and buckets of water.
   6. Display a picture of a worker, ask the children questions about the picture and write down their response. Read their responses to the family at the end of the day.
   7. Dramatize careers.
   8. Read stories about different workers.

How People Keep in Touch
A. Ways of Communicating
   1. Discuss ways of communicating without talking.
   2. Use facial expressions and have the children guess the feelings of each other.
   3. Use body language.

4. Talk about community communications like mail boxes, TV's, radios, telephones.
5. Visit areas in the community where communication originates.

How People Travel

A. How People Travel
1. Discuss how to get from one point to another.
2. Experiment with distance.
3. Discuss vehicles and categorize them.
4. Classify modes of travel according to speed.
5. Discuss problems like pollution and gas shortages.
6. Make vehicles out of boxes or clay or draw pictures of them.
7. Take a trip on different vehicles.

How The Community Changes

A. You Change
1. Take snapshots of the children throughout the year.
2. Keep lists of how they grow and change during the year.

B. The Community Changes
1. Bigger-New Homes-larger trees, etc. Use old pictures going back a year, 5 years, 10 years, 20 years, or more.
2. Read "The Little Chestnut Tree" story by Lisl Weil. Good lead-in for ecology.
3. Read "Who Built the Bridge?" by Norman Bate. Afterwards, pick a new building going up and take pictures of the different stages of construction.

C. The Seasons Change
1. Make four-season pictures.
2. Collect and mount pictures of seasonal scenes.
3. If you have a tabletop town set up have the children make Christmas decorations and other seasonal changes.
4. Make a mural of the different seasons.*

Developing Thinking Skills

It is helpful to a gifted or talented child to learn the processes of problem solving and to be taught how to effectively use the thinking skills that will strengthen productive efforts. Two of the thinking practices are identified as divergent and convergent thinking. Both these thinking skills come naturally to most people, as can be observed in young children. It is true, however, that the gifted may tend to utilize one more than the other and may need some wise direction and practice with each. There are many educational methods, games, and activities that are designed to help with each of these thinking skills.

---

*From J. G. Searle, *Helping Your Child Get the "Most" from the Environment*, Unpublished. Courtesy of the author.

Divergent Thinking

Divergent thinking may be defined as the ability to study a problem and develop a number of solutions or alternatives. The divergent thinker is not limited by the conventions or stereotypes imposed upon and accepted by others, therefore, this child is challenging to the patience and adaptability of the teacher. Divergent thinking has been discussed in some detail earlier in this chapter as "brainstorming." If a gifted child tends to think convergently most of the time, it is very healthy to introduce some divergent thinking activities to help the child gain new insights and possibilities. When the child cannot initiate divergent thinking activities and experiences a block in thinking or problem solving, he or she needs to be taught the value of brainstorming with a friend or associate. This activity can be fun and productive and can also foster good personal and cooperative relationships. When approaching a friend with a divergent or brainstorming task, one should be careful not to give the friend one's mental set. For example, one would not say to one's friend, "I am seeking a theme for a poster for April, and I cannot get past 'April Showers.' " Now the friend has April showers predominately in mind and may have difficulty brainstorming. It is wiser to simply state the problem and ask for suggestions: "I am seeking a theme for a poster for April. Will you help me consider possibilities?" Also, from the beginning one should tell one's friend that ideas are needed but not a solution at this time. Both persons are to share ideas as fast and freely as they come, just for the fun of it. Thus the problem solver is not obligated to accept and follow through with the idea(s) offered by the friend but may incubate the possibilities, prioritize, and select the option that is most personally appealing.

Many class activities can be designed around open-ended, free-choice, divergent tasks. Children can be encouraged to make original cards, stories, or projects; create dramas, productions, or dances; invent humor to be shared; seek different answers to a known problem; freely use blank paper and pen, crayon, or paint; discover and explore; change the location, setting, or environment for learning; or create a new game.

The teacher can ask questions such as What other ways could a person use this item? How many people are involved in the production of a can of soup? Questions need to be open-ended and not designed for yes and no answers or the finding of a given solution known by the teacher.

Parents are wise to introduce divergent thinking tasks during travel, at home, or perhaps at the supermarket (Sucher, 1981). They may ask questions such as How many things can you see that are square? Red? Rough? Horizontal? Soft? Plastic? Where could you go to see a bird? Fish? Monster? Train? Butterfly? Policeman? Many responses to a given question can be sought, which really challenges children's thinking.

Paper and pencil games are fun for the divergent thinker. The following are examples of paper and pencil games that should exercise a child's divergent thinking.

WHAT CAN YOU SPELL? Several letters can be placed on the paper and the children can see how many animals, foods, names, etc. they can spell.

L G D _____

M A B _____

K I F _____

H B E _____

N R C _____

T O S _____

OLD TO NEW (Monson, 1981) challenges children to find new uses for old items such as discarded containers, empty boxes, broken toys and so on. For each of the following objects, they should identify as many uses as they can think of, trying to think of some uses that others have not thought of, list all the ideas that come to mind even if they seem silly or impractical. The objects may be changed to suit the leader's purpose.

Empty Milk Cartons

1. _____   7. _____
2. _____   8. _____
3. _____   9. _____
4. _____   10. _____
5. _____   11. _____
6. _____   12. _____

Old Automobiles Tires

1. _____   2. _____

---

*These and following activities from Jay A. Monson. Unpublished. Courtesy of the author.

3. _____   8. _____
4. _____   9. _____
5. _____   10. _____
6. _____   11. _____
7. _____   12. _____

PICTURE MESSAGES (Monson, 1981) allow children to produce original visual symbols for standard everyday words and directions. Signs along our highway often use pictures to give directions to drivers. A good picture should enable the driver to recognize its meaning instantly. Children should imagine that they are designers who have been asked to design symbols for each message below. They are to draw their pictures in the spaces provided and make up their own messages.

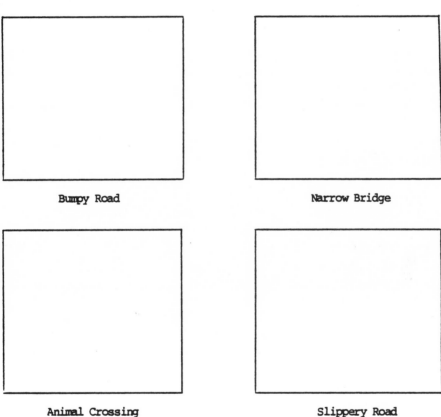

Bumpy Road   Narrow Bridge

Animal Crossing   Slippery Road

TOM SWIFTIES help children to consider alternate solutions and to strive for fast, humorous responses. After some practice they can originate sentences with fun, dual response endings.

DIRECTIONS: Below are a group of short statements. Each statement needs to be completed with an adverb. The adverb should be chosen so that it serves a dual purpose: (1) it indicates the manner of speaking characterized by the speaker's mood or intent; and (2) it reflects indirectly the content of the message. There are no right or wrong answers except that the adverb chosen should reflect this dual response: style and content.

EXAMPLES: "I always buy items in large quantities," said the merchant *grossly*. In this case the word "grossly" can refer both to the uncouth manner of speech used by the merchant, and also "gross" can refer to a large number of items.

"I dislike going out at night," said the young woman *darkly*. Again in this case, the word "darkly" can refer to the manner of speaking and to the fact that nights are dark.

1. "It's time for your shot," said the nurse _____.
2. "I have a hard time walking," said the crippled man _____.
3. "Please give me a soft drink," said the customer _____.
4. "I designed the St. Peter's Cathedral in Rome," said Michelangelo _____.
5. "I feel very awkward on the dance floor," said the young man _____.
6. "I become very uncomfortable while traveling across the desert," said the Arab _____.
7. "While you were asleep I took out your appendix," said the surgeon _____.
8. "I love the feel of cotton," said the little girl _____.
9. "I always travel First Class," said the tycoon _____.
10. "Hurry and complete your project," said the art teacher _____.

MORE TOM SWIFTIES (answers at end of chapter).

1. "I just bought a foreign car!" Tom announced t _____.
2. "Nyeah, Nyeah, let's have some turtle soup," Tom said m _____.
3. "I forgot what my wife wanted from the store," Tom said l _____.
4. "I'm so happy that I can float," Tom declared b _____.
5. "Block that kick!" Tom shouted d _____.
6. "I've got a code in da nose," Tom muttered s _____.
7. "Did *you* ever fly a plane?" Tom asked t _____.
8. "My paint canvas is blank," Tom said a _____.
9. "I hate quizzes," Tom stated t _____.
10. "This cream is bad," Tom said s _____.
11. "Better order 12 dozen of the blasted things," Tom said g _____.
12. "I always shop here," Tom announced p _____.
13. "Columbus, you were wrong," Tom stated f _____.
14. "I prefer unposed photos," Tom remarked c _____.
15. "It's a copy machine, It's a copy machine," Tom said r _____.
16. "Try on this negligee," Tom suggested t _____.
17. "All campers to their shelters," Tom announced i _____.
18. "Let's not cut the Valentine," Tom agreed w _____.
19. "I read *Newsweek* from time to time," Tom said p _____.

Convergent Thinking

In convergent thinking, ideas are brought together in an orderly manner; the best solution or answer is sought and relationships are noted. The child who tends to think convergently is easier to work with, for this child thinks in an orderly, logical, and constructive manner. The child who thinks divergently more often than not will benefit from convergent tasks, games, and activities that cause him or her to seek relationships and to bring things to orderly conclusions.

Most of the tasks in the classroom are convergent tasks, wherein the student is asked to find the correct answers, solutions, or results. Hopefully, the teacher does not do all the thinking and solving for the student. Gifted children need the opportunity and freedom to seek solutions on their own in their own learning styles.

Many convergent games and activities are available to the student. Examples of convergent assignments, games, or activities used in a classroom setting might be worksheets, problem sets, written assignments, research tasks, quizzes and exams, inquiry learning, group investigations, bulletin board projects, puzzles, and reading tasks.

Parents might implement similar covergent tasks, including puzzles, word games, logo and construction sets, color books, game books, problem-solving questions that involve deriving answers and organizing facts, and domestic responsibilities to be accomplished at home allowing the child to solve the hows.

Many problem-solving and logic puzzles or riddles help in teaching sequencing, order, and organization.

LATE FOR WORK (Monson, 1981).

		Should be No.
A.	Take a cold shower	_____
B.	Slam it behind him	_____
C.	Finish dressing	_____
D.	Dry himself	_____
E.	Open the front door	_____
F.	Snatch a towel	_____
G.	Put on his underwear	_____
H.	Rush madly out	_____
I.	Throw back the covers	_____
J.	Run down the block	_____
K.	Grab his overcoat	_____
L.	Jump out of bed	_____

THREE-DIMENSIONAL MAZES are fun ways to teach convergent thinking, for children must follow the principles and rules to experience success. There are many types of three-dimensional mazes, each offering a different type of challenge.

RINGS AND THINGS. The arrows lead you round and round through the rings.
Try not to get dizzy. Note: Stay *inside* the tube.*

*Reproduced by permission of the publisher from the book: *3-DIMENSIONAL MAZES, Volume Two* by Larry
Evans © 1977, Troubador Press, 385 Fremont St., San Francisco, CA 94105.

AQUEDUCK OR WATER OFF A DUCK'S BACK. Follow the water through the aqueduct as it pours from channel to channel. Flow from the urn to the swimming duck. Note: If you try to work backwards, BE CAREFUL. The water falls down only.*

TWO-DIMENSIONAL MASTER MIND (Simpkins, 1981) is a paper version of the Master Mind® game in which each side of the paper represents a game board. Two people can play at the same time or they may take turns.†

---

*Reproduced by permission of the publisher from the book: *3-Dimensional Mazes, Volume Two* by Larry Evans © 1977, Troubador Press, 385 Fremont St., San Francisco, CA 94105.
†From Katherine E Simpkins. Unpublished. Courtesy of the author.

1. Person number one thinks of four letters from A to F (ABCDEF), places them in any order desired, and writes them in the four larger circles in the bottom rectangle. The answers are covered so that the other person does not see them.

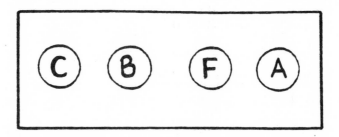

2. Then person number two may write any four letters (A-F) in any order in the first guessing line.

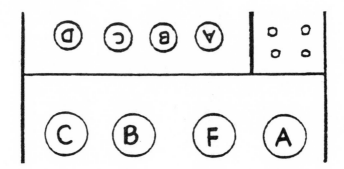

3. Person number one gives person number two feedback in the four tiny circles on the edge. There is no specific or relevant order to the placement in the tiny circles, but the circles are filled in as follows:

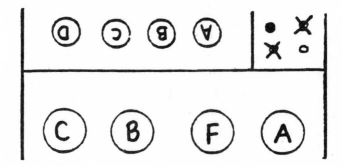

4. Person number two may guess as many times as he or she needs to and should use logic and deduction to find the correct letters in the correct order.

PENT-TAC-TOE is another convergent game of strategy, problem solving, and manipulation.

Materials: Two pencils and a piece of paper on which a 5 × 5 grid has been drawn.

Object: Each player tries to get four *X*s or *0*s in a row, horizontally, vertically, or diagonally. The first to achieve this wins.

Rules: Each player takes turns adding his *X* or *0* to the grid and the first to achieve four in a row will win.

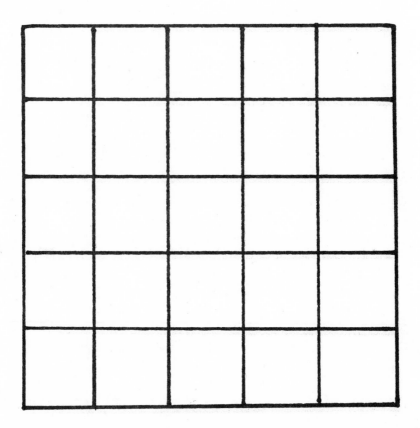

For more advanced students, convergent thinking tasks may be sought from sources like *Games for the Superintelligent.**

1. Three boxes are labeled "apples," "oranges," and "apples and oranges." Each label is incorrect. You may select only one fruit from one box. How can you label each box correctly?

2. A snail is at the bottom of a well thirty feet deep. It can crawl upward three feet in one day, but at night it slips back two feet. How long does it take the snail to crawl out of the well?

3. What is the next letter in the following sequence:

   O T T F F S S ?

4. What do the following words have in common:

   deft, first, calmness, canopy, laughing, stupid, crabcake, hijack?

5. You have ten gray socks and twenty blue socks in your bureau drawer. If you reach into it in the dark, how many socks must you take out to be sure of having a pair that matches?

6. Zoo Story

   Man: How many birds and how many beasts do you have in your zoo?

   Zookeeper: There are thirty heads and one hundred feet.

   Man: I can't tell from that.

   Zookeeper: Oh, yes you can!

   Can you?

7. A missionary visits an island where two tribes live. One tribe always tells the truth. The other always lies. The truth tellers live on the western side of the island and the liars live on the eastern side of the island. The missionary's problem is to determine who tells the truth by asking one native only one question.

   The missionary, seeing a native walking in the distance, tells a nearby native, "Go ask that native in the distance which side of the island he lives on." When the messenger returns he answers: "He says he lives on the western side of the island." Is the messenger a truth teller or a liar? How can you be sure?

COMMERCIAL RESOURCES. There are many books, games and materials available on the market today that can be very useful to the teacher for strengthening problem-solving and cognitive skills. A few examples of available games follow.

Convergent — Clue®, Master Mind®, Monopoly®, Rubik's Cube®, Battleship®, Logo®, riddles, Careers®, and crossword puzzles.

Divergent — The Ungame®, make-your-own puzzles, printing sets, Imagine®, and Stacks®.

Answers to Problems

MORE TOM SWIFTIES

1. Triumphantly	5. Defensively
2. Mockingly	6. Secretly
3. Listlessly	7. Airily
4. Buoyantly	8. Artfully

9. Testily
10. Sourly
11. Grossly
12. Patronizingly
13. Flatly
14. Candidly

15. Repeatedly
16. Temptingly
17. Intently
18. Wholeheartedly
19. Periodically

LATE FOR WORK

a. 3
b. 10
c. 7
d. 5
e. 9
f. 4

g. 6
h. 11
i. 1
j. 12
k. 8
l. 2

GAMES FOR THE SUPER INTELLIGENT

1. The Apples and Oranges Puzzle. Both the ordinary person and the bright person see one thing clearly right away; That if, for example, a fruit is picked from the box marked "Apples," it can be either an apple or an orange and will therefore tell nothing about whether the box should be marked "Oranges" or "Apples and Oranges." Since the same is true if a fruit is picked from the box marked "Oranges," it is tempting to conclude that the same will also be true of the third box, "Apples and Oranges." But the bright person does not take that supposition for granted. Instead, he goes ahead and tries it. Suppose, he thinks, I pick a fruit from "Apples and Oranges" and it turns out to be an orange — then what do I know about what's in that box? Well, for one thing, since we have been told that all the boxes are wrongly labled, we know that it is not "Apples and Oranges." Therefore, it must be oranges. Then the remaining boxes contain apples and apples and oranges. But which contains which? Simple. Remember once again that the boxes are all mislabled. Simply switch the two remaining labels and the problem is solved. The bright person has succeeded because he does not assume the problem cannot be solved simply because it cannot be solved in one way or even two ways he has tried. He tries every alternative.

2. Twenty-Eight Days. On the twenty-eighth day the snail reaches the top of the wall. Once there, it does not, of course, slip backward.

3. The next letter in the sequence OTTFFSS is E. The letters are the initials of letters of One, Two, Three, etc.

4. All of them contain three consecutive letters of the alphabet.

5. Three.

6. There are ten birds and twenty animals. The problem may be expressed in equation form as follows, letting A represent animals and B represent

birds: A + B = 30, 4A + 2B = 100.

7. The messenger is a truth teller. If the native in the distance lived on the western side of the island and was, therefore, a truth teller, he would say so. If, on the other hand, the native in the distance lived on the eastern side of the island and was, therefore, a liar, he would say the same.

CHAPTER SEVEN

MATHEMATICS

Can you answer the following questions?

1. Can you list seven characteristics of potentially gifted children in the area of math?
2. What is a procedure to follow in identifying children talented in the math area?
3. In setting up a math program for gifted children what should the goals be?
4. What should be the components of a math curriculum for gifted children?
5. Which teaching approach is considered essential to working with gifted and talented youngsters in math?
6. What traits are necessary for the teacher of math?
7. Can you list six to eight resources for teaching computer and calculator skills to gifted children?
8. What are five publications that could be helpful in developing a math curriculum for gifted children?

IT would not be unusual to find gifted children in the elementary classroom who are two to three years above their age-mates in the area of mathematics. This situation usually creates a dilemma for the child, the classroom teacher, and the regular public school program. Stanley (1977) indicates that many gifted children in a regular math program learn the material being presented to the other children instantaneously, resulting in boredom, frustration, and the development of poor attitudes toward the math task. Martinson (1972) reinforces the idea of boredom, indicating that if the gifted child is working at the same level as the rest of the class then he or she is in all probability reviewing material that has been learned or understood for two or three years. Teachers and administrators face another dilemma, that of attempting to provide a stimulating environment for the accelerated learner while still maintaining an ongoing program at a level commensurate with the abilities of the school population that they are charged to educate.

Hersberger and Wheatley (1980) proclaim that it is highly inappropriate for gifted students to study a computationally oriented curriculum, characteristic of what would be found in the public school system. They contend that students need to be challenged with interesting problems requiring originality of thought and that to do less than this is to stifle a most valuable natural resource. Hersberger and Wheatley outlined some primary goals that should be considered in a gifted mathematics program at the elementary level. These goals, which could also be considered within the public school system in general, are

1. Development of problem solving skills.
2. Development of thinking learning skills.
3. Stimulation of intellectual curiosity.
4. Exploration of advanced topics.
5. Participation in determining problems to be investigated.
6. Development of spatial ability.
7. Development of visual intuitive thinking.
8. Development of logical analytical ability.
9. Development of healthy concepts.
10. Development of computational ability. (P. 38)

As a part of these goals, Hersberger and Wheatley specified that spatial ability and visual intuitive thinking are important in the imagery building activities that are necessary for understanding and utilizing mathematics. While most mathematics programs in the public school concentrate primarily on computation, mathematics curriculum for gifted children must take into account higher level cognitive thinking and higher order reasoning skills (Payne, 1981). Therefore, the math curriculum must have goals (similar to those specified above) that will provide children with more in-depth treatment of basic content as well as more involved and challenging exercises.

IDENTIFICATION OF CHILDREN WITH MATH ABILITIES

Along with the characteristics of gifted and talented children discussed in earlier chapters, students who excel in mathematics also have good logical and abstract reasoning abilities. They display good problem-solving skills and display creative thinking abilities. Initially the teacher will identify the mathematically gifted child through the child's computational skills; however, this is not always the most accurate means of identifying students who have talent in the area of mathematics. Payne (1981) indicates that characteristics of these talented students include

1. Having the ability to work independently
2. Being self-directed

3. Displaying a level of curiosity and interest in the "whys" as well as the "hows" of the mathematics process
4. Having the ability to concentrate for long periods of time
5. Displaying a willingness to entertain complexity
6. Being stimulated by problem-solving situations
7. Displaying good short-term and long-term memory

Seven distinct characteristics of gifted math students are also outlined by Greene (1981). She feels that by looking more critically at potentially good students, differentiation between the good "exercise-doers" and those children who are truly gifted in math can be made. This differentiation would ensure that special programs for the gifted would not be diluted. Greene's (1981) seven characteristics of a gifted math student are

Spontaneous formulation of problems. When given a problem situation the child may generate questions about it while proceeding to answer those questions. Greene (1981) provides the case of Marcie to illustrate this characteristic.

> One day Marcie's fifth-grade class was reading about the Statue of Liberty. The article stated that "the Statue's mouth is 36 inches wide." Marcie became curious about the length of the arm of the statue that holds the flaming torch. Her teacher suggested that this information could be found in a reference book in the library. Marcie, however, said that she could compute the length. Marcie proceeded to measure the width of her own mouth. She found that her mouth was about two inches wide, or $1/18$ the width of the statue's mouth. Marcie then measured the length of her arm, multiplied this length by 18, and thus was able to approximate the length of the statue's arm. (P. 15)

Flexibility in handling data. A variety of nonstandard approaches to problem solving will be used by the gifted child. Often the child will apply previously learned information in finding simpler strategies for solving problems.

Data Organization. The gifted student sometimes organizes data into lists or tables as a means of locating patterns and relationships between data.

Mental agility of fluency with ideas. This characteristic is best illustrated by the story of Dana (Greene, 1981), a fifth-grade boy in a high-ability classroom. He was given the following problem:

> Mrs. Johnson traveled 360 km in 6 hours. How many kilometers did she travel each hour?
>
> Expecting the students to solve this basic problem by dividing the total number of kilometers travelled by the number of hours, the teacher was surprised when Dana, one of the brighter students, did not respond by raising his hand. Rather, Dana stared at the transparency with a perplexed look. When questioned, Dana indicated that the problem was not clear. He pointed out that the problem did not state that the same number of kilometers were travelled each hour. Therefore, the solution could be any set of six numbers that add to 360. "There are an infinite set of such sets," stated Dana. (P. 16)

Originality of interpretation. The gifted child will demonstrate an ability to "depart from the obvious" and to see things differently than other children.

Ability to transfer ideas. The gifted child will apply information learned in one context to solving problems in another.

Ability to generalize. A gifted child will usually examine a situation thoroughly, observing relationships that exist between phenomena, and then generalize those relationships.

Considering these characteristics, it is important that the teacher look beyond computational skills in identifying those who are to participate in a mathematics program for talented children. Even though computation and a fundamental understanding of computational rules are necessities for productive participation, these skills are probably less important than the attitude and interest of the child in participating, the child's ability to work independently, and whether or not he or she is stimulated by the curriculum and/or environment in which the math program is being conducted.

DEVELOPING A MATHEMATICS CURRICULUM

In the development of the mathematics curriculum several components are proposed in the literature. The intent herein is to summarize what those components could be, as well as to provide a guide that could be used in the development of such a program. Many authors (Waverick, 1980; Hersberger and Wheatley, 1980; Payne, 1981; and others) have indicated that a fundamental part of the math curriculum is development of *basic computational skills*, including mastery of numbers, numeration, and the ability to add, subtract, multiply, and divide up to a two- and three-digit level of difficulty. Payne (1981) suggests that the curriculum should provide an in-depth treatment of basic content to include computation rules. *Fractions and decimals* are another component of the math curriculum. As fundamental skills in understanding fractions and decimals are developed, they become a launching pad for participation in higher levels of math as well as a means through which problem-solving skills can be developed. Another important math component is *basic geometry*, so that dimensionality, areas, and volumes can be understood. The field of *probability and statistics* is another math component, which provides a practical method that the child can use in collecting, analyzing, and presenting data. In learning probability and statistics children are exposed to the basics of the research process and the application of math skills in a functional way. Skill in *estimation* is helpful for the talented math student. Estimation is important in understanding large numbers as well as in understanding the concepts involved in science and other mathematical processes. *Enrichment activities* are also suggested as supportive components of a mathematics program for talented students. Possible enrichment programs could include studying the history of mathematics, looking at ancient numeration systems, learning about nondecimal systems or old algorithms, discussing in formal logic, and pursuing the logical nature of mathematics itself.

An emerging component of a math curriculum is the utilization of microcomputer technology. The curriculum should focus on developing *computer literacy* within its students. This not only should include the application of microcomputers in simple problem-solving activities, i.e. utilization of the computer with existing software programs in solving standard calculations, but also should provide a curriculum in which the child learns to apply a computer language such as BASIC in actually programming the computer (Shanahan, 1981).

The following were suggested in the Roeper Review of the G/C/T for planning math programs for all age levels:

1. Send letter to all parents about what the gifted students will be learning and doing.
2. Give students the answers to problems and have them come up with the problems.
3. Contract with each student.
4. Use parents from community as aides and/or resources.
5. Have left-brain and right-brain learning material on hand so each student will benefit and will learn material the best way for him/her.
6. Allow students to pair up.
7. Subscribe to a current mathematics magazine.
8. Allow students to move along at own pace.
9. Use computer games (i.e. Canper Math® — Apple II; Cash Register® — Atari; Typing Fractions® — Pet; Scramble® — TRS-80.)

TEACHING APPROACHES

Once the components of the curriculum have been identified, the teaching approaches and methods need to be considered. There is consensus within the literature as to which approaches should be considered in teaching math to gifted and talented children. The most favored approach is one in which the child is placed in a *problem-solving* situation. As Wavrik (1980) indicates, the goal of mathematics instruction is to produce students who can solve problems. In essence, this means that they must be placed in a position to analyze a problem, apply their understanding of mathematical ideas in planning how to solve that problem, and then work interactively with the problem until it is solved. Of course, actually placing the student in a problem-solving situation is more easily said than done.

Most traditional math programs provide a memorization approach for learning basic facts from which basic problems are solved. Payne (1981) indicates that more challenging exercises that go beyond the rote application of these mundane problem-solving tasks are needed. For example, Payne (1981) suggests that if regular students are learning how to determine the area of flat planed figures, talented students may be challenged to find the areas of irregularly shaped figures or to break a polygonal figure into simpler component parts. If a third grade class is attempting to solve a simple one-step problem such as "Caroline spends 42¢ for a pen and 79¢ for a pack of paper, how much does she spend?" this type of one-step problem could be expanded for gifted children to include how much two, three, four, or more pens would cost and "How much change would Caroline receive from a five-dollar bill?" In other words, problem-solving tasks can be more complex and involved when they are given to the gifted and talented individual. The way to enhance problem-solving skills is to provide an opportunity for the student to work on realistic situations and problems.

It is essential to the success of a good math program that the environment in which the program is to be conducted be productive and healthy. The environment includes the physical surroundings, the psychological atmosphere in which the program takes place, the actual resources to be used, and the teacher skills that are necessary in implementing the program.

The *physical environment* should provide opportunities for students to move about freely in ample space and explore the resources (including other students) within the classroom some freedom to work independently or in small groups, and a great variety of different projects or problem-solving activities. The children should be encouraged to explore, to investigate, and to challenge each other and the teacher.

This leads to a good *psychological atmosphere*, the emotional and attitudinal setting within the classroom. It is important that the child feel comfortable with and confident of himself/herself, the teacher, and his or her personal interaction with classmates. A good psychological climate may be established by the teacher if expectations are firm, friendly, and fair. Ridicule and humiliation should hold no place in the classroom setting, and the actions and feelings of the students and the teachers should be treated with respect and courtesy. If integrity and supportive attitudes are fostered by students and teachers then each may relax and get on with the more important and more challenging aspects of learning and problem solving. The environment should, however, provide structure and balance as well as specificity of goals — goals that can be realistically met and evaluated in terms of achievement. Math achievement should be evaluated not only by the teacher but, more importantly, by the children themselves.

Resources are an obviously critical component of the math program. These resources should include a great variety of textbooks and activities that involve problem-solving situations ranging from simple computation to the design and development of research projects for investigating ideas of interest to the students. Also, the resources should include, as much as possible, up-to-date technology, i.e. calculators and microcomputers that are available and being utilized extensively in almost every area of human effort.

Finally, the *teacher* should be competent and confident. Of course, this is an expectation for any teacher in any classroom; however, in working with talented math students the teacher must be even more confident and competent in the areas in which he or she will be teaching. Needed teaching skills will vary depending upon the actual curriculum involved, but the characteristics described earlier in this text should be the leading criteria upon which a teacher is selected for teaching a gifted and talented class. In other words, the teacher must possess appropriate technical and academic skills, demonstrate competence in teaching, and be confident of his or her ability to apply those skills in actually working with talented children. As Hersberger and Wheatley (1980) point out, the probability is quite high that the teacher's mathematical knowledge will be taxed or exceeded in working with gifted and talented children. It is also important for the teacher to be comfortable in encouraging students to generalize and to abstract. Another important quality is that the teacher be open and willing to allow students to explain the reasons behind what they have done and are doing. Teachers must provide that extra impetus so that the students' abilities can be challenged, as well as the example from which the students can model and explore even more in the application of their mathematic skills.

The ultimate goal of the mathematics curriculum is that the gifted and talented child reach his or her potential and that, having worked through the curriculum, the child may have developed higher levels of thinking and reasoning skills going beyond mere understanding of basic mathematical computation.

The remainder of this chapter is divided into activities that can be utilized in working with preschool, elementary, and secondary students. These are presented merely as ideas and activities that could be used by parents in the home or within the public school system as a means of supplementing the basic components discussed previously in this chapter.

PRACTICAL MATH EXPERIENCES

For Preschool Children

The following are ideas or activities that can be implemented in the home and in familiar surroundings and that lead a child to concepts of mathematics and measurement.

SAND PLAY. From the different containers used in sand play (buckets, cans, cups, and liquid bleach and detergent bottles), a variety of concepts can be learned. The different shapes and sizes can teach wide, narrow, thin, tall, short, full, empty, flat, round, big, and little.

Sand is also useful in learning about volume. The concepts of how much, how much more, how much less, and others are easily illustrated. Also, the child can easily make comparisons between the containers and the amount of sand each can hold. Which holds the most? Which one the least? Are there any which hold the same amount?

The child can estimate how much sand each container will hold and then measure each. This information can also be shown on a simple graph that the child can draw.

SHOPPING EXPERIENCES. Shopping experiences can provide the student with an opportunity to learn and to read numbers, to identify prices, and to learn comparisons. While shopping a child can also be taught weights and measures (pounds, ounces, cups, pints, quarts, gallons, etc.) and the concepts of half, whole, large, medium, small, etc.

Concepts of quantity and groupings can be learned, such as a dozen eggs, a pound or cube of butter, a quart of milk, etc. Shapes and colors can also be identified in a store setting, and depth and volume perception sharpened, through consideration of the displays and the layers and rows of goods.

COOKING EXPERIENCES. Cooking experiences are useful for learning the following concepts: volume (measuring the ingredients), time (how long does it need to cook?), temperature, fractions (fill it half-full, one quarter-cup, etc.), and ordinal numbers (first we put in the sugar, second we put in the butter. . .).

MEASURING EXPERIENCES (LENGTH). Using a box of ribbons or string of different lengths, the child can find the shortest ribbon, find the longest ribbon, and put them in order from shortest to longest (sequencing).

Several children can cut pieces of ribbon or string the length of their waists, and then each child can *compare* the length of his string with that of the others. Other body measurements may be compared as well. (Who has the longest foot, widest shoulders, tiniest toe, etc.). Or objects in the home may be measured using strings, dowels, handspans, etc. and counting how many lengths it takes to measure them. In this way vocabulary words important to math will be learned, such as across, around (circumference), top, bottom, four-sided object (perimeter), quantity, and number sequencing. Different measuring mediums (dowels, books, handspans, short strings) may be used to find equivalence. (How many book lengths equal three handspans?)

Finally, a clock can be used to teach number sequence and time. This can be related to getting up, playing, eating, etc.

GEOMETRY (SHAPES). Attention can be focused on the shapes of things in the home — shapes in the floor and ceiling; shapes of doors and windows or individual panes of glass; shapes of clothes; shapes of cars, buses, and trucks; and shapes of fences, walls, and gates. The parent can ask the thought question,

"Why do you think it is this particular shape?" Vocabulary words resulting from these activities are straight, curved, vertical, horizontal, round, circle, square, rectangle, triangle, cylinder, edge, and corner.

SORTING ACTIVITIES (SET IDENTIFICATION). Different objects found around the home can be sorted in a variety of ways. Toys, buttons, rocks, writing instruments, cups, scraps of material, etc. can be sorted by type (all the dolls, all the trucks, all the stuffed animals), color (all the red buttons, all the white ones), or material (all the plastic things, all the paper, all the metal). Many other classifications are also possible, and it is easy to incorporate the word "set" into the activity.

One final note: According to the Nuffield Foundation (1967), discussion is a *vital* part of these experiences. The teacher must work *with* the child — the child can't do it alone. Recording the results of the activities can also be valuable if it enhances the experience and uses pictorial representation (this can introduce a child to graphs) or the child's own words.

Other activities for the preschool gifted child, suggested by the Nuffield Foundation, include activities in the home such as mind teasers (What could you do if. . . ? How could you make a train from these items? etc.), drawing parallels (if a child enjoys piece puzzles, a parallel with the parts of a pumpkin that make a whole product — the skin, stem, pulp, seed — can be drawn), and calculating the unit price of items in a store and the amount of change expected. Field trips, with activities such as calculating the number of telephone poles passed and computing the estimated time of arrival by speed and distance, are also recommended by the Nuffield Foundation.

They also offer suggestions on how to provide for the development of the total child. To encourage his or her moral and emotional development, they offer questions such as Is it worse to steal 10¢ or $1? Why? If one rabbit has five bunnies, another seven, in two years, how many will each have? Is one happier than the other? To stimulate intellectual growth, they suggest that parents provide a learning environment (math books, calculators, etc.) and give answers and let the child work problems. Generally broadening activities are also recommended, such as taking the child on a nature hike and showing how bugs fit together in the ecology puzzle.

For Children of Elementary School Age

These suggestions also come from the Nuffield Foundation.

1. Using a farm supply catalog, the child should decide what supplies will be needed. The child can then calculate the quantity and cost of these supplies.
2. The parent can supply sheets of simple problems in adding, subtracting, multiplying, or dividing. The child is to see how many problems he or she can do in 10 to 60 seconds.

3. Using picture books or magazines, the child should see how many different shapes he or she can find — squares, circles, triangles, hexagons, etc.

4. The parent should give "answers" and then have the child find all possible problems.

5. The parent could give the child a hand calculator and its instructions booklet with the challenge to learn the processes available on that calculator.

6. The child could make at least twenty equilateral triangles all the same size and then design an icosahedron shape (twenty sides) by gluing the sides together. He or she can also experiment with the triangles and create new shapes.

7. The child can be challenged to arrange eight 8s in an addition problem so that the sum will be 1,000.

$$
\begin{array}{r}
888 \\
88 \\
8 \\
8 \\
8 \\
\hline
1,000
\end{array}
$$

8. The parent could ask the child to write to 100 in Roman numerals.

9. The child could be challenged to devise a mathematical poem without listing the answer. For example:

> A number pair are we
> Our product 32
> We differ by just 4
> We'll tell you nothing more
>   Who are we? (8, 4)

10. The child can be given a road within the state in which he or she lives and asked to convert miles to kilometers and measure the distance from large city to large city, the length and breadth of the state, or the distance from town to town.

For Older Students

Again according to the Nuffield Foundation, the parent could challenge the child as follows:

1. Given five metric measures of length, create your own picture. Example: .8 mm, 12 cm, 2 dm, 8cm, 5 mm.

2. Given five English measures of length, create your own picture. Example: 2", 3-1/2", 5", 1-3/8", 3/4"

3. Given $100,000, invest in real estate from the newspaper want ads in

such a way that your investment will increase each year.

4. Given plane geometry figures such as a triangle, square, trapezoid, hexagon, rectangle, etc., create a robot-monster. Describe its qualities, powers, and characteristics.

5. Given solid geometry figures such as a triangular prism, tetrahedron, sphere, cylinder, etc., create new packaging for a soft drink, cereal, margarine, and chocolate syrup.

6. Create five-three-step equations with answers that are whole numbers. All four operations, integers, decimals, and fractions may be used.

7. Create a money system that will simplify the money exchange problems in foreign travel.

8. Name the three most important mathematical discoveries of all time. Justify your choices.

9. Name three women who have made a contribution to the field of mathematics and discuss their work.

10. Name and explain five practical uses for geometry in today's world. (Above from Roeper Review G/C/T)

11. Plan a hypothetical future marriage and calculate the total costs — ring, announcements, flowers, clothing, reception, honeymoon, etc.

12. Calculate what it will cost you to live when you are out of school and on your own — rent, transportation, food, clothing, recreation, etc. — and balance that against the type of wage you will require. (This is an insightful task for many reasons.)

For All Ages

The following activities are examples of a problem-solving approach and provide math experiences for use with any age child. The important aspect of a math program should be challenging the child to apply the maximum level of his/her capacity. The National Council of Teachers of Mathematics has identified the development of problem solving as its primary objective for the 1980s. Problem solving places the child in a situation of having to exercise different levels of thinking skills (divergent and convergent) in conjunction with mathematics talent.

BRAIN GAMES (Clark, 1979).

1. Use three numbers — 4, 5, and 6, to fill in the squares so that whichever way you add, up, across or diagonally, the total will be 15. Each number may be used 3 times.

2. Split 100 into four parts so that when you add 4 to one part, you get the same answer as when you multiply 4 by another part, or subtract 4 from another part.
3. Can you determine what the next number will be — 6, 8, 12, 20. . . ?
4. Can you use the numbers 1 thru 9 so that whichever way you add (horizontally, diagonally, vertically) the total answer will be 15?

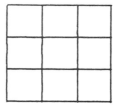

5. A maze similar to the one below was presented at the world's fair nearly a half a century ago. When a person entered the maze they received a ticket. The ticket was punched at each gate the person passed on the way to the center of the maze. In the center was a small building with the number 138 over the entrance. A person having a card with 6 numbers (only six gates could be used) that totaled exactly 138 won a prize. What are the 6 gates that total 138? For example: If you selected gates 25, 3, 50, 10, 5, 20, your total would be 113 (Loomis, 1977).

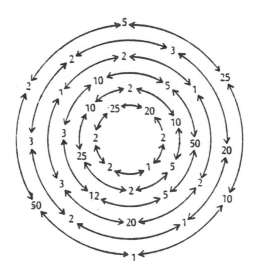

ANSWERS TO BRAIN GAMES
1.   4   6   5

```
   6     5     4
   5     4     6
```
2. Four parts include 64, 20, 12, 4.
3. 36 — Double each number and subtract four to get the next.
4.
```
   4     9     2
   3     5     7
   8     1     6
```
5. Both 50, 20, 20, 3, 25, 20 and 50, 2, 1, 50, 10, 25 add up to 138.

MATH FOR ABLE LEARNERS. Rathmell and Leutzinger (1981) make the following comment on helping children learn basic facts through a problem-solving approach.

> As children begin computation, they can benefit from learning to add and subtract mentally as well as with paper and pencil. The following examples also emphasize problem solving, even as children are learning basic facts:
> What pairs of numbers have a sum of 7?
> What pairs of numbers have a difference of 4?
> List sets of three numbers with a sum of 14.
> As children learn to compute with two- and three-digit numbers, more complex problems are possible.
> List pairs of numbers with a sum of 136.
> I'm thinking of a number. Adding 5 to this number gives the same answer as subtracting this number from 89. What is the number?
> I'm thinking of two numbers. The sum is 30 and the difference is 6. What are the two numbers?
> Keep in mind that there are many ways to derive the answer to a problem. Often it is easier to compute mentally by using the tens or hundreds first, rather than working from right to left as we do with paper and pencil. For example, to add 34 and 26 you might think that $30 + 20 = 50$ and $4 + 6 = 10$, so $34 + 26 = 50 + 10$, or 60. (P. 48)

Schulman (1981) provides a multiple-solution problem situation for talented children.

> Most students begin this problem by thinking of two one-digit numbers that when multiplied produce a six in the ones place. The fact $6 \times 6 = 36$ is usually generated first. Some students continue to work backwards, others divide by six to find the missing factor. Once the solution $161 \times 6 = 966$ is found, gifted students are often motivated to search for other examples that meet the problem conditions. Some students ask, "Are there any ways to see if a number is divisible by another number?" this leads to an introduction of rules of divisibility.
> There are five solutions to the multiplication problem in figure 1: 1×966, 2×483, 3×322, 6×161, and 7×138. (P. 49)

In an attempt to change the story problem format, Rathmell and Luetzinger (1981) give three examples.

> 1. Fill in the blanks with numbers, then solve the problem.
> Dan has _____ boxes of apples. He sells _____ boxes. How many does he have left?

2. Write a question, then solve the problem.
Lisa has 7 oranges. Todd has 4 oranges.

_____

_____

3. Write a story to match the number sentence 4 + 6 = 10 _____
_____. (P. 54)

Humphries (1981) proposes the two-person game *Nim* as a method of developing problem-solving skills.

> *Nim* is believed to be Chinese in origin and can be played with bits of paper,
> coins, chips or other objects on a flat playing surface. Playing pieces are placed in
> rows as shown in figure 5. Players take turns removing any number, from one to all,
> of the playing pieces from any one row. Play continues until all of the pieces have
> been removed. The winner is the player to remove the last playing piece. (The game
> can be reversed so that the player to remove the last piece is the loser.)
>
> Challenge: Devise a strategy to insure that you will always be a winner. (Hint:
> Keep a record of moves and winners, then look for a pattern.) Try adding another
> row of six playing pieces and play the game as before. Will the addition of this fourth
> row change your strategy? Why? Why not? (P. 63)

Mathematics Resources for Teachers and Parents

Obtaining resource materials for setting up the mathematics program
should be greatly facilitated by the following lists, selected for use by both
parents and teachers.

1. Publications

Arithmetic Teacher is a monthly publication of the National Council of Teachers
of Mathematics. This is an excellent journal, complete with ideas for stimulating math development in youngsters. Recent editions feature activities
for able learners, and the February, 1981 issue (Vol. 28) was devoted entirely to the challenges posed by the able student.

Boxes, Squares, and Other Things: A Teacher's Guide for a Unit in Informal Geometry,
by Marion I Walter. Reston, Virginia: The Council, 1970.

*Especially for Teachers: ERIC Documents on the Teaching of Mathematics, 1966-
1980*. By Suydam and Higgins. Columbus, Ohio: ERIC, 1981.

Mathematical History: Activities, Puzzles, Stories, and Games, by Mitchell Merle.
Reston, Virginia: The Council, 1978.

Mind Benders — Deductive Thinking Skills, by Anita Harnadek. Troy, Michigan: Midwest Publications Company, Inc., 1978.

Sourcebook of Applications of School Mathematics, by the National Council of
Teachers of Mathematics. Reston, Virginia: The Council, 1980.

Techniques a Problem Solving Elementary Problem Out Set, by Greenes, Carol, and
others. Palo Alto, California: Dale Seymour Publication, 1980.

Warm-Up Mind Benders — Deductive Thinking Skills, by Anita Harnadek. Troy,
Michigan: Midwest Publications Company, Inc., 1979.

Most new editions of Basal Mathematics texts (Ginn, Allyn and Bacon, MacMillan, and so on) have set aside activities especially designed for able learners.

2. Programs

ESP for the Gifted. The Exploratory School Program (ESP) was implemented by the Akron Public Schools for the gifted and talented in mathematics and science in grades 1-6.

Mathematical Talent: Discovery, Description, and Development, by Julian C. Stanley, Daniel P. Keating, and Lynn H. Fox (Eds.). Baltimore: Johns Hopkins University Press, 1974.

Minnesota Talented Youth Mathematics Project: Evaluation Report, by Peggy A. House. St. Paul: Minnesota State Department of Education, 1977, 1978, 1979, 1980. Mimeographed.

3. Computer/Calculator Information

Addition with Carrying. ARARI, 8K, cassette (requires joy stick). Greenwich, Connecticut: Program Design, Inc., 1980.

Area of Triangles. Apple II, cassette. Philadelphia. School District of Philadelphia Board of Education. Division of Instructional Systems.

Calculation Activities for the Classrooms, by G. Vermont and P. Mason. Toronto: Copp Clark Publ., 1977.

Cash Register. ARARI, 16K, cassette. Greenwich; Connecticut: Program Design, Inc., 1980.

Compu-Math Decimals and Fraction. Apple II, diskettes. Canoga Park, California: Edu-Ware Services, Inc.

Games With the Pocket Calculator, by Thiagarajan, Sivasailam, and Harold D. Stolovitch. Menlo Park, California: Bymax, 1976.

Language Practice — Approximate Measurements 2. Applesoft, BASIC, 16K, cassette. Fresno, California: CourseWare Magazine 1 (May 1981).

Problem Solving Kit for Use with a Calculator, by W. Judd. New York: Science Research Association, 1977.

Scramble — Division Drill. TRS-80. Level 2 BASIC, 16K, cassette. Fresno, California: CourseWare Magazine 1 (January 1981).

Typing Fractions — Approximate Measurement 1. Pet. BASIC, 8K, cassette. Fresno, California: CourseWare Magazine 1 (March 1981).

CHAPTER EIGHT

READING AND LANGUAGE ARTS

Can you answer the following questions?

1. What are some goals of a reading and language arts program?
2. How could you identify children talented in reading and language arts?
3. Can you list some curriculum components of a reading and language arts program?
4. What are some good teaching approaches for reading and language arts?
5. How can you develop critical reading skills?
6. What are some good teaching activities for language arts development?

READING and writing activities in the regular classroom curriculum can be very "boring and sterile" (Witty, 1971) to a child who has already mastered the skills prior to entering school. More often than not the gifted or talented child who enters the classroom has well developed skills in reading and language arts, yet the teacher is often either unable to acknowledge and identify the existence of these skills or has not developed a curriculum that will facilitate further development at a level commensurate with the child's ability to perform.

The purpose of this chapter will be to outline the goals, curricular components, and teaching activities that could be utilized in developing a program for teaching reading and language arts to the gifted and talented child. Reading and language arts are really two separate teaching entities yet are so closely related to each other in the overall curriculum program that it is hard to separate them. This is especially true when the activities used in teaching one topic directly overlap with teaching the other. Therefore, when distinctions can be made between reading and language arts development they will be so identified; however, the curricular components, the educational goals, and the learning activities specified in this chapter could essentially be used in either or both areas.

GOALS OF THE READING AND LANGUAGE ARTS PROGRAM

Several authors contend that the reading and language arts programs in most regular school curriculums malign and in fact retard the performance capabilities of the gifted and talented child (Malone, 1974; Carroll and Laming, 1974; Switzer and Nourse, 1979). This statement is accurate in the sense that the public school systems are actually in the business of educating to the mean; that is, they may not be well prepared or equipped to assist students on either end of the learning continuum. Students who are too advanced or too delayed to fit into the educational mainstream sometimes perish by the wayside. Carroll and Laming (1974) indicate that, paradoxically, our culture emphasizes conformity to the average for those very students (the gifted and talented) who may be the most capable of coping with radical change and solving some of the culture's most difficult problems. In any event, the reading and language arts programs in most schools are poorly equipped or not flexible enough to adapt to the learning needs of the gifted and talented child. This stems somewhat from the teachers' inability to identify those students who are most capable of performing at higher and higher skill levels.

One of the primary goals of a reading and language arts program should be *early identification* of student abilities. Early identification is important in assisting the teacher to make appropriate curriculum choices and provide the most appropriate activities and curricula to foster the child's gifts and talents. Another goal of the program should be the development of the child's *creative potential*. In other words, the school atmosphere (the learning environment) must be such that the child's potential is enhanced and the creative abilities of the child are emphasized. Another goal that is mentioned regularly throughout the literature is the child's mastery of *basic skills*. When reading or writing there are certain basic fundamentals that must be learned; therefore, it is important to insure that one of the goals of the reading and language arts programs for gifted and talented children is the laying of a solid skills foundation and that the basics are mastered by the students (Boothby, 1980; Switzer and Nourse, 1979; Torrance, 1965; and Mindell and Stracher, 1980).

Mindell and Stracher's (1980) process model provides the focus of a reading and writing program for the gifted; it includes

1. The goal of a language program for gifted children is to enable them to think and act creatively.
2. Creative thought and action are predicated upon a basic language education which emphasizes both skill and advanced thinking ability in all aspects of reading and writing.
3. The first step in setting up a program is to evaluate each student's functional abilities in the areas of reading and writing. (P. 72)

While these goals may appear general, they do provide a meaningful basis from which a curriculum program can be developed. The important concept in the development of any curriculum for the gifted child should be differentiation from the normal curriculum to the point that acceleration, depth, breadth, and creative opportunities are emphasized far beyond the conventional curriculum in the regular school (Mindell and Stracher, 1980).

IDENTIFICATION OF CHILDREN TALENTED IN READING AND LANGUAGE ARTS

As mentioned, one of the fundamentals of a good reading and language arts program for the gifted would be early identification of those children who would best benefit from an advanced or accelerated curriculum. While it may appear quite easy, the identification of those children who display unusual gifts in the area of reading and language arts is not. Some children may, for example, score quite high on a standardized test of reading or language arts development. This may help to initially sort out those who have the talents from those who do not, but the tests themselves do not provide enough diagnostic data from which to plan an appropriate program. This dilemma is similar to that which Stanley (1976) found in his assessment of math abilities among children. He noted that standardized tests, while identifying children scoring in the 99th percentile, did not discriminate among those children with good divergent thinking skills. It was not until these children were tested further with advanced instruments or with advanced concepts that those who were indeed talented in the math area were identified. Essentially the same problem exists with identification of children in the reading and language arts area. Standardized tests (*see* Chapter One) merely provide one small bit of information that can be utilized in identifying or specifying who the potential candidates may be for a gifted and talented program in reading and language arts.

The teacher will have to rely upon other devices or means of identification. One tool that is quite valuable to the teacher is simple observation of specific behaviors in the classroom. This necessitates that the teacher know and understand some of the characteristics of students who may have gifts and talents in the reading and language arts area. These characteristics would include some of the following behaviors:

1. Having unusual ability and expressed interest in reading and language arts
2. Beginning to read and write before the usual ages or grades at which those activities take place (reading before first grade and writing coherently before the end of the first grade)
3. Expressing a high level of language development and verbal ability (usually the first indicators)
4. Displaying advanced skills in written expression

5. Showing a seemingly unusual capacity for processing information
6. Demonstrating observable flexibility in processing ideas
7. Displaying an observable ability to generate original ideas and solutions
8. Showing an unusual ability to utilize abstract terms and thoughts in making generalizations or solving problems

Mindell and Stracher (1980) were able to specify some behaviors that occurred in advanced young readers and writers that may be characteristic or revealing of children who have gifts and talents in those two areas. They suggest that advanced readers master the basic decoding process very quickly and that, essentially, they need no further instruction in that area. This is not to imply that further instruction within the basics of reading development is unnecessary, but the gifted child has an unusual propensity for developing decoding skills and utilizing them much more readily than his/her regular age-mates. Another characteristic identified was advanced vocabulary, this being one basis of identifying talented students.

Therefore, identification of the child with gifts and talents in the reading or writing area should include the utilization of standardized tests to determine advanced acquisition of learned skills in each of these areas and should also include a very astute observation of the aforementioned characteristics. Through an analysis of both of these sources of information the teacher should have a substantial data base from which to confidently select students who are most likely to benefit from a challenging reading and language arts program and develop more and more individual potential within these areas.

CURRICULUM COMPONENTS

A reading and language arts program curriculum can be developed from the following components selected from the literature. While vocabulary usage may differ, it is interesting to note that most authors identify one essential component of both the reading and the language arts curricula, to insure that the child has mastered the *basic skills*. For example, basic skills in reading may require a well-developed *vocabulary*, both verbal and reading; good *comprehension* of materials and topics read; and some *word analysis* or phonic analysis (decoding) skills that can be utilized in attacking new words for reading and understanding. In writing, the basics would include understanding the elements of *grammar, punctuation,* and *spelling*. Each of these skills would vary according to the age and the express ability of the child, but the fundamentals of writing must be taught and understood by the child.

Another important component of the curriculum is that the *creative abilities* of the child should be enhanced and exercised. Creative abilities can be expressed in both reading and language arts activities. *Thinking skills* (convergent and divergent) are also important factors in reading and writing. The reading content should allow the student to think convergently to bring together what has been read into a complete whole or to diverge from the content to new ideas, new possibilities, and new solutions. The same thinking tasks apply to writing. The child should be allowed to write convergently utilizing bits of information or data to recall or reconstruct and be encouraged (even placed in situations) to think divergently, generating and writing new ideas.

A final component that is found throughout the literature (Switzer and Nourse, 1979; Martinson, 1968; Trezise, 1977; Clark, 1979; Boothby, 1980; Daniel, 1982; Royer, 1982; and others) is that reading and writing programs should be *enjoyable*. Reading and writing should not be just for the purpose of expression and evaluation of skills but should be an enjoyable extension of the overall development of the child. As Martinson (1968) nicely states, the child's independent reading should be truly independent, and one component of the independent reading program should be just that — independent choice and time. The same holds true for writing. The child should be encouraged to write for the sheer enjoyment of expressing him or herself.

The curriculum for reading and language arts for the gifted should be differentiated from the regular school curriculum. It must be a curriculum that is neither sterile nor boring and one that will not cause the child to regress from skills and interests already developed. Activities that will exercise advanced thinking skills and that are applicable to problem-solving situations must be used to exercise the child's gifts and talents in these areas. Teachers of reading who have gifted and talented students must have a well-rounded idea of the available literature for use with the gifted and talented child and an understanding not only of children's literature but of how to select pieces of literature that can be used in a variety of ways for stimulating the development of both critical and creative reading skills in these children. Royer (1982) suggests that a writing curriculum for the gifted and talented should employ the objectives outlined in Bloom's *Taxonomy* (Bloom, 1956). Royer suggests that by following this taxonomy, coupled with the real interest of the child, writing assignments can be more efficiently developed, organized, and evaluated. In essence, teacher adherence to the taxonomy will assist students in developing or exercising their creative writing abilities. This same system outlined by Royer (1982) can be applied to reading assignments. The following is an outline of how Royer proposes using Bloom's *Taxonomy* in generating topics for writing assignments:

1. Students are asked to *identify* or *define* a current problem which needs addressing.
2. Utilizing the *knowledge* level of the taxonomy, the students are requested to answer or to identify what facts are pertinent to the problem under investigation.
3. Utilizing the *comprehension* dimension, students are asked to clearly define the current problem and to state why this particular topic may be a problem.
4. In utilizing the *application* dimension of the taxonomy students are asked to provide or identify outside information which could be used to help solve this prob-

lem, as well as to determine how this information might best be used.

5. During the *analysis* part of the taxonomy students are asked to specify solutions that have been proposed to solve this problem as well as to specify how those solutions relate to the primary issues within the problem.

6. *Synthesizing* is developed by having students outline or specify the information that has been useful in solving the problem as well as specifying how the problem could be solved.

7. Finally, *evaluation* is then incorporated by having students make decisions or summarize the literary decisions and evaluations that have been made regarding the existing problem. All information collected is discussed in regards to which solutions appear to be appropriate and why. (P. 30)

To summarize the critical components of the curriculum, an emphasis is placed first on the importance of having the child demonstrate an understanding of the basics as well as insuring that those basics are taught and understood on each level of development. In other words, the child should be learning the basics, and these should be assessed as the student progresses from one level of development to the next. Secondly, the creative abilities of the child should be enhanced. Critical thinking skills of the student (convergent/divergent thinking) as they apply to problem solving must be exercised and facilitated throughout the curriculum process. Third, a part of the curriculum should focus on sheer enjoyment — enjoyment of reading and enjoyment of writing with their inherent value to the child's self emphasized and expressed. Finally, in setting up a curriculum, a model such as that proposed by Royer (1980) following Bloom's *Taxonomy* (Bloom, 1965) should be used as one way of insuring that the child has an opportunity to experience as well as to exercise different cognitive processes.

TEACHING APPROACHES

This section will present a series of teaching approaches that can be used in the development of a reading and/or language arts program. Many of the activities listed under a given section or area could be utilized within *either* the reading or language arts program. The activities suggested could be used at any stage of development as long as the child has developed some verbal and written language abilities; all the activities presented are activities that could be used at any age at any time. As Daniel (1982) points out, "Writing is a skill or a craft, an art that is always becoming, yet never perfected. There is no child who can form words and letters that is too young to begin to write, nor any writer who is too old" (p. 56). Surely this comment can be extended to the reader. As long as the child has either writing or reading skills the following activities and concepts should apply. The only attempt at distinctions will be in terms of those activities that can be used for reading development and those for developing a language arts or writing program.

TEACHING ACTIVITIES FOR READING

Understanding the Basics

One of the tragedies of reading instruction for the gifted child is that it is usually a boring and somewhat pedestrian task (Switzer and Nourse, 1979; Trezise, 1977). This is mainly due to the child's prior mastery of many of the basic reading skills. On the other hand, a lack of these skills could be an equally detrimental experience for the child. The initial step in any reading program, therefore, is to assess the present skill levels of the child. The basics of reading, including word decoding, vocabulary, and comprehension, are the foundation skills that should be assessed before deciding placement of children within a reading program. It is an unfortunate situation if children are placed either too high or too low in reading levels that are not commensurate with their ability to perform. Most often the gifted child in the regular school program is placed in a reading situation that is well below his or her reading capabilities and interests, but just as unfortunate is the assumption that the child has accelerated skills, which may result in a placement beyond the child's capacity to perform. Therefore, it is essential that a good diagnosis or understanding of the child's basic reading skills be made.

Mindell and Stracher (1980) provide a comprehensive analysis of reading skills in which a child's word reading, decoding, spelling, and vocabulary can be easily assessed. The assessment begins with some basic standardized reading tests, used mainly to insure that the teacher or program planner is able to identify the child's functional entry level into the reading program. (For standardized tests used in assessing reading skills, *see* Chapter One). Using these test results, the child's word analysis or decoding skills, plus his or her vocabulary and comprehension skills, may be determined for appropriate selection and placement in a reading program.

Boothby (1980) suggests that in developing reading programs in either the critical or creative area vocabulary development is a must. She suggests that helping gifted children enrich or learn new vocabulary be done through experiencing the *connotative power* of words, developing *figurative language*, and studying *etymology*. In developing the connotative power of words, children can discuss and list groups of words that evoke certain feelings. For example, words could be categorized as mysterious, scary, or happy; using poetry and prose is another way to help children identify words that evoke images or connotation. Advertisements can be a source of figurative language as well as connotative words, which can be discussed in terms of how particular words are used to sell a product or to induce a potential buyer to purchase a product. Having students write their own advertisements would be one method of reinforcing their understanding of both the connotative power and the figurative use of words. The history of words, etymology, is another way of developing a critical and creative reading vocabulary for the child. O'Rourke (1971) suggests a number of activities for studying etymology. In essence, having children discover the historical development of a word not only increases their understanding of that word but provides another basis from which new vocabulary can be enriched.

Comprehension is another basic that is a must for furthering the reading development of children. Comprehension skills should be consciously and systematically taught (Trezise, 1977). One way to facilitate teaching comprehension is to have students with similar interests work in groups, read the same or similar material, and discuss with each other what they consider to be the author's purpose, the author's treatment of the topic, the believability of the plot and characters found within the book, and how different books deal with a similar topic in different ways. Comprehension is an obvious, basic component of good reading; however, comprehension needs to be practiced and exercised to ensure that students do indeed understand what they have read. Gifted students can extend beyond just reading for comprehension into the area of critical and creative reading by an in-depth analysis of purpose, appropriateness, and themes.

Developing Critical Reading Skills

In developing critical reading skills, Boothby (1980) suggests the use of the *Directive Reading-Thinking* activities by Stauffer. Boothby feels that these activities promote critical thinking through prediction and problem solving. Comparative reading is another activity for developing critical reading; for example, the children might be asked to compare what different authors say on a particular topic (inflation, world hunger, capitalism) or individuals (Abraham Lincoln, Thomas Jefferson, Rousseau, Freud). Having children compare different newspapers and investigate how each paper has accounted for the same event (i.e., sporting event, national tragedy, or a current event of some sort) allows the children to contrast and discuss how different authors utilize different language patterns, feelings, and even expressions of personality in their writing. Trezise (1977) suggests that reading is basically a thinking process — one in which visual symbols are transformed into meaning. Reading can be a convergent as well as a divergent thinking task. Children can convergently discuss the similarity between authors, themes, treatment, and believability of what has been written. Divergently, children could launch from what they have read into new thoughts and possibilities. Trezise (1977) suggests the use of the Hilda-Tabatha discussion strategies as a means of helping children develop new thoughts and ideas from the reading they have just completed. To do this, students are asked to make inferences about the reading. "How did the characters feel?" "Why do you feel they felt that way?" "Has anything happened to you like what happened to them?" Trezise utilizes an example from a work by Platt (1971) entitled *Hey, Dummy* to develop divergent thinking. He first suggests that a convergent activity involving the discussion of the story itself could immediately follow the reading. From this discussion an attempt could be made to capitalize upon the experiences of the children by having them apply their own experience to the story itself. Asking them to determine how they felt or what they have experienced related to the story content should evoke a discussion of some depth.

The teacher can help the child become a critical reader by suggesting ways in which something can be done with what is read. This, again, is more of a divergent task but requires the child to critically analyze and think through utilization of the information read. Torrance (1965) suggests several methods in which children can be encouraged to do this

1. Have the child reproduce what is read imaginatively.
2. Have the child elaborate on what is read.
3. Have the child transform and rearrange what is read.
4. Push the child beyond what is read through discussion and follow through on ideas and questions suggested by the reading.

Creative Reading

Creative reading involves applying divergent thinking to the reading task. In essence, creative readers attempt to foster their own ideas, feelings, attitudes, and values from what they have read. In other words, they attempt to develop new ideas or express feelings and attitudes based upon their reading (Trezise, 1977). Creative reading is best exemplified when the story read is dramatized, set to music, danced, or interpreted in some way through the performing arts or when a theme, a situation, or even a character from the reading is used in a new and different way (Bolding, 1980). To develop creative reading skills children could be encouraged to rewrite what has been read into a play or to dramatize in some way the meaning of the content simply to express openly their attitudes and feelings concerning what has been read.

Boothby (1980) suggests that creative reading is a divergence through personal integration with expression as the goal. Torrance (1965) indicates that teachers can foster creative reading by preparing the child for the reading assignment. Teachers should attempt to heighten the child's expectations and anticipation prior to the actual reading, as well as to encourage the child to be prepared to use what is read in some meaningful way. Heightening the child's expectations can be accomplished by encouraging predictions about what is to be read and the possible outcomes that may result in the story itself. Once these have been made prior to the reading they can then be compared to the actual content of the text.

Reading for Enjoyment

Martinson (1968) and Witty (1971) strongly suggest that children be allowed to read books that correlate with their individual interests and that allowances be made for them to read independently. Independent reading should be encouraged and reinforced. One means of helping students to increase their vocabulary, strengthen their reading, and improve their writing and language arts skills is to help them gain a love of literature and a knowledge of the variety of literary options available. For example, many of the gifted and talented have enthusiastically discovered science fiction, which may involve them in the medieval and mythical past with the unicorn, winged and fire-breathing dragon, noble heros and heroines, orcs, hobbits, and other mystical and fantasy characters. Or, since science fiction involves a wide time span, many prefer the futuristic fantasies of space travel and the imagined occupants of distant galaxies. It is amazing to note how much may be learned about the medieval past or about modern technology and electronics through science fiction, for the authors are generally not allowed to deviate far from known facts or realities, but they may creatively project their plots around conjecture as to what may be beyond the known in early earth history or in future technology, occurrences, and peoples. Connoisseurs and consumers of science fiction are very critical and exacting in their high expectations regarding consistency, validity, and reality when dealing with known technology within the stories. Another interesting characteristic in science fiction, medieval or futuristic, is that good and evil are generally clearly discernible and consistent.

An extension of science fiction literature is the area of role-play games. These may be founded on either medieval settings or space travel. In either case, if the observer will analyze what occurs in these games it will be noted that the participants must cooperate and pull together with other players for the game to move properly. They must study the scripts and be prepared cognitively to understand their own character's strengths and limitations and those of the other players. They must accept a knowledgeable group leader, who helps to keep order and direction and serves as a reality check and judge within the game, and the participants must become involved and be willing to keep within the basic game rules. When a game is in progress and going smoothly it is amazing to note the language development, technical insights, awareness, and mental gymnastics of each one of the players. It is, in fact, rather impressive. It is also exciting when gifted students choose to either try their hand at writing science fiction or try developing a game of their own. A lot may be learned cognitively, socially, emotionally, and in terms of integrity. Much may also be learned in language development, creative thinking, creative writing, and sheer enjoyment of this fantasy area.

Some of the gifted and talented are simply not interested in science fiction and find more enjoyment in historical literature. In this area they may read about people, places, and events out of the past. As they gather information and insight they enrich their own perspective. Many other types of literature are also available in abundance: biographies, mysteries and detective stories, westerns, spy and intrigue stories, adventure and exploration sagas, and gothic and romance novels. One can also move away from fiction to the many fine books available on science, nature, and different cultures, and of course to the great classics as well.

There are so many advantages to enjoying literature. The reader is exposed to language arts, as discussed earlier in this chapter, but also to studying problem-solving approaches, the customs and behaviors of different people, personal interaction skills, relationships and behaviors. The reader may vicariously visit many lands and be exposed to many emotional insights. It does not take long for the reader to become discriminating as to the type of books he or she finds most enjoyable and most acceptable, and with the help of good teachers the student can learn to consider values and the benefit of reading the classics and broadening his or her horizons with a variety of literature. Again, it is important to encourage independent reading and to expand the interests of children, exposing them to different types of literature — literature of high quality — either by reading to them or by having the materials available for their selection and personal use.

Poems and prose should also be available either in the classroom, from which the teacher can read, or as a nearby resource, from which materials for personal reading and enjoyment can be selected by the child. Having the child not only read but write poetry can be useful for developing a child's interest in this area. Further, Switzer and Nourse (1979) suggest correlating books with filmstrips, films, and television programs as a means of motivating and creating interest for the child. Reading for enjoyment must be considered a viable part of the reading program. It is important for the teacher to provide time and materials through which reading enjoyment can be fostered.

Hershaw (1981) suggests the following activities for use or adaptation with any piece of literature. The activities are designed for students in the intermediate grades of elementary school and for students in the junior high school. Students could be asked to —

1. Make a crossword puzzle that fits the pattern of words and clues from the story
2. Write a story using words from a vocabulary list derived from the story. The story should be about a topic that is unrelated to the piece of literature being used
3. Pretend that they are one of the characters in the story and write two journal entries for two different days that they are the character
4. Make a two-minute speech as if they are one of the characters in the story
5. Make a mobile depicting some aspect of the story, using anything *except* paper and crayons

6. Make a diorama depicting a scene from the story, using only "living things" such as twigs and grass in their creation
7. Write a character sketch describing a character in the story
8. Make puppets to represent the characters in the story and present a puppet show using the puppets and relating an event from the story
9. Present a television or radio commercial selling the story
10. Make a book jacket for the story; the scene on the front should depict an event in the story that made them feel happy, sad, angry, etc., and the flap summary should describe the same scene
11. Write the next chapter for the book
12. Write an event from the story in play form and perform it for the group

TEACHING ACTIVITIES FOR LANGUAGE ARTS

Understanding the Basics

Like reading, the language arts activities of writing and oral expression are based upon some fundamental concepts. These concepts include an understanding of punctuation, word usage, spelling, handwriting, and organization of thoughts. It is suggested that at the beginning level children be assessed as to their skill aquisition in each of these areas. The writing skills — spelling, punctuation, grammar, and so on — that the child understands and uses and the oral expression that the child has relative to these same areas of word usage should be observed and measured. (For more information on assessment of spelling, grammar, word usage, punctuation, etc., *see* the list of tests provided in Chapter One.) Too often gifted children are not taught some of the basic fundamentals of good writing composition. This should not be overlooked; nor, on the other hand, should the writing task become mundane and repetitive. Children should know the fundamentals of good writing. Once that has been established, writing can then be more functionally managed. Daniel (1982) outlines several beginning activities that should be considered in a language arts writing experience for gifted children. First is to help the child make accurate observations. One exercise that can be used in making accurate observations is to have the child select some architectural detail of a building and then describe it in words. This activity forces the child to look carefully at the piece of architecture as well as to find words that transfer what is seen into what is thought, changing a visual image into a verbal image. The next activity Daniel refers to is organization. This can be accomplished by having the children recall an experience to which they have all had a great deal of exposure (i.e. a sporting event, television program, or a movie attended together) and then ask them to discuss their observations about that particular activity. This is a brainstorming exercise that initially has no limits. The ideas as they are expressed are written down. Once a great number of ideas are expressed, the children are then asked to organize these different thoughts into categories, associations, or generalizations that may be observed in the unordered information. After the initial associations have been completed, new associations and new sets of generalizations may begin to emerge. Another similar activity to promote organization is suggested by Irmscher (1979). Students take a magazine and cut out pictures they like. The pictures are then assembled to make a personal statement — in effect a collage that represents the child or tells something about him or her. The children are instructed not to decide what the collage will say until after they have selected the pictures that appeal to them.

Mindell and Stracher (1980) suggest that assessment of spelling, vocabulary, paragraphing, and composition skills be made prior to beginning a language arts program. Spelling should identify the decoding errors as well as the specific spelling errors that the child may be making; is the child unable to differentiate between different sounds such as "ch" and "sh," for example, or does he or she not understand the rules for plurals and vowels? Having the child write a pargraph or a short story will help in the analysis of the child's vocabulary, paragraphing skills, and understanding of organization, clarity, and logic of thought in writing. Helping children to understand these basic components of language, along with helping them to develop and improve their observation and organizational skills, should result in improved writing and oral language abilities.

An outline for teaching the language arts skills is provided below. This is simply an outline of possible basic topics that should be taught or reviewed by students.

A. Mechanics (review five to ten minutes periodically)
   1. Vocabulary
      a. Descriptive words
      b. Action words
      c. Root words (planning)
   2. Production
      a. Capitalization
      b. Punctuation
   3. Sentence structure
      a. Phrase
      b. Simple, compound, complex
      c. Construction of a paragraph
   4. Organization
      a. Arrangement of ideas within a paragraph
      b. Three main ideas — beginning, middle, ending
B. Expression
   1. Giving information

    a. Listing advantages and disadvantages
    b. Sequential order of information
    c. Letter of reference
  2. Promoting ideas
    a. Advertising a product
    b. Comparison of items
    c. Television script
    d. Letters to a friend
    e. Job application
  3. Expressing feelings
    a. Emotions
    b. Subject matter
    c. Five senses
  4. Creative writing
    a. Poetry (haiku, prose)
    b. Journal (ways to do things, jot ideas and dreams)
    c. Research report
    d. Newspaper report

Critical Writing and Thinking Skills

Critical writing is precise and accurate. It is highly dependent upon the children having a good understanding of the basics of written and oral language and their ability to apply the skills of grammar, punctuation, organization, and logical reasoning in the writing task. Procedures discussed earlier (Royer 1982) that employ Bloom's *Taxonomy of Educational Objectives* (i.e. knowledge, comprehension, application, analysis, synthesis, and evaluation) are suggested as a means of helping develop children's critical writing and thinking skills. Applying these objectives can stimulate both convergent and divergent writing behavior. These objectives place the child in a situation where basic skills can be applied and the child's creative process exercised. To utilize Royer's procedures the following steps are suggested. The child should —

1. *Identify* a problem that exists and needs to be addressed. This could be a current event, something of importance to the individual child, or a problem that is pertinent to the community or nation.
2. *Collect* information (knowledge) about that particular problem, answering the question, "What are the facts pertinent to this problem?" Answering this question increases the child's knowledge about the problem.
3. Attempt to *develop* an understanding or comprehension of the problem. What is the current problem, and why is this a topic of concern? Are there still questions to be answered in order to gain a better understanding or comprehension of the situation?
4. Attempt to identify possible solutions or strategies in solving the problem.

What outside information can be used to help solve this problem, and how? This is an *application* step.

5. *Analyze* what solutions have been proposed for this problem and which of these solutions relate to the primary issues within the problem itself.

6. *Synthesize* all the information gathered, including the analysis, application, and knowledge, into information that would be useful for solving the problem.

7. *Evaluate* what strategies and solutions appear to be most appropriate, why, and why not.

In all of Royer's (1982) steps both convergent and divergent thought processes are exercised. The child converges information, identifying facts and solutions, and then is exercised divergently, answering the why or why not and predicting or projecting what could or might happen given each solution. Royer suggests that this procedure allows children to use a variety of thinking skills, making them more independent thinkers, which may result in more creative composers and writers.

Creative writing is an exercise in which students can go beyond merely demonstrating good writing skills by projecting themselves into the writing activity — their feelings, attitudes, and ideas. Creative writing can be both informative, factual writing such as a report or a projective exercise in which logic and reason are used to express answers to existing problems, to project solutions to new problems, to determine new methods and solutions to new problems, or to determine new methods and procedures for solving old problems. The following activities develop both creative writing and oral expression within the child.

THE "SIXTY-SEVEN IN ONE" ACTIVITY (*Teaching Gifted Children*, 1981) is an illustration of a method that involves the child in thinking using a problem-solving approach. This activity places the child in a situation in which he/she can apply creative abilities in solving problems. Written reports can be very time-consuming or even boring to the child and can be restrictive of the creative or written expressive abilities of each individual. The "Sixty-seven in One" activity described below is an example of how the child may produce a factual report without violating his or her creative writing abilities.

Begin by explaining that there are different ways to show that you understand a concept or that you can apply a skill. Suppose that you had researched the pollution problem in your town. Some of the ways you could report your results include an interview between a businessman and an EPA official (real or simulated), a map of the problem areas, a crossword puzzle of words pertinent to pollution control, a written report analyzing the influence of pollution on your town.

Share the following list with the students (each student should have his or her own copy). Invite questions about the meaning of any unfamiliar terms (diorama, or time line, for example, may be unfamiliar) and encourage any additions to the list:

Activity calendar   dialogue   mobile

advertisement	dictionary	mosaic
analysis	diorama	mural
autobiography	display	newspaper
banner	dramatization	observation
booklet	drawing	papier-mâché
cartoon	design	pattern
characterization	film	paragraph
chart	game	picture
chart story	graph	play
collection	interview	poster
comparison	letter	problem
construction	list	puppet
crossword	magazine	puzzle
design	map	questions
diagram	mask	report
scrapbook	story	test
sequence story	survey	time line
skit	symbol	transparency
song	tape	weaving
speech	telegram	three-D object

This list of activities could be incorporated into contracts for subsequent independent projects. Any student or group of students should specify in their contract which and how many of the different activities will be applied until work has begun. The contract should specify the days on which each of the individual activities will be completed, how each one will be evaluated, and the criteria for grading.

Copies of students' completed projects, collected in a file, provide a pool of ideas for future student research. As students have the opportunity to experiment with novel ways to report their findings, they will develop new forms to be added to the list of sixty-seven.

Some other activities that can be used for older students in a creative writing experience may include the following. The teacher can —

1. Publish a class newspaper. This allows the students to write about themselves — a subject they know a great deal about.
2. Have students rewrite newspaper articles or editorials using the same facts but taking an opposite view.
3. Utilize students' interest and creativity to write and perform short plays or radio and television scripts. With the advent of readily available tape recorders and videotaping machines this suggestion is easily implemented.
4. Practice stream of thought writing, an old technique but a very useful one. In this activity the students are directed to put on paper their random thoughts. This is an excellent way to simply get the children to start writing.
5. Publish a classroom literary journal. This journal would include voluntary student contributions. This activity can give many students an opportunity to participate since students can write, illustrate, and edit the journal.
6. Stimulate writing by using provocative pictures taken from newspapers,

magazines, or comic books. Students are asked to write their reactions or feelings about one or a series of pictures.

In developing oral expression the teacher could consider activities initiated by such things as good literature, problem-solving activities, and humor. To foster the development of oral expression the following guidelines and activities can be used. The teacher should —

1. Provide both hands-on and vicarious experiences about which the students can then orally express themselves
2. Capitalize on the words used in the various formal and informal activities in the class
3. Cultivate an interest in words
4. Teach children to communicate effectively over telephone
5. Upgrade sharing time
6. Capitalize upon the use of the "language experience" approach by which group or individual stories can be created or recorded
7. Provide opportunities for storytelling
8. Have students practice making simple, but concise, announcements
9. Stimulate informal conversation and discussion
10. Have students practice giving directions to and from places as well as directions for doing or making certain things
11. Teach social skills for introducing one person to another
12. Teach the children to do simple choral readings
13. Help students enjoy various kinds of dramatizations
14. Begin the practice of communicative oral reading to an audience
15. Have students conduct interviews
16. Help students compose puns, limericks, haiku, etc

The following are some specific activities for developing children's written and oral expressive abilities.

WHAT COULD THEY DO?

Materials: Pictures of objects or the objects themselves, such as an onion, a trash can, or a doorknob.

Procedure: Show each object and have the children make up an oral short story about what the object might reveal if it could talk.

CHAINMAKER

Objectives: Children need to increase verbal fluency and ability to give a variety of responses to the same problem.

Materials: Cards containing the picture or name of a city helper such as a policeman or ambulance driver.

Procedure: Have children go through the following steps:

1. They form a circle or chain.
2. The teacher chooses a leader to begin.
3. The leader stands in the middle of the circle and holds up a card.
4. He/she points to someone who tells what the helper does for people.

5. Each time the card is held up, a new way of helping must be given for that worker.
6. If someone cannot offer a new way, the chain is broken.
7. The broken link earns his/her way back into the chain by giving a correct answer when another link becomes broken.

TELL A TALE

Objectives: To aid in developing creative oral expression.

Materials: Six folders with a variety of pictures in them and a tape recorder.

Procedure: Give out folders containing pictures to the students, but tell the students in advance not to open the folders until called upon. The teacher or student begins telling a story. She points to a student with a folder who then looks at his picture and continues telling the story. His part should be related to his picture. The rest of the students do the same as it comes their turn. The last child ends the story. Tape the activity and play it back for the students.

WORD CHARTS

Objectives: Children need to use and manipulate words.

Materials: Chart paper.

Procedure: Have children select a category and then find as many words in that category as they can through the week and make books or charts. Example: Elephant words are plod, clomp, weighty, hugh, immense. Funny words are laugh, giggle, silly, joke, happy, clown. Soft words are cuddly, fuzzy, furry, snow, peaceful.

MAGIC CIRCLE. This is an idea adapted from Bessell and Palomares (1971). All children are seated in a large circle on the floor.

Rules: All statements are accepted.
       No one's ideas are put down.
       Only one child talks at a time.
       Every child gets a chance to talk.

Sometimes the teacher initiates the conversation by a question, and sometimes a child does. Example: "What animal would you be if you could be any animal in the world and why?" "What keeps me from growing into a giant?"

The teacher can either join the circle or let the children converse alone. The circle can continue until the teacher stops it, or it can be a timed exercise.

ACTIVITIES FOR GETTING TO KNOW CHILDREN

Autobiographical Sketch. Prepare questionnaire for students to answer. It could include

1. Name
2. Where were you born?
3. What are your parents' names and occupations?
4. Tell anything you would like about your family.
5. What is your favorite pastime after school? Weekends?
6. Tell about your hobbies (two).
7. What do you do with your free time?

8. What do you plan to do ten years from now?
9. Who is your best friend? Why?
10. How do you feel about school?
11. Are you happy about yourself?

Heros. Have students describe their hero and tell why they have chosen that person. Extension: Have students describe their best friend, bullies in other classes, etc.

Pictures. Set up room with a variety of pictures, animals, rockets, people, scenes, activities, etc. Have students take a picture and tell what thoughts or feelings they have about it, why the picture is important to them, and/or why they chose it.

Bulletin Board. Introduce a new board, then brainstorm and list on the board any words or thoughts students have about its message or impact. Have them take turns explaining why they chose that word or idea.

Story-telling. Have students choose a story from a supplemental reader to read silently and retell to class orally. Extension: Have the student be the hero and change the crisis and climax of the story orally or describe the roles of various characters.

Success Sharing. Students can be divided up into groups. At an opportune time have students publicly share some of their successes. What successful activity have they done this week? What achievement do they remember before they were ten? What is an important accomplishment in their life between ten and fifteen years?

Bragging. Divide into groups of five or six. Students have five minutes to boast about any accomplishments, awards, talents, or characteristics they choose. Evaluate: How did they feel about bragging? Was it comfortable? What boasting did they like best? Is boasting good?

Success Box or Bag. Have students decorate a box. Have them put success symbols in it, such as papers, medals, certificates, or anything that shows success and accomplishments. Have students share at end of the day or weekly what they have achieved or learned.

POETRY. Poems are a fun creative writing experience. Common poems like haiku and cinquain are fun to use. A *cinquain* is a special kind of poem which has five lines and follows this format.

1. *Name* of something or someone. (noun)
2. *Two words* that tell what it does. (verbs)
3. *Three words* that describe it. (adjectives)
4. *Your own thought* about it. (a short sentence about line one)
5. *Repetition of the name* or a word that means the same thing as the name. (synonym)

My Mother
Mother
Cleans and teaches

Happy, helpful, loving
She is my mother.
Mrs. Brown.

Borrow a "poem bone" and write a poem. For example, take a poem or idea such as

The Funniest Thing
What's the funniest thing you can think of?
A clown
My cat dressed in my sister's clothes
Funny jokes
What's the funniest thing you can think of?

Take out some of the words and have the child fill in the blanks.

The _____ Thing
What's the _____ thing you can think of?
What's the _____ thing you can think of?

_____
_____
_____

What's the _____ thing you can think of?

Happiest, saddest, ugliest, prettiest, scariest, best, etc., can be used in the first and last blanks. Be creative! Another good poem bone is show below.

A Present
My Dad gave me a present.
I gave that present to Randy.
What was that present? Candy!
Yummy
Scrumptious
Fattening
Candy.

A Present
My _____ gave me a present.
I gave that present to _____.
What was that present? _____!

_____
_____
_____
_____.

A *haiku* is a Japanese form of poetry that does not rhyme in English. It generally has seventeen syllables (in the order five, seven, five) and is often a description of nature or events which make a comment.

The bright hued feather
Blowing past my windowpane
Was an autumn leaf.

Clerihews are poems about people. They have an *aa, bb* rhyme pattern. Here are two examples from Monson (1981).

PAUL REVERE	*a*
Rode out on a night so clear	*a*
And warned all he found	*b*
That the British would soon be around.	*b*
WILLIE MAYS	*a*
He had his days;	*a*
With a trade to the Mets,	*b*
I've lost all my bets	*b*

A good poetry activity is to give students clerihews in which some of the lines have been left for them to finish.

Bugs Bunny	*a*
Is so funny,	*a*
_____	*b*
_____.	*b*
Albert Einstein	*a*
Was so fine,	*a*
_____	*b*
_____.	*b*
Cheryl Tiegs	*a*
In fashion leads,	*a*
_____	*b*
_____.	*b*

Then have students try writing some clerihews from start to finish.

Limericks are funny poems with an *aa, bb, a,* rhyme pattern. Here are some examples:

There was a young man in a boat	*a*
Who said, "I'm afloat! I'm afloat!"	*a*
When they said, "No, you ain't!"	*b*
He was ready to faint,	*b*
That unhappy old man in a boat.	*a*
I wish that my room had a floor	*a*
I don't much care for a door,	*a*
But this walking around	*b*
Without touching the ground,	*b*
Is getting to be quite a bore!	*a*

Students can be given limericks in which some of the lines have been left out for them to finish.

There was an old lady named Crockett	*a*
Who went to plug in a socket;	*a*
_____	*b*
_____	*b*

And came roaring back down like a rocket!   *a*
Then have the children try writing their own limericks.

Concrete Poems are drawings with words. First, children should think of an object that they enjoy — it can be anything tangible. Next, they should make a list of words that describe that object. Finally, they should use the words to form the shape of the object. For example:

FRUITY-MMM, SMOOTH AND MELLOW, SATISFYING, DELICIOUS, JUICY, YELLOW,

PICTURES. Pictures can be excellent story motivators. The teacher or the child can draw or cut and paste a picture on the top of a piece of writing paper. Then one can discuss or write about the picture, ask questions about the picture, or have suggested titles to go along with the picture. Here are a few examples, but don't limit the child to these illustrations.

Frog
Hoppy toad
Sitting on a Lilly Pad
Happy in the sun
Will it hop off soon?
Why is it smiling?

A family
Five members
What are their names?
Where do they live?
They look happy
The Harrison Family.

A glass of water
Warm or cold?
Who drank the top half?
Are you thirsty?
Could a fish swim in it?

Suggested Bibliography for Teachers of Reading and Language Arts Programs

Anderson, V.: *Reading and Young Children.* New York, Macmillan, 1968.

Binder-Scott, L.: *Learning Time with Language Experiences for Young Children.* New York, McGraw-Hill, 1968.

Burrows, A., Jackson, D., and Saunders, D.: *They All Want to Write,* 3rd ed. New York, Holt, 1964.

Coody, B.: *Using Literature with Young Children.* Dubuque, Iowa, Wm. C. Brown, 1979.

Croft and Hess.: *An Activities Handbook for Teachers of Young Children.* Boston, Houghton Mifflin Co., 1975.

Dallmann, Martha.: *Teaching the Language Arts in the Elementary School.* Dubuque, Iowa, Wm. C. Brown, 1970.

Dorsey, Mary E.: *Reading Games and Activities.* Belmont California, Fearon, 1972.

Ehrlich, H., and Grastry, P.: *Creative Dramatics Handbook.* Philadelphia, School District of Philadelphia Instructional Services, 1971.

Freeman, Frank N.: *Starting to Write.* Zaner-Bloser Co., 1969.

Heyman, Marjorie Rowe.: *Enriching Your Reading Program.* Belmont, California, Fearon, 1972.

Jacobs, L. (Ed.): *Using Literature with Young Children.* New York, Teachers' College, 1965.

King, J., and Katsman, C.: *Imagine That: Illustrated Poems and Creative Learning Experiences.* Pacific Palisades, California, Goodyear, 1976.

Larric, N.: *A Teacher's Guide to Children's Books.* Columbus, Ohio, Merrill, 1963.

McIntyre, B.: *Creative Drama in the Elementary School.* Itasca, Illinois, Peacock, 1974.

Monroe, Marion: *Learn to Listen, Speak and Write.* Glenview, Illinois, Scott Foresman and Co., 1960.

Northwestern Regional Educational Laboratory: *CHILD: Coordinated Helps in Language Development.* Portland, Oregon, Copy-Print Centers, 1971.

Osborn, Keith S., and Haupt, Dorthy: *Creative Activities for Young Children.* Merrill-Palmer Institute, 1964.

Pilon, B. A.: *Teaching Language Arts Creatively in the Elementary Grades.* New York, Wiley, 1978.

Possien, W.: *They All Need to Talk: Oral Communication in the Language Arts Program.* New York, Appleton-Century-Crofts, 1969.

Schaff, J.: *The Language Arts Idea Book: Classroom Activities for Children.* Pacific Palisades, California, Goodyear, 1976.

Schimmel, N.: *Just Enough to Make a Story.* Berkley, California, Sister's Choice, 1978.

Schubert, Delwyn (Ed.): *Reading Games that Teach.* Creative Teaching Press, 1965.

Sealy, L.: *Children's Writing: An Approach for the Primary Grades.* Newark, Delaware, International Reading Assoc., 1979.

————: "The Gray Velvet Rabbit," *Learning Time With Language Experiences for Young Children.* New York, McGraw-Hill, 1968.

Veatch, J., Sawicki, F., Barnette, E., Elliott, G., and Blakey, J.: *Key Words to Reading: The Language Experience Approach Begins.* Columbus, Ohis, Merrill, 1973.

CHAPTER NINE

SCIENCE

Can you answer the following questions?

1. What are five characteristics of children with potential in science?
2. What is RETAL and its purpose?
3. What should be some components of a science curriculum for accelerated children?
4. How would you enrich the science program?
5. What are some good resources for materials for the science program?

OVER the years, interest in science and especially in science programming for the gifted and talented has been somewhat cyclical. With the launching of Sputnik by the Russians in 1957, interest in science escalated, and educators were motivated to develop a number of approaches for working with gifted science students (Abeles, 1977). As education moves into the mid 1980s with renewed interest in teaching the basics, the emphasis on science education may begin to wane. However, there is no question that the sciences (i.e. social studies and health, natural, and physical sciences) are fundamental educational needs of all children, especially the gifted and talented. The sciences by their very nature stimulate inquiry and creative efforts that are fundamental to the thinking characteristics of gifted and talented children. The neglect of a science program, limiting inquiry and self-expression, will destroy the achievement motivation of many young gifted students (Whitmore, 1979).

Education in the sciences necessitates the learning of certain fundamental tools and skills. The science student is almost forced into higher levels of divergent thinking. Further, the science student explores, finds, and utilizes newer vestiges of self-expression and self-development. Therefore, this chapter will highlight some of the procedures relative to the identification of those children who would most benefit from a science-oriented program, will identify the curriculum considerations that should be made in developing a science program in the public schools, and will present program ideas that can be used or implemented in the public school system for elementary and secondary level students.

IDENTIFYING CHILDREN WITH SCIENCE ABILITIES

All of the characteristics of gifted and talented students previously discussed in this text (*see* especially Chapter One) combine to emphasize the benefit of student placement in a science curriculum that incorporates productive and competitive interaction with other exceptionally bright children. Kopelman, Galasso, and Strom (1977) suggest students who are creatively gifted in sciences have the following characteristics:

1. They are strong and sincerely motivated toward learning and achieving in science.
2. They are able to work well independently in the laboratory, library, and class-rooms.
3. They are curious and ask questions about phenomena they encounter.
4. They are very much interested in getting answers to questions suggested by their work and by their teachers.
5. They ask many questions.
6. They are stimulated by problem-solving approaches to learning.
7. They are good at identifying significant problems in a mass of information.
8. They are readily able to induce, deduce, and make connections between related ideas.
9. They often see different approaches or come up with "off-beat" ideas.
10. Their creativity and achievements often extend to many other areas.
11. They relate well to their peers and elders.
12. Many of them have long-term goals well established. (P. 82)

There are some specific characteristics that should be considered in the identification of these gifted science students. Del Giorno (1977), in her discussion of how students are selected for a special science program in the public schools, suggests that several people involved with the science program and the school recommend those students who would most benefit from participation in the science program. For example, the science department chairpersons, guidance counselors, and principals could be asked to make recommendations regarding those students interested in and desiring to attend a science program. These students could be asked to describe in letter form their scientific interest. This letter would not only reflect the students' interests but serve as a means of evaluating the students' capabilities for entrance into the program. Del Giorno indicates that in many cases students go beyond what is requested and submit a detailed report of their science activities as well as specific goals for scientific projects they wish to pursue within a science program.

Kopelman, Galasso, and Strom (1977), in describing how students are selected for the science program at the Bronx High School, indicate that students have to pass an examination designed by the Scholastic Testing Corporation of Bensonville, Illinois. The exam consists of verbal and mathematic segments. The verbal testing is comprised of objective questions in vocabulary, sentence completion, and reading comprehension. The reading comprehension is based on the interpretation of scientific and technical information. This study indicates three criteria that could be used in identification of students for a gifted science program: high achievement and aptitude in science and mathematics; motivation and interest in science projects as demonstrated by requesting entrance into the science program, and finally creative science abilities as identified by a teacher's direct observations and evaluative devices.

A child who has demonstrated achievement capabilities in math and science as measured by selected standardized tests would be considered a potential candidate for a special science class. Recommendations of teachers and/or other professionals pertaining to the conducting of scientific projects and the intense interest and motivation of the child in attending a science class or a set of courses would have to be considered as prime criteria for entrance into a science program. However, as stated earlier, science itself should be considered a critical component of the overall education program of all children. Science should not be put off for later grades but be made an important part of the child's curriculum early in the child's school program.

CURRICULUM CONSIDERATIONS AND COMPONENTS

The question is what and how to teach science to the gifted learners. The literature is replete with different approaches to working with the child in this area. However, in summary, all the approaches could be outlined by the following:

1. Provide an opportunity for the child to explore.
2. Let the child express ideas freely and openly.
3. Provide the necessary information, tools, equipment, and atmosphere in which the child can experiment and investigate.

There are many variations of this particular theme throughout the literature, but in essence all science programs have these three elements in common.

Whitmore (1979) suggests that the curriculum should be based on real world problems. These problems can be the basis of developing new knowledge as well as learning new tools and skills necessary to solve the problems. The curriculum should also offer an opportunity for the child to explore the many contributions of different disciplines (i.e. political science, sociology, anthropology, history, economics, and psychology).

Many authors suggest different curricular components for a science program. The following descriptions provide a sampling of some of those proposed models. First, Del Giorno (1977) outlines RETAL (Research Team Approach to Learning) as a method of helping students develop critical and divergent thinking skills in the science area. This approach groups children and provides them specific roles and tasks to perform for the purpose of investigating a particular research topic using the scientific method. In essence, it is a cooperative approach. It involves the students in finding out the underlying phenomenon that they are investigating or the underlying why, where, how, and when of the problem. RETAL is composed of a team of three persons: the *researcher* who defines a problem and makes a preliminary search into the literature; the *technician* who plans the experimental design as well as carries out the investigation; and the *recorder* who is the coordinator of activities, records and interprets the data while the other team members are involved with research, and is responsible for the dissemination of that new information.

RETAL assists students in developing critical and divergent thinking skills by having them work through the research or scientific process. This process involves (1) *making a proposal*, which is a description of a problem requiring a review of the literature, a statement of purpose, the review of literature that provides a rationale for conducting the study, and the limitation of the study itself; (2) *designing the research techniques* or strategies, stating hypotheses, outlining the procedures and methodology to be used in reaching the end result, and identifying the statistical tests or procedures that may be used in helping to determine the effectiveness of the methodology; (3) *implementing the experimental design*; (4) *interpreting and reporting the results*; and (5) *preparing a research report* that clearly identifies each of the above elements plus projects new directions for the research in this area.

Abeles (1977) suggests that science education for the gifted could involve both *acceleration* and *enrichment*. Acceleration in science means providing a student with instruction in a given area earlier than the regular sequence for the average student. Acceleration as proposed by Abeles (1977) may work as outlined below:

Grade	Average Student's Science Program	Accelerated Student's Curriculum
7	Life Science	Life and/or Physical Science
8	Physical Science	Earth Science
9	Earth Science	Biology
10	Biology	Chemistry
11	Chemistry	Physics
12	Physics	Advanced courses in astronomy, geology, or human physiology and advanced placement in science

The use of acceleration tables is a means of self-pacing. The opportunities provided by self-pacing allow children to move ahead more rapidly according to their ability rather than in comparison to other classmates or in accordance with a normal curriculum schedule.

Acceleration is also found in the modular approach. This is an approach in which a course of particular interest for the student can be produced by selecting a series of modules (i.e. information, lessons, outlines, texts, and other resources) and putting them together into an instructional sequence that satisfies the interest and development of the child. The other approach suggested by Abeles involves enrichment of a science program by the adding of activities, mini-courses, or full courses that would not normally be found in the science program of a given school system.

Rose (1978), Harrison (1981), and others suggest using the Enrichment Triad Model proposed by Renzulli (1977) as a basis from which the science curriculum could be developed. In this model, three types of enrichment activities are proposed; type I and type II activities would be appropriate for all learners, and type III activities become the most important for gifted students.

Type I enrichment consists of *general exploratory activities* that provide experiences to help the child learn or become familiar with new information or new types of vocabulary. Essentially this type of enrichment exposes the child to a variety of topics in the science area and facilitates freedom to explore those topics in an environment that provides opportunity to expand curiosity and interest. Type II enrichment consists of instructional techniques necessary to learn *problem solving*. These techniques are designed to help the student acquire skills necessary for dealing with content, tools that the student will use to solve the scientific problems encountered. Type III enrichment activities are those in which the child becomes the actual investigator, the researcher, the scientist and in which an attempt is made to solve or investigate *real problems*. Whereas in type I and II activities the student is engaged in consuming information and learning information, type III activities focus on the production of new knowledge and new information. It is this distinction that Renzulli (1970), Harrison (1981), and Rose (1978) feel distinguishes the science program for gifted from other science programs in the public school system.

Knutsen (1979) proposes two lessons from which the science curriculum could be developed. Lesson one requires the student to employ brainstorming activities and divergently produce ideas. Brainstorming, as discussed earlier, includes having the children discuss and explore the idea or problem or activity they are involved in and then having the teacher provide some examples about the particular idea or activity. For example, the teacher might say, "Name everything you can that is round, hard and black," and then ask the students to brainstorm all the things that come to their minds concerning such an object. In brainstorming the rules are:

1. Criticism is not allowed. Any child can say anything, and it should be accepted.
2. Children can build on the ideas of others but must not comment positively or negatively on the ideas. In other words, they should expand on another child's ideas without making a value judgement.
3. All ideas are accepted.

Following this first lesson, the brainstorming activity from which all the ideas have been written down, the children next review the ideas and set up criteria for evaluating them. Some possible evaluative questions are "Does the idea solve the problem or create new ones?" "Is it practical?" "Is it safe?" "Will it last?" "Is it beneficial?" "Is it expensive?" and "Is it worthwhile?"

Once the criteria are established and all the different ideas relevant to that object, issue, or problem are scrutinized, then the students can move on to lesson two. Lesson two consists of "the formula" for creating units of science for the gifted. Here the teacher becomes a group facilitator and the students become project directors. The formula is as follows:

1. Presenting the problem
2. Defining/delimiting the problem
3. Gathering basic tools
4. Collecting data
5. Forming hypotheses
6. Designing experiments
       Isolating variables
       Running control groups
7. Making specific job assignments
8. Presenting results
9. Drawing conclusions
10. The Zinger

Knutsen (1979), provides more detail for how the formula is employed, using molds as an example. In *presenting the problem*, the teacher usually asks a basic question derived from the brainstorming session. Children may be asked by the teacher, "What are molds?" "Why or how do they grow?" In *defining the problem*, students break the problem down into small component parts, again employing brainstorming techniques, answering the questions of what are molds, how do they grow, how are they identified, are they plants or animals, and so on. *Basic tools* are then identified relative to this particular problem. The vocabulary necessary to further explore this problem is identified. *Collecting data* may be accomplished by reading about or observing, in this case, molds; all information students have collected is then identified and listed by a group leader or by the teacher. Children review the data and discard irrelevant bits of information. In *designing experiments* the problem is directly addressed. What are molds?

Are molds plants or animals? Students explore or discuss methods in which they might be able to answer their questions. The students are allowed to test their experiment unequivocally by *controlling for those variables* that will or could affect the outcome. In the example of molds, if the students know that dampness makes mold grow, they will attempt to eliminate other possible causes, to ensure that that part of the investigation does in fact occur without contamination. Again, students are encouraged to brainstorm the possibilities that could affect their experiment. Students then determine who will take care of what parts of the experiment — who will record data or observe, who will participate within the experiment itself, etc. — *making specific job assignments*. Students next decide what would be the most appropriate way of *presenting their results*. Daily charts, anecdotal records, photos, and such may be discussed as options. In *drawing conclusions*, students should decide which of the activities, experiments, variables, or results are the most conclusive and can then relate the results to the experiments to prove or disprove their hypotheses.

The Zinger is a disguised evaluation activity on the part of the teacher, which is derived from the information developed from the experiment itself and from the discussions by the students. In terms of the lesson on molds, the teacher could ask, "How can you make mold grow faster?" "How can you kill mold?" or "How can you prevent mold?" The idea of the Zinger is to take the information that has been gathered by the students and create questions that solicit answers indicating how well the child understands or understood the problem and the information generated from studying that problem.

In summary, the science curriculum for gifted and talented children should involve the three basic components identified earlier — student exploration, expression, and experimentation within an atmosphere that nurtures divergent thinking skills in relationship to real world problems. These problems should extend beyond the regular school curriculum and be a challenge to the students that are identified as gifted and talented. The science curriculum must be different in this respect and should challenge the gifted child beyond that which all other curricular expectations have done to that point in the child's life.

SCIENCE ACTIVITIES

For Elementary Children

Following is an example of a natural science program for multigraded elementary students. This program, developed by Duchek (1982), provides an example of the different elements that could be included in a science curriculum. The format of this program is such that it could be used in several areas of natural science study such as geology, pond life, weather, plants, reproduction, sea life, tidepools, and so on. The teacher's imagination will be the only limiting factor in developing a curriculum to follow this format. Also, it will be noticed that throughout the program the child is allowed to expand, express, and experiment.

Natural Science Program on Conservation of Trees and Forests

OBJECTIVES. The main objectives of this program are to develop skills in the scientific methods of observation, data classification, hypothesis formation and testing, organization of material (findings) for meaningful reporting, and, last but not least, an appreciation of the beauty and variety that may be found in the natural surroundings.

TEACHER PREPARATION

1. Visit the local Forest Ranger Office for free and fun materials on forestry and conservation. If you are in a convenient area, it may be possible to have a ranger visit the classroom or for the class to take a field trip.
2. From the school or local library, check out all the books you can locate on the topic. Books of differing reading levels are a must for a multigraded gifted class or for a regular classroom. Don't hesitate to check out both very elementary (basic) and very challenging materials. Good illustrations are a must for all levels.
3. Prepare a center where leaves may be either examined with a microscope/magnifying glass, measured with either metric (preferred) or standard equipment, or pressed or dry-mounted.
4. Make a display chart of several varieties of leaves. An unlabelled chart is more flexible since it can be used on several levels of study, such as mere identification of the tree or, for the older or gifted student, the classification of veins, and borders.

INTRODUCING THE UNIT

1. For most elementary students, try to obtain a copy of Shel Silverstein's delightful book, *The Giving Tree*, and read it to the class. Older students might enjoy Joyce Kilmer's *Trees*, or you may select a favorite of your own. Discuss the benefits we derive from trees, both spiritual and practical.
2. From the above discussion, preferably after children have had time to think about it, hold a brainstorming session. Depending on the class focus, this might be concerned with the benefits we receive from trees as a natural resource, the life cycle of the tree, or its place in the ecosystem.
3. Arrange a class nature walk and make it clear that trees are the specific point of inquiry. Be sure that children have the opportunity to see the likeness and difference that exists between different varieties. Children could collect leaves, seeds, nuts, or pine cones to use for further study in the classroom.

ACTIVITIES

1. Each child should select a local tree for in-depth, long-term study. A diary or record based on the tree, reporting the changes due to temperature and season is a useful activity. This report could cover the total environment of the tree and the life forms which utilize the tree, such as birds, insects, animals and fungi. This diary might be kept daily for the first weeks, monthly thereafter.

2. A leaf collection should help the child develop an understanding of attributes and classification.

3. Each student should prepare a report on some particular element of the unit. Possible topics would be the place of the tree in the balance of nature, ecosystems, life cycles, conservation, natural resources, the history or geographic distribution of a particular tree, folk heroes (Johnny Appleseed), or in-depth studies of leaf variations and classification, the process of decay, or the tree's usefulness to man. Each child should be encouraged to develop his own area of study and method of inquiry.

4. A graphic display should be developed by each child to support his written report. This could be charts, graphs, murals, posters, and/or dioramas.

ENRICHMENT

1. Films are very useful for nature study as they enable the viewer to see complete processes that are not usually available to the intermittent observer. Two films, *A Walk in the Forest* and *Succession, From Sand Dune to Forest*, are highly recommended. A study of your particular film collection will be the deciding factor, of course.

2. A classroom visit by a forest ranger or other person engaged in the forest or orchard industry is desirable.

3. A field trip to a local forest, nursery, or orchard will give the children a further dimension for their study and give concrete examples. Input from personnel in these fields is pertinent, up to date, and usually of a practical nature.

4. Games of various types can help children utilize facts for better retention. These may vary from mere naming of trees to more complex levels depending on pupil age and ability. *Forest Resources*® is a game available free from the Forest Service that stimulates thinking about the management and conservation of our natural resources.

CORRELATED ACTIVITIES

1. *Art*: crayon relief drawings of leaves, press leaves between waxed paper and iron, make fossil leaves by pressing leaves into plaster of Paris in a shallow dish (paper clips or hairpins stuck in back make good hangers), make a mural of trees or a forest (a good project for total class involve-

ment), or paint a tree's portrait.

2. *Language Arts*: write the biography of a tree, write a concrete poem for a tree or leaf, write a haiku, produce a puppet play about a tree and its animal friends, or compile a booklet called "101 Uses for a Dead Tree."

3. *Social Studies*: map the areas where different types of trees flourish (depending on grade and ability, this could be local, state, national or world), make graphs or charts showing where different varieties grow (altitude, climate, etc.), learn the state trees, develop charts or posters depicting the flora at various stages of the Geologic Time Scale, study dendrochronology (tree ring dating) and illustrate its uses for archaeology.

4. *Math*: measure leaves (length, width, and diameter), use a pencil point to estimate tree heights, estimate the number of logs or boards you would need to build a house (or fence or fort) using some given standard length and width, calculate the perimeter and area of local forests (parks, etc.) using local maps, price lumber locally and figure the construction costs for various structures.

EVALUATION

1. Reports (both written and oral)
2. Findings and results of investigation in the form of charts, graphs, and anecdotal records
3. Questions by the teacher relative to measuring what and how much the child has learned
4. Students' answers when asked to project what will happen to forests and trees if current trends of conservation continue and what will happen without forests and trees

These activities are of varying age and grade levels and could easily be adapted for regular classroom use. In a regular classroom, gifted students would be expected to extend the activities to fit their ability and interest. When students compile their research in the form of illustrations, posters, and oral or written reports, they enrich the unit for the other students and act as catalysts in the learning process. Needless to say, they also extend their research and organization skills.

Some additional science activities useful for elementary children are as follows:

SCIENCE THROUGH COOKING. Science at a young age level is an awareness process and, therefore, a time to explore materials (foods, ingredients, etc.). Since measuring and stirring are a part of science as well as of cooking, the success of the science task often involves how well measuring and stirring have been understood and practiced. A cooking task can help teach the effect of ingredients upon one another and upon the final outcome. Many different types of cooking tasks can be implemented, each designed to teach a different science principle, including popcorn, yeast bread, carbonated beverages, melting marshmallows, or freezing ice. Each can teach valuable science principles.

THE STUDY OF FARM ANIMALS is a natural science task in which students study animals, their growth patterns, sounds, habitats, means of protection, food, coverings, or usefulness. Farm animals can be contrasted with zoo animals or animals in the wild. Often helpful with the study of animals is a multimedia approach in which books, films, models, and stories are used, and then animals can be brought to the classroom or the class can go on field trips.

PLAYING WITH MACHINERY. Children love to see how things work. Introducing household tools (screwdrivers, pliers, hammer, saw, scissors, etc.) initially to see how and where they work and to learn their proper use is a good primary task. The teacher can then bring in simple machinery or machines to study, such as machines used in the kitchen (can opener, mixer, toaster, waffle iron, etc.), machines used for travel (car, boat, plane, bus, etc.), and machines that help (the doctor, dentist, farmer, etc.). Children can practice the wise use of these machines, learn how they work, or construct models of them.

EXPERIMENTS WITH MAGNETS AND WEIGHTS. Children can learn a lot from studying magnetic attraction, gravity, and the use of weights. Magnets and a trip around the room to see what attracts and what does not can be a good beginning. Each child can acquire a magnet, some pins or nails, and other objects to test. Good lessons can be taught with objects of differing weights. A scale to weigh objects can be informative; children can weigh the different objects in the room, including themselves, their shoes, etc., and make comparisons to be noted or graphed.

THE WEATHER. Children can study the types of clothing needed for different types of weather, weather symbols, weather predictions, and basic temperature gradients. They can follow the weather report on television or in the papers and can keep a chart of weather conditions and temperature changes. A visitor who is knowledgeable in weather forecasting would be a good resource person, or the children could visit a weather station and hear of the factors involved.

FINGERPRINTING is a fascinating topic for many children. They can read about it, visit a police station, have their own fingerprints taken, take the fingerprints of others in their class, and then see if they can identify the differences.

THE SOLAR SYSTEM. The location of stars and planets can be studied, the names and distances of those bodies learned, and a planetarium visited. THE HUMAN BODY — lungs, heart, ears, eyes, and how these and other parts function — makes a fascinating study. THE FIVE SENSES —touch, taste, smell, hearing, and sight — can trigger many interesting discussions, as can MAKING A SUNDIAL and studying time or light sources, or learning about GEOLOGY AND ROCK FORMATIONS.

Another approach to scientific activities is that of inventing. Shlesinger

(1982) proposes that gifted and talented children are an untapped resource of inventors. He feels that there is no great mystery involved in inventing, that in fact it is another approach to problem solving. Shlesinger states that a six-year-old first grader has more stored information than all of the computers on earth, but unfortunately, adults tend to underestimate the amount of information a child has. In helping first graders to become inventors, the teacher has only to show them how to correlate information and put it together in a workable fashion so as to produce a technical or practical solution to invention problems.

Many gifted children are particularly talented in the sciences, and their special skills may enable them to produce complex inventions at a very early age. Invention actually depends a great deal on observation, on recognition, and on utilization of special knowledge of skills.

Shlesinger (1982) indicates three areas of problem identification leading to inventions.

1. Listening for complaints from people that indicate problems needing solutions
2. Looking for difficult and inconvenient situations, and
3. Becoming aware of breakdowns and injuries.

A history of the item or phenomenon needs to be pursued, and then future development can be considered. The collecting of data is an important part of the inventing process. Studying the advantages and disadvantages of a problem also helps. Once children have identified relevant data and have added it to the classification and historical records, they must use imagination (divergent thinking processes) to produce solutions to the problem. Shlesinger describes children as "inspired believers": if told that they can invent new solutions or objects, they believe this and only seek instruction and direction. Often the gifted and talented child is a natural inventor and produces many new objects or activities in his/her range of interests.

For Secondary Students

The following is an example of a science curriculum designed around the Renzulli (1977) model as proposed by Harrison (1982). This program is in operation in the Provo School District, Provo, Utah. It involves several different elements of curriculum adaptation for the gifted and talented youngster and can include pull-out, acceleration, and enrichment programs, and (in some degree) mentorships as well as other curriculum adaptive possibilities.

Type I Activities
General Exploration
Rationale: Regarding inquiry, a period of time is needed in which the inquirer simply encounters the materials within the environment. Many believe that one of the primary functions of a teacher is to provide for these encounters. Such exploration is structured only by the properties of the materials and the experiences of the

learner. During this activity, the learner comes to wonder, hypothesize, and experiment with ideas.

Time required: Large blocks of uninterrupted time.

Material needed: Numerous components related to a specific principle, e.g., principle — electricity; components — batteries, cells, wire, light bulbs, circuit breakers, etc. Or one can use the materials in a specific setting, such as tide pools and beach items. Books and equipment for research should be available.

Organizational pattern: Freedom of movement is needed; working singly, in teams, or in self-evolving small groups.

Teacher function: Provisioner, resource person, facilitator.

Procedure: After setting up guidelines for movement, care of materials, and group structure, students should be allowed to freely explore the materials.

Evaluation: Students may be asked to collect data on their observations, hypotheses, and conclusions throughout the experience (clipboards are good for mobile data collection), or have group sharing at the end of the experience.

Interest Centers

Rationale: Gifted students need opportunities to explore areas of their interest and become aware of areas unknown to them. By establishing centers built around specific disciplines, and by covering numerous areas of basic knowledge at various times, both exploration and awareness can be accomplished.

Time involved: Ongoing, large blocks of time.

Material needed: The centers should be open-minded and exciting, and they should facilitate understandings of how people in a given field contribute to society; for example, an archeology center could incorporate instructions on organizing a dig, journals or books from famous digs, how the findings have changed our view of history, what experiences archeologists have, information on nearby sights now being excavated or worth excavation, films, tapes, etc.

Organizational pattern: Open structure with simultaneous activity, freedom of movement, and with field trips provided.

Teacher function: The teacher may organize centers or help students to organize their centers, resource persons should be available.

Procedure: Students work at centers singly, in teams, or in small groups. The center indicates the procedure to follow.

Evaluation: Journals, projects, oral reports, or conferences may be utilized. In some cases, students may explore several interest centers without evaluation.

Group Exploration

Rationale: Often through discussion with others and sharing of interests, students can become more aware of different ideas and areas. It is also possible to set up situations where exploration as a group creates more data and excitement (such as demonstrations, group movement, group energy exchanges; these have more impact when more people participate.

Time involved: Variable.

Material needed: Materials may be specific to the demonstration or to the students.

Organizational pattern: Jigsaw groups, changing to counter groups and back to teach in the jigsaw group.

Teacher function: Group facilitator, demonstrator, occasional discussion leader; can be assumed by classroom teacher or student. (Sharan, S., and Lazarowitz, R. H., 1980)

Procedure: Jigsaw group dynamics as proposed by Sharan and Lazarowitz

(1980). This activity involves small independent learning groups where each student learns to cooperatively help and teach each other. The class members are divided into small (5 to 8 people) groups. This constitutes the jigsaw (family) group. A group leader is selected and each member of the jigsaw group has a different topic or a small portion of a main topic (A, B, C, D, E). The group leader has everyone read or share only their topic titles or objectives with the others in the jigsaw group. Then everyone separates into counter groups with other members throughout the class. Each counter group will now have the same topic (AAAAA, BBBBB, CCCCC, etc.). The counter group spends time together reading, researching, and discussing the material, preparing each other to effectively report their topics later. The counter group may also develop 3 to 5 content questions for use on an exam. (The procedure of the counter group gives students different points of view, a vested interest in and practice with open communication, and the development of interpersonal relations.) At a pre-determined time everyone in the class returns to their original jigsaw group (A, B, C, D, E). The group leader selects a time keeper, and each person is given a specific amount of time in which to teach his or her material to the jigsaw group being careful to cover the main principles likely to be on an exam.

Research on this strategy has shown that: The jigsaw has positive interpersonal effects, cooperative groups perform better than competitive ones, students learn more than when in competition, attitudes toward school improve, there is a substantial improvement in the performance of minorities, and even in heterogeneously grouped classes, high ability students benefit.

Evaluation: Self-evaluation of experience.

Speakers

Rationale: By bringing experts with a variety of skills into a class, the students not only have the chance to hear and ask questions, but they also have the opportunity to be exposed to fields of study through the enthusiasm of people actively engaged in creating and using that kind of knowledge.

Time involved: Variable; weekly to several times a year.

Material needed: Dynamic people, knowledgeable in their field.

Organizational pattern: While these presentations can be made to the total group, it is often more successful to announce the speaker's subject in advance and invite interested students to sign up. Presentation would then be conducted in the discussion area of the room, while students who have no interest can work in other areas.

Teaching function: The teacher is an organizer, provider of related resource people and materials for preparation and follow-up.

Procedure: Dependent on the speaker.

Evaluation: Optional, may serve as many resource experiences.

Field Trips and Visitations

Rationale: A great deal of the world cannot be recreated inside a classroom. Students can learn naturally, in integrated ways in the setting of the specific events. For example, a trip to an island can provide experiences in math (arranging the trip, transportation, expenses, meals, etc.), science (climate, geology, astronomy, land and sea, flora and fauna, navigation, food preparation and preservation, tide data, etc.), language (journal writing, communication with planning groups, letters to authorities requesting permission, etc.), social science (government jurisdiction and involvement, economics, ecology, etc.), and interpersonal relations. All of these and more have great built-in motivational impact.

Time involved: Variable; one day, a series of visits, or a week long journey.

Materials needed: Transportation and financing; if camping, all necessary gear.

Organizational pattern: Adult to child ratio according to age and designation.

Teaching function: Pre-trip planning and facilitation of arrangements; organization of trip; group leader and facilitator during trip; post-trip follow-up.

Procedure: This will depend on the goals of the trip and should be decided in cooperation with the students and their parents. Parents can be allowed to take students to museums, concerts, and other places either during or after school hours. Torrence (1968) calls such provisions "time-outs." He believes strongly in such leave taking. Encouraging parents to become involved in school activities is important for both home and school.

Type II Activities — Discussion and Problem Solving
Brainstorming

Rationale: A greater fluency of ideas is believed to produce ideas of higher quality. This strategy allows groups to explore ideas without judgment or censure. All ideas receive acceptance and consideration. Unusual ideas or take-offs from ideas already suggested are encouraged.

Time involved: Fifteen to thirty minutes. The session may last as long as the group continues to offer ideas. Follow-up activities may take another thirty minutes or could lead to a longer project.

Materials needed: None.

Organizational pattern: Small group with a facilitator.

Teacher function: The teacher may serve as the group facilitator.

Procedure: A focus for the group should be given and the rules of brainstorming stated: (1) No criticism allowed; all ideas are accepted. (2) Make your ideas as unusual as possible; give as many as you can. (3) Build on ideas you got from others. (4) No evaluation until the session is completed. The facilitator lists all ideas on the board with no comment. Only after the fifteen to thirty minute time period are the ideas discussed. The teacher may then help the group evaluate the ideas against the criteria for selection which they must devise. The ideas may serve as the basis for further development by individuals.

Evaluation: The more ideas, the better. Be sure to use the ideas for a purpose; the outcomes should seem meaningful to the students. If you use real problems, they will have more meaning.

Inquiry

Rationale: Aiding students to become independent in their thinking requires the development of many skills (making careful observations, asking good questions, thinking of alternatives, comparing, discovering relevant data, summarizing, and generalizing from data, to name a few). Inquiry sessions give students practice in these skills. Suchman (1961, 1962) developed an inquiry model from his understanding of the scientific model of thinking. While it may oversimplify human thought by leaving out important areas, it is quite useful in teaching many important processes. The inquiry model consists of data collection, data organization, hypothesizing, hypothesis testing, and back to data collection, all in a continuum. Suchman's program gives students practice in solving problems by establishing the properties of all objects or systems involved in the problem, finding which objects or systems are relevant to the problem, and discovering how they function in the solution. Sessions are designed to help students learn to formulate and test their own theories and to become aware of their own learning processes. The outcomes lead not so much to new answers, and never to wrong or right answers, but to new and more productive questions.

Time involved: Forty-five minutes to an hour.

Material needed: Films, filmstrips, or materials to set up a dissonant event.

Organizational pattern: The classroom must have resources, trust between students and teacher, and the sense of freedom for inquiry. The group should be composed of seven to ten students depending on age (the younger, the smaller the group).

Teacher function: The facilitator must have the ability to: inquire; create classroom conditions that are accepting; clarify; probe for data, intent, prediction, and statements of theory; and be silent (teacher's silence is critical in allowing students to think through the problem).

Procedure: The facilitator sets up a dissonant event, either on film, tape, or by demonstration. The rules for the session are: (1) Students must ask questions that can be answered yes or no. (2) Students, when recognized by the facilitator, may ask questions until they wish to yield. They indicate this by declaring that they "pass." (3) The facilitator does not answer statements of theories or questions attempting to gain approval for a theory (whether the facilitator accepts the theory or not). (4) Any student may test a theory at any time. (5) During inquiry, students are not allowed to discuss among themselves unless they call for a conference. This may be done at any time. (6) Inquirers may consult resources in the room at any time. The inquiry continues until all theories are satisfactory to their originators. The facilitator then debriefs the session, helping the students to become aware of the processes they were using, which questions provided useful data, and how they might gain more information next time.

Decision-Making, Alternative Thinking

Rationale: Gifted students may function in society as change agents, innovators, and reconstructionists. Our societal problem solvers will come from this group. By being exposed to many ways of viewing problems, students may find better solutions. Give students experiences that allow them: (1) To become aware of bias in thinking, the difference between belief and fact. (2) To see that each conflicting viewpoint may be valid. (3) To see the importance of sources of information. (4) To experience the importance of cooperation and consensus in group action. (5) To seek many alternatives before deciding on solutions.

Type III Activities — Investigation Beyond

Beyond Content

In some academic content areas, though not all, gifted students will be from two to eight years ahead of other students at their grade level. Here are some suggestions for letting them investigate beyond:

1. Core curriculum: In small groups, or individually, gifted students could take a particular period, concept, person, or object and, using it as a central theme, investigate the history, art and music, social, cultural, economic, etc., conditions. By actually "living" through the creation of this person, object, period, or concept, the student will understand and appreciate inquiry far more.

2. Independent study/seminar program: Offers pupil assessment and individualized planning, open curriculum guides, and a variety of resource people. This program combines the use of independent study, advance course work, advance placement in colleges, and special seminars for gifted students on an individual basis.

3. Mentor programs: Some students are so advanced they need a challenge of an outstanding expert. Others need to interact with an expert to find the motivation and excitement for extending their grasp. On and/or off campus contacts

can be arranged.

4. Publishing: Gifted students should be encouraged to publish their work, either in established journals and magazines or in ones that are school or class produced. Editing for publication teaches far more about grammar, punctuation, and spelling than skill drilling and sentence diagramming.

5. Resident expert: Encourage all gifted students to become resident experts on the one area in which they are most interested. Call upon their expertise, let them help you and others in the school with problems in their area of knowledge.

6. Conceptual framework and systems: Be sure to expose gifted students to conceptual frameworks that you use to organize your thinking. Encourage their participation in new problems — yours, theirs, the schools, the community's — by the development of systems or conceptual frameworks. Be sure there is a way for the students to share their creations. Example: a group of fifth and sixth grade students were studying the land use in their area. They obtained advice from architects, city planners, and engineers who paid regular visits to their classroom. After several months, one group devised a plan for development that excited them. Their teacher arranged for them to present their plan, with maps and graphs, to the planning board of the county. Later, the students were notified that a portion of their plan had been adopted. They received a commendation from the county for their work.

High school, junior college, or university placement: In many areas, high schools, junior colleges, and universities are making classes available to upper elementary gifted students. Some allow participation in regular classes, some in specially designed classes. In some cases, parents can organize after school and weekend classes. These classes have saved many bored youngsters from giving up on a school as a place to learn.

Beyond Process

Resource skills: Gifted students need a way to get to information and ideas far sooner than more typical learners. They must be able to move efficiently on their own into areas not yet explored. They need to become familiar with the skills of historical research, descriptive research, and experimental research as tools for future learning and thinking.

Kopelman (1977) outlines the program utilized at Bronx High School of Science, a specialized high school for gifted students. The program is outlined here as a means of illustrating the contents of what a science program at the secondary level could be, but it must also be kept in mind that this is a specifically designed program for a specifically identified population (the gifted and talented), and as such for implementation in a regular school program several adaptations would have to be made. The following is an outline of the program:

NINTH YEAR. All students are given the opportunity to learn techniques of the scientist by a hands-on approach. Here they use microscopes, microbiology techniques, and so on. Students are led to speculate on what they see and hypothesize about what will eventually happen. They are asked to design simple experiments answering questions such as "What is the effect of temperature on the growth rate of various types of bacteria?"

TENTH YEAR. The Socratic method of teaching is used during this year, with an emphasis on recognizing problems and setting up hypotheses. The laboratory experiments are performed by students, and teachers meet with students individually to discuss the hypothesis and problem selection for individual research.

ELEVENTH YEAR. During this year a student is expected to conduct an individual piece of research. Each student is individually guided by a teacher or a team of teachers as to the practicality of his or her proposed research activity. Students are expected to do extensive library research and to read scientific papers, as well as to abstract from those papers relevant information; students learn to use the *Biological Abstracts, Index Medicus*, and other specialized journals in conducting their research. Again students meet individually with a teacher to discuss their progress, which is presented either orally and/or in written form. A final, scientifically written report is the concluding activity for this eleventh year. The eleventh year consists of forty weeks in which the student attends two eighty-minute classes on alternate days and one forty-minute class at the end of the week. Laboratory time is also made available to the student before the start of the day and at any time during the day in which the student has free time. The teacher is always present within the lab. It is interesting to note also that the best papers written throughout the year are compiled and published in the high school's annual departmental publication, entitled *The Journal of Biology*. This is a student publication and highlights much of the creative work arising from the Bronx High School of Science program. (For information concerning this program write to the Project Director, The Bronx High School of Science, 75 West 205th Street, Bronx, New York 10468.)

The possibilities for effective science lessons are limitless; the teacher has but to look around in the schoolroom or at home and be creative in exploring possibilities. Sometimes letting the children brainstorm possible science projects can be helpful and enlightening; there is so much to learn about life that children have many options.

Finally a quotation from Harrison (1981) summarizes the considerations in developing a science curriculum.

> The needs of gifted students are often in the content areas. They are not so much deficit needs, but rather needs for challenge in specific areas of strength. Providing more of the same level of content will rarely fulfill this need; ways need to be found to accelerate and enrich the concepts and processes in each content area of strength. Generally, our main goal should be to go beyond mastery of standard content processes to develop in these students a greater understanding of the concepts underlying a specific discipline. In both mathematics and in science, we often find the computational and rational applications emphasized exclusively, so that the excitement found by the practicing mathematician or scientist is missing. Firing the imagination and creative ability of gifted students requires inclusion of the intuitive aspects of math and science. Only in this way can we help students view such subjects as dynamic, with real problems yet to be solved. These, after all, are the students who will contribute most to the expanding fields and disciplines. We must present them with an expanding, potentially limitless world view.

Suggested Bibliography in the Area of the Sciences

Abruscato, J., and Hassard, J.: *The Whole Cosmos: Catalog of Science Activities*. Salt Lake City, Goodyear, n.d.

Alberti, D. J.: *The Correlation of Activity-Centered Science and Mathematics*. Hayward, California, Activity Resources Co., 1975.

Althouse, R., and Main, C.: *Science Experiences for Young Children*. New York, Teacher's College, 1975.

Babcock, Hyrum J.: *A Science Activity Program for Elementary Schools*. Dubuque, Iowa, Wm. C. Brown, 1961.

Carmichael, V.: *Science Experiences for Young Children*. Los Angeles, Southern California Association for the Education of Young Children, 1969.

Cobb, V.: *Science Experiments You Can Eat*. Philadelphia, Lippinscott, 1972.

DeVito, A.: *Creative Sciencing: A Practical Approach*. Boston, Little, Brown, 1976.

Games for the Science Classroom: An Annotated Bibliography. Washington, D.C., *National Science Teacher*, 1977.

Gega, P. C.: *Science in Elementary Education*, 4th ed. New York, Wiley, 1982.

Good, Ronald G.: *Science — Children: Readings in Elementary Science Education*. Dubuque, Iowa, Wm. C. Brown, 1980.

Harlan, J.: *Science Experiences for the Early Childhood Years*. Columbus, Ohio, Merrill, 1976.

Hillcourt, W.: *The New Field Book of Nature Activities and Hobbies*. New York, Putnam, 1970.

King, J., and Schippers, J.: *Preschool Science Activities*. Stockton, California, University of Pacific, 1972.

Nelson, Leslie Welddemar: *Science Activities for Elementary Children*, 7th ed. Dubuque, Iowa, Wm. C. Brown, 1980.

Nickelsburg, J.: *Nature Program for Early Childhood*. Reading, Massachusetts, Addison-Wesley, 1976.

Podendorf, I.: *101 Science Experiments*, rev. ed. Chicago, Children's Press, 1972.

Romey, W. D.: *Inquiry Techniques for Teaching Science*. Englewood Cliffs, New Jersey, Prentice-Hall, 1968.

Schmidt, V., and Rockcastle, V.: *Teaching Science with Everyday Things*. New York, McGraw-Hill, 1968.

Skelsey, A., and Huckaby, G.: *Growing Up Green*. New York, Workman, 1973.

Stone, A., Geis, F., and Kuslan, L.: *Experiences for Teaching Children Science*. Belmont, California, 1971.

Strongin, H.: *Science on a Shoestring*. Menlo Park, California, Addison-Wesley, 1976.

Sund, Robert B.: *Teaching Science by Inquiry in the Secondary School*. Columbus, Ohio, Merrill, 1967.

Victor, Edward: *Science for the Elementary School*, 4th ed. New York, Macmillan, 1980.

CHAPTER TEN

VISUAL AND PERFORMING ARTS

Can you answer these questions?

1. What is the importance of a visual and performing arts program?
2. Can you list some of the curriculum components recommended for a visual and performing arts program?
3. What are some activities appropriate for the gifted student in the following areas: visual arts, music (vocal or instrumental), dance, and drama?
4. On a national level, what are some programs available for stimulating and developing gifts and talents of children in the visual and performing arts?

THE importance of a visual and performing arts curriculum for the gifted and talented child (and for any child) cannot be understated. The arts provide an outlet for the child's aesthetic nature, as well as contributing to the enjoyment of life in general. Therefore, in this chapter, information will be presented relative to children gifted in the visual and performing arts; the curriculum components involved in the areas of the arts; the identification of children within these two areas of giftedness; activities for children that can be used for stimulation, enrichment, and development of their talents in these two areas; and finally, national programs that have been developed for stimulating and developing those visual and performing art talents in gifted and talented children or prodigies.

Fisher (1973) points out that the term "prodigy" for many years suggested a child who was peculiar, unhealthy, perhaps even a freak, and has for this reason been a term avoided in educational circles. Instead, a euphemism is used — "gifted child." One saying has it that a child prodigy is "a youngster who is too young to be as old as he is." Fisher prefers this definition: "Prodigy: A person who shows early signs of extraordinary talent or exceptional ability" (p. 10).

It will be difficult at best within the confines of this chapter to discuss how the talents of a visual or performing prodigy may be further stimulated and developed. However, information will be given as to the procedures that can be followed for identifying the prodigy in the arts; the enrichment activities that may be used as a stimulation to help young gifted students to appreciate the visual and performing arts; and finally, the resource programs to which a prodigy may be sent for the development of his or her gifts and talents.

CURRICULUM COMPONENTS

In developing a curriculum at any level for the visual and performing arts, it is important to keep some basic things in mind. First of all, exceptionally talented children must be identified and encouraged. Gallagher (1979) indicates that the development of procedures and measuring devices with which the identification of gifted children can be made is a necessary component for eventual program planning. (Several testing instruments are mentioned in Chapter One and later in this chapter in relationship to specific gifts and talents.) Hildreth (1967) indicates that the aesthetically gifted need to be challenged if their natural facility is not to turn into glibness. Anderson (1959) indicates that study in the arts should be initiated in elementary school and certainly no later than high school to be effective.

Some unfortunate components of the regular school arts program are highlighted by Szekely (1981); he identifies five pitfalls that a gifted and talented youngster may encounter in the public school system.

1. Not having teachers with sufficient training in the arts to recognize and guide gifted children within the performing arts areas
2. Children receiving recognition for success in one area, which encourages that child to repeat that success rather than to experiment in other areas of growth
3. Challenge being unavailable within an arts program
4. Parents being fearful that the child's potential choice in the visual arts or performing arts area will lead to a difficult life or parents being indifferent or antagonistic toward the arts and artists in general, either of which may discourage their talented child from pursuing a career in this area, and
5. Isolation from their peers and adults being experienced by many gifted and talented children because they may be different

Other potential problems may be found in the reluctance of school administrators to spend money for special programs for artistically gifted children. In some instances they may consider these programs much too expensive or as detracting funds from other projects that would serve more individuals. Administrators may feel that in fact the regular arts program as it is presently constituted is more than enough to promote the natural unfolding of talents in children — regardless of their gifts.

In spite of the perplexing problems that are confronted by the curriculum planner, some helpful components in the curriculum for the gifted must be considered. Szekely (1981), in outlining the Art Partnership Network, proposes some objectives for curriculum in the visual and performing arts

1. to develop in the child a more complete understanding of the nature of art and art making
2. to develop the child's independence
3. to challenge the gifted child
4. to provide companionship and support to the child during his or her endeavors within this area
5. to develop a balance between self-confidence in the skills already manifest and a willingness to risk the unfamiliar that leads to expansion. (P. 68)

It would be good if the public school system would allow flexible time schedules so that the young artist could be allowed to work during the most productive times, usually in the morning hours, but as Szekely (1981) indicates, these hours are most often devoted to the academic subjects equally important to the creative mind. This is a dilemma, but in any event schools should be willing to provide the necessary physical space and facilities in which to encourage the artistically gifted child. Further, the enrichment of gifted and talented children should include allowing them the opportunity to travel to exhibits, museums, concerts, and other real experiences that allow them to witness and participate in the visual and performing arts. Resources within the school should be increased as much as possible to include reproductions of classical works of both music and the visual arts. Books and magazines and autobiographies of great artists should be made available. The curriculum should challenge the children to develop their own artistic abilities as well as to enrich their lives with visual and performing arts resources. Finally, Lowenfield (1979) suggests that if the curriculum is such that it expects a great deal from the young artist, then a great deal can be achieved.

THE VISUAL ARTS

The importance of the visual and performing arts in the overall curriculum of the child should not be considered separately from the rest of the child's learning and life development. An attempt should be made to assess children's art work, as this should enhance their learning programs in other areas. Art is an extremely helpful activity in developing a child's confidence, concentration, willingness to learn and ability to abstract, analyze problems, and be more observant in all facets of life (Szekely, 1981). A discussion of those arts that are visual in nature includes painting, drawing, design, graphics, sculpture, photography, and the like.

Szekely (1981) provides a checklist for the identification of visual artistically gifted children. The checklist of nineteen items asks if the child demonstrates the following characteristics:

1. a sustained involvement in creating or in viewing works of art
2. interest in reading about or in collecting art related materials
3. multiple art interests
4. interest in the sensuous qualities of art works
5. interest in keeping visual records of written planned art or art ideas
6. unusual powers of observation and recall of visual detail and overall structure
7. imagination exhibited in a wide range of new ideas
8. advanced technical skills in an art medium
9. a highly developed capacity to organize art works in various mediums
10. awareness of the medium's possibilities as well as its limitations
11. adaptability from one creative situation or medium to another
12. ability to execute self-initiated problems and see them through to conclusion
13. ability to explore freely, experimentally, and playfully
14. satisfaction in the challenges of creative problems, difficult tasks, and displaying the capacity for art, organizing creative ideas
15. tolerance of difficult moments in creation
16. a capacity for self-evaluation and the setting of high standards
17. realistic appraisal of present achievements along with positive plans for future action
18. willingness to assume leadership in the arts program
19. interest in entering a profession in the arts or in becoming an artist. (P. 70)

Identifying children for inclusion within a program for students gifted in the arts may on the surface appear to be quite easy. However, there are many children who hide their talents so they will not be considered "different" from others. It is extremely helpful to spend some time in identifying gifted artists at an early age or at least within the elementary school ages or grades in order to encourage them to pursue their talents in an appropriate program. Once identified, the potential artists can then be encouraged through one of several programs outlined later in this chapter to pursue and develop their talents to their fullest potential.

ENRICHMENT OF VISUAL ARTS PROGRAMS

The task of an enrichment or appreciation program is to stimulate the aesthetic abilities of the children as well as to exercise their cognitive capacity in some regard. Following are some activities designed primarily for art appreciation but which, with astute observation on the part of the teacher, may help to uncover a hidden talent in the visual arts area. The first activities are designed for young children in the elementary grades, particularly the early elementary grades.

ART NARRATIVES. To stimulate art appreciation, the teacher may begin with a picture such as Van Gogh's "The Harvest" and then add a brief narrative.

Van Gogh lived in a country called Holland and had many brothers and sisters. When he became a man, Van Gogh went to work with some poor miners. He wanted to help them as much as he could, so he provided them with everything he had. He began to draw sad pictures of these poor miners and this began his art career. Van Gogh moved to France and began to paint pictures that were happier pictures. "The Harvest" is a picture painted in France, and it shows people working on the farm. It also shows that Van Gogh used, or liked to use bright colors in his paintings — yellows and oranges.

Following are some other discussions that could be used with young children to stimulate appreciation of specific paintings (Kohler, 1982).

"Bedroom at Arles" by Vincent Van Gogh

This picture is called "Bedroom at Arles." It was painted by Vincent Van Gogh. This is a picture of the bedroom of the house where Van Gogh lived when he moved to France. Van Gogh was very poor, and many times he did not have very much to eat because he spent all of his money to buy paints and brushes. He wanted more than anything else to be able to paint.

"Lady at the Piano" by Pierre Auguste Renoir

This picture was painted by Pierre Auguste Renoir. It is called "Lady at the Piano." Renoir liked to paint the people he saw around him. Renoir liked to look at other people's paintings and learn from the pictures that other artists made. When Renoir was old, he had arthritis. This is a disease that made his hands crippled, and he could not hold a brush. Renoir loved to paint so much that he would have someone tie the brush onto his hand so he could still paint.

"Mona Lisa" by Leonardo Da Vinci

This picture was painted by Leonardo da Vinci. He lived in Italy a long time ago. Da Vinci was a very smart man. He liked science and drew pictures of new things. Da Vinci drew a picture of a flying machine before any airplanes had been made. He was the first one to draw pictures of the parts on the inside of the body.

This picture is called the "Mona Lisa." Da Vinci painted this picture of a woman he knew. He gave her a little smile. It makes the woman look like she is thinking of something special. She seems to be smiling at you.

"A Girl With a Broom" by Rembrandt Harmenszohn Van Rijn

Rembrandt Harmenszohn Van Rijn painted this picture. He lived in a small Dutch town. Rembrandt drew in school all the time and did not do his work. His father sent him to live with an artist so Rembrandt could learn how to paint. He became a great artist. Rembrandt got married, and he was very happy. He painted pictures of people and made lots of money. Then his wife died. Rembrandt stopped painting pictures of people. He did not have any money, and he had to sell his house and everything he had. Rembrandt still painted.

This painting is called "A Girl With a Broom." Rembrandt wanted people to focus on the girl's face. He made the rest of the picture black.

"Still Life With Soup Tureen" by Paul Cezanne

This picture was painted by Paul Cezanne. He lived in France. Cezanne's father was a banker, and he wanted his son to be a banker, too. Cezanne wanted to be a painter. His father let him go to Paris to learn how to paint. He painted people at first, but he liked to paint the things he saw outside better. Cezanne also liked to paint the things he saw around him at home.

This picture is called "Still Life With Soup Tureen." A soup tureen is a big bowl that you serve soup in. This picture shows some things in Cezanne's house. A still life picture does not have any living things in it.

"The Gleaners" by Jean Francois Millet

This picture was painted by Jean Francois Millet, who lived in France. When Millet was a little boy, he loved to paint. He took lessons from other painters who lived by his home. Later, Millet went to art school in Paris. He liked to paint pictures of people working.

This picture is called "The Gleaners." After the wheat is cut and picked up, there is a little wheat left on the ground. The women are picking up the little pieces of wheat that are still on the ground. Millet knew that work was good, and he wanted to show other people how important work was in his pictures.

"Blue Boy" by Sir Thomas Gainsborough

This picture was painted by Sir Thomas Gainsborough. He lived in England. Gainsborough liked to draw pictures when he was little. His father sent him to school in London to learn to paint. He liked to paint pictures of people and of the things he saw outside. Gainsborough became famous, and many people came and paid him to have their pictures painted.

This picture is called "Blue Boy" because the boy has on blue clothes. The boy in the picture was a butcher's helper. Gainsborough liked the boy's face so he put the pretty clothes on the boy and painted this picture. People like this picture of a poor boy in fancy clothes.

"Three Musicians" by Pablo Picasso

This picture was painted by Pablo Picasso. He lived in Spain. By the time Picasso was fourteen, he had learned to paint very well. He decided to paint in a new way. First he painted pictures that were all blue. Then he began painting pictures with boxes and squares. This kind of painting is called cubism. Picasso liked to do many kinds of paintings.

This picture is called "Three Musicians." The men are made out of boxes and lines. One man is playing a violin, one man is playing a flute, and the other man is playing a piano. Cubism painting is called modern art.

Yunghans (1981) outlines a pull-out program for gifted elementary students. The goals of this type of program are that the child will:

1. be able to communicate thoughts and feelings through art expression.
2. become sensitive towards their own experiences and progress in developing empathy for others.
3. be able to solve problems involved in giving visual form to ideas through art media.
4. selectively appreciate form and objects made by people in the visual arts and in nature.
5. consciously use knowledge and skills to improve the quality and sensitivity of a technological society. (P. 50)

Yunghans's program was essentially an art enrichment program in which students were pulled out of the regular curriculum once a week for ninety-minute sessions and were given twenty class sessions taught by professional artists from within the community. The program consisted of five units.

Unit One, Beginning Oil Painting. In Unit One children were given the opportunity to learn about the Alla-Pringla method of painting and to demonstrate or experiment with a basic pallet of paint. They then demonstrated knowledge of the method by a spontaneous painting utilizing the eight basic color pigments.

Unit Two, Weaving on Cardboard. In this unit children were given the opportunity to learn the skills of constructing a simple cardboard loom with the purpose of creating a wall hanging.

Unit Three, A Field Trip to an Art Institute. This provided an opportunity for children to learn to compare and contrast different art media and art productions observed in the art institute.

Unit Four, Latch Hooking. Students were given instruction on how to execute latching in a creative exercise on rug making.

Unit Five, Story Illustration. A story was read to the students, and at the conclusion they were asked to illustrate one of the scenes in the story using at least two different media for illustration.

There are many other programs that can enrich and educate the talented young prodigy in the arts, for example:

PHOTOGRAPHY PROJECTS. A good resource person in photography can help a group of interested students to make their own camera from a cardboard box or tin can, learn to take pictures properly, develop their own pictures, and learn to discern light and shadow effects, exposure time, etc.

SCULPTURING. Students can begin by sculpturing soap, and when they have learned some of the principles involved they can move to sand sculpture (using wet sand as a mold for wax or plaster of paris), ice sculpture, molding in plastics or ceramics, wood sculpture, clay sculpture, and eventually stone.

MOBILES. Principles of balance, movement, and eye appeal can be taught with the production of a mobile. Mobiles can be made from nearly anything. To begin, children could make a mobile from coat hangers, bottle lids, and thread, fishing wire and sea shells, thread and leaves, or paper objects hung from thread or yarn.

GRAPHICS PROJECTS. Students can be invited to design a new can label or advertising display. They could make up their own stationery motif or logo, packaging, or rubber stamp. The possibilities are numerous.

HOME MOVIES. While it may be a bit expensive, much can be learned from making a movie, for a theme must be selected, a script must be written, the exact sequence of shots and actions mapped out in detail, the props gathered, the people selected and rehearsed, the equipment acquired, the weather considered, the lighting prepared appropriately, the filming scheduled, the film developed, and then the editing done (which takes hours). It is wise to have a knowledgeable resource person to be advisor to this project.

PRINTING PROJECTS. Students can work on making their own greeting cards or Christmas cards. They can learn the principles of printing and copying machines. They can have fun with color and design as they apply it to a real project.

There are other activities in advanced placement programs that have proven worthwhile. Hurwitz (1978) proposes the following:

> Some art teachers work with a few students of high ability and interest, absorbing them into their regular classes. Others create separate Advanced Placement classes in art, using this as an opportunity to expand resources such as art materials, books, slides, reproductions, etc. Many high schools have A.P. programs in academic areas and a designated A.P. chairperson, so a good place to begin is by working through your local A.P. head. However, teachers, and even students, often operate their own without assistance or intervention from any higher authority.

For more activities in the arts, one needs only to contact a local high school or college art department and brainstorm with one of the teachers. Many different projects can be developed to meet the needs and interests of the students in the gifted program. This is also a good time to consider all the resource people in the area (other teachers, parents of the children, retired neighbors, community service organizations, and professional groups). The wise teacher could have the students do the investigating initially and have them propose the programs or activities in which they would like to participate and learn.

THE PERFORMING ARTS

Music, dance, and drama will be the performing arts discussed in this section. While all children can benefit from programs in these areas, it is important to identify those individuals whose gifts and talents specifically lie in the performing arts, so they may receive the support and programs appropriate to meet their needs and strengthen their talents.

In the area of music, there have been several measuring instruments developed by which musically inclined students can be appropriately identified. These instruments (discussed earlier in Chapter One) include the Seashore Measures of Musical Talent (1919, revised in 1960) plus a number of other music ability and aptitude tests, such as the Music Aptitude Profile, by Gordon; Measures of Musical Ability, by Bentley; and the Wing Standardized Tests of Musical Intelligence. Dorhout (1981) provides a good condensed outline of these instruments for identifying musically gifted children. Unfortunately, definitive measures for identifying gifted or talented children in drama or dance are not as readily available. However, the checklist provided by Shelsky (1981) for identifying the gifted visual arts child could be easily adapted for use with young people interested in the areas of drama and dance.

Musical Talents

Musical talents are usually viewed in terms of composing, conducting, or performing. According to Fisher (1973), *composing* is a much more internal process than either painting or writing. Many young people simply have a keen ear for organizing sounds heard and imagined and have gained the technical training and insights necessary for putting those musical ideas on paper. The youthful efforts of gifted composers will usually lack the maturity of approach and universality of emotion that mark the great musical masterpieces, for they lack the experience that a mere twenty years of life will seldom offer.

Some of the same qualities that make up a good composer are manifest in the gifted *conductor* who can internalize the music and who can coordinate, feel the flow, and direct the movement of the piece. This prodigy is no less impressive in the ability to perform.

Young prodigies gifted in *performance* are more numerous than other gifted and talented musicians, more dazzling, and more difficult to understand and assess than composers or conductors. Even with the knowledge and expertise of modern psychology and personality analysis, the scientific world is far from understanding how a child of tender years is able to compress motor skills, memorization, musical understanding, and emotional sensitivity into his or her short life. It is also amazing that a child can present his or her talent to the critical testing of public performance (Fisher, 1973).

In the areas of performance, young prodigies may excel in vocal expression or in violin, piano, or almost any other musical instrument. They can excel in the classics or in nonclassics such as blues, folk, or rock music. The fact is that they are very good indeed at what they can do and have abilities far beyond their years.

Menuhin (1973) wisely indicates that in discussion of the musically gifted child, the uniqueness of the gift is not as crucial to consider as the presence of favorable supportive influences such as good parents, high spiritual and moral standards, enlightenment and humility, encouraging environment, learning of self-discipline, good health and vitality, foresight and vision — all of which are important if the gift that resides in every child is to find expression, for these children thrive on a wholesome environment, encouragement, inspiration, clean air and water, and nutritious food. It was these simple and real things that have accounted for the proliferation of so-called musical "prodigies" in the past. This represents another emphasis on personal balance and health.

Enrichment for Music

Some activities suggested by Sanderson (1982) for stimulating music appreciation and/or expressions of talents in young children are as follows:

Recognition of musical instruments:
1. Records may be played, such as "Benjamin Britten's Introduction to Instruments of the Orchestra" with filmstrip or "Carnival of the Animals" by Camille Saint Saens. After listening to such records the students should be able to distinguish the different instruments in the orchestra and should have an understanding of the parts these instruments play in the orchestra.
2. The teacher may play such records as "Grand Canyon Suite" or "Peter and the Wolf." Before playing these records, he or she should discuss with the students the different instruments involved and the characters they will portray. This is a fun way to teach an appreciation for good music.

Building rhythm and musical instruments: Students build instruments and then may accompany themselves, other students, or the entire class. Additional instruments could be made as interest indicates. Examples:
1. Tambourines may be made by putting pebbles, pennies, or bells in between two paper plates and then stapling them.
2. For a wind instrument, use an empty paper towel roll. Paper punch a hole in one end and cover that end with waterproofing spray. Cover the opposite end with wax paper and attach with a rubber band. An instrument can be decorated creatively by making it look like an animal, train, or car, painting it, or just leaving it plain.
3. Drums can be made with an empty oatmeal carton decorated, or wet leather or hide can be stretched over a hollow object.
4. Combs with wax paper on them make good instruments.
5. If a wood shop is available with an assistant, the teacher can teach the child to cut, sand, paint, and put handles on wood blocks.
6. For chimes, cut pipes different lengths to get the musical scale. One can either hold by hand or attach to a wood stand.

Appreciation for different types of music: The teacher could have children listen to different types of music each day — classical, country, rock and roll, blues, jazz, etc. A good variety should be used so that the students get a definite feel for each type. Children can write down how each type of music made them feel and which one they enjoyed the most or the least.

Field trips: Classes can take special field trips to encourage music appreciation. Places to be visited might include the symphony, the ballet, a musical instrument factory, concerts, the opera, band practice, a musical play, or a choir production.

Conducting: The teacher can teach children about time signatures and methods of conducting then have them conduct the class in singing and also in the playing of musical instruments. A program in which the students that have accomplished this skill conduct their own numbers might also be developed.

Writing original songs: After students learn about major and minor scales and note values, they could be encouraged to write their own melody and share it with the class. They might write songs about famous people and events in history with lyrics to go with them. The teacher can create accompaniments for songs that do not indicate the chords to be played and encourage transposing music by changing the key.

Classroom orchestra: Students can form a classroom orchestra using rhythm instruments, melody instruments, autoharps, recorders, etc. They could take turns being the conductor.

Musical Activities Suggested for Secondary Students

Many of the same activities will serve the elementary and secondary students; however, some activities are more appropriate for more advanced or secondary students.

1. Developing the ability to play an instrument, perfecting a talent already manifest, or learning to play a different instrument from one's area of talent.

2. Joining a band, orchestra, or other small group for the enjoyment as well as the experience of using the skill and learning to blend with others.

3. Working with a resource person or talented teacher who can challenge one to increase one's knowledge and skill.

4. Teaching younger children to play an instrument or to sing properly. One excellent means of learning occurs when one is striving to teach the principles to someone else. This can tie in with some economic benefits if the gifted student can teach for pay, at home or as a teaching assistant.

5. Being part of productions, assemblies, and class programs in which one's talent can be shared and needs to be prepared for excellence.

Dance Talents

The dance prodigy is another wonder in the performing arts. This young person is amazing in terms of discipline and control of body movements. From early youth some individuals manifest this rare gift for expressing rhythm, form, and movement. Through practice and exercise, some talented young people have mastered the art of movement to an amazing degree. This skill is not only a physical discipline but a matter of timing, a sense of design and form and space, and a relationship with nature and the cultural pulse; it relates to emotional expression and is a form of nonverbal communication.

Dance Activities

Henshaw (1982) has suggested some ideas for challenging the talented dancer. He or she might be asked to

1. Categorize a list of dances according to the skill required, costumes and equipment needed, and age of the person best able to perform them.
2. Develop a dance routine for a handicapped person.
3. Research how dance has evolved and changed through the years (in the United States or another country). Predict how dance may change in the future.
4. Evaluate what would happen if students did not train to be successful dancers or there was no dancing at all.
5. Design a disco for the 1800s. Explain what changes there might be.
6. List all the dance styles that best develop coordination, muscle tone, or rhythm. Rank them in order of priority.
7. Create a totally new dance style. Give it a name. Where would such dancing take place? What would people wear? What kind of music is most appropriate?
8. Plan a dance marathon for school.
9. Use the jigsaw idea (*see* Chapter 9) for teaching basic dance steps to a class.
10. Use modern dance or interpretive movement to show how someone or something feels.
11. Decide, as a new owner of a dance studio in your hometown, which dancing style you will teach and why.
12. Draw animals at a dance. Which animals would be best suited for which dances?
13. Discuss which famous dancer of the past did more to influence the public's attitude toward dance.
14. Research careers available in dance. What requirements are there for each? What training is necessary?
15. Select a favorite song and choreograph it so that your actions tell the

story without the words.

16. Discover what aerobic dancing is. Why is it so popular today?
17. Choreograph a dance, structuring the situation as appropriate to the time and circumstances. For example, a dance could be created to fit a piece of music, a mood, or a theme.
18. Write a set of dance instructions specific enough to be interpreted by another dancer.

Drama Talents

The prodigy in drama is another amazing and enlightening individual. Drama can be expressed through speech, mime, or the combination of speech and mime. The gifted child in drama can portray many emotions and can cause others to laugh, cry, fear, ponder, question, and experience the gamut of emotions. The drama prodigy often has an amazing ability to memorize, to communicate and convey messages, to articulate, to create visual imagery, to spontaneously produce amazing entertainment, to perceive and step into another role or personality, and to interact with others in a make-believe or role-play setting. There are many benefits from a child's involvement with drama, for through drama a person can act out feelings in a socially acceptable way, can try certain behaviors and peform successfully (which strengthens self-confidence), can become more sensitive and perceptive about the feelings and behaviors of others, can improve speech patterns and increase vocabulary, can gain personal poise and discipline of the body and behavior, can improve personality traits, and on and on. There are dangers if the child dwells too much on fantasy and an unrealistic world, but most children manage to deal with fantasy and become more creative problem solvers as a result of their early formal or informal experience in drama. For those who are gifted in this area, some healthy opportunities for performance and expression are needed. Many lessons can be enriched in the classroom if someone comes dressed in the costume and make-up appropriate to the setting and relates the lesson's story in the first person. Many times role-play situations can bring a lesson or principle into focus more clearly. The child gifted in drama will enjoy and flourish in these settings. Most children are comfortable and effective in drama situations, although the "television generation" has learned to be spectators rather than actors and may be self-conscious and embarrassed in acting situations. If given the right setting and a fun and psychologically comfortable environment, however, it does not take most children long to get involved. For the drama prodigy, such situations are part of their life-style and means of communication.

Drama Activities

Some suggestions for drama activities for the elementary age group might include

Finger puppets for preschoolers are helpful in encouraging self-expression and the fun of being an actual part of a story being enacted.

The making of *simple puppets* from small paper bags or stockings can enrich a puppet show and can motivate a shy or nonverbal child to speak out as a different personality that he or she has created.

Inviting children to make up their own *fairy tale* or story and put it into a play for the family or for their class members can be fun and creative drama activity.

Extemporaneous speeches can be a good exercise especially if based on nonsense. For example, a child may be invited to give a speech on "Why black jellybeans are better than green ones" (it doesn't matter if the child prefers green, the challenge is to defend the black ones) or "Why is round better than square?" "Why is cold better than warm?" etc.

Role-play situations are always good drama experience. Each child is given a situation and then asked to act out his or her responses in relationship to the other person's role.

Mime is another fun drama activity. This is nonverbal communication. The child acts out an object or story or situation without sounds or lip movements. A lot of facial and body expression is required with this activity, which helps to develop communication skills as ideas are conveyed to the viewer.

The game of *charades* is old but effective in teaching self-expression and drama skills. In this fun game a person is in essence using mime to tell the title of a book, movie, or song; to convey a slogan, object, or emotion; to name a person, place, or thing; or whatever the ground rules are as established at the beginning of the game.

Some suggestions for gifted drama students in the secondary school might include

Debate teams. Confidence and self expression are musts in the debate situation. Many gifted teens enjoy a formal debate experience.

Readers' Theater is a fun and enjoyable experience. In essence, the participants simply read the play from the script as they go. This can be rehearsed and studied in advance or it can be spontaneous. It can be full or part costume and use some props or none at all.

One-act plays or full-length plays can be produced. Gifted drama students enjoy the entire production process wherein they may be director, prompter, set director, props person, make-up artist, costume director, advertising and program manager, or actually one of the cast members. It is an involved and enjoyable experience if set up properly.

Mini-plays to convey a historical account for a class setting can be fun. If given the time and creative freedom, the gifted teen can do wonders in getting a message or account across.

To be *emcee* or *announcer* or *participant* at the school assemblies is good experience, or to act out a commercial or advertisement for a coming school event at lunchtime or in class can be a good experience.

Regarding drama activities, the teacher is only limited by his or her own imagination and creativity. Once again the local college's drama faculty, libraries, and other resource people could be consulted.

PROGRAMS IN THE VISUAL AND PERFORMING ARTS

There have been several programs that have emerged over the last twenty years as examples of what can be done to provide stimulation and development for talented children in the visual and performing arts area.

THE NORTH CAROLINA SCHOOL OF THE ARTS (NCSA) opened in 1965 in Winston-Salem, North Carolina, with approximately 226 students. This school provides programs in dance, design and production, visual arts, drama, and music. The primary purpose of the school is providing both a secondary and a college education to promising youngsters in the performing arts. In 1982, there were approximately 735 students from around the world attending. However, almost 50 percent of these students came from within the state of North Carolina. The NCSA is an example of what can be done when a state provides atmosphere, resources, and support for the arts in an attempt to develop artistic talent. Further information about this school and its entrance requirements can be obtained by writing to the North Carolina School of the Arts, Winston-Salem, North Carolina. It should be noted that admission to this school is based upon an assessment of talent and professional career promise through an audition and/or review of a child's art portfolio.

The curriculum of the PENNSYLVANIA GOVERNOR'S SCHOOL OF THE ARTS consists of art, music, theater, dance, creative writing, and photography. This school is designed to provide students with intensive individualized instruction to strengthen their abilities. The students are selected on the basis of demonstrated talent and commitment, and a rigorous system of application and audition is used to identify the most promising students. Students receive intensive instruction with master artists and teachers in each of the identified areas. The Pennsylvania Governor's School is another example of what a state government can do to provide a supportive atmosphere and education for its artistic in-state constituents. A cooperative effort between the Pennsylvania Departments of Performing Arts and Special Education was necessary to develop and finance this program, and it is an example of what can be done within almost any state.

In Houston, Texas, the HIGH SCHOOL FOR THE PERFORMING AND VISUAL ARTS initially began in 1971 with 175 tenth grade students and now has been expanded to a full senior high program with each class consisting of approximately 200 students. Most of its students come from within the state of Texas, but it also includes students from several other states and foreign countries. In addition to improving and developing their individual artistic talents, all students take a regular high school curriculum. A rigorous application and selection process is employed, with prospective students taking a battery of aptitude tests. The program emphasizes music, visual arts, media arts, dance, drama, and instrumental and vocal music. Many of the students have received national recognition in music and the arts and several of the dance students have participated in national and international repertoire groups (i.e. Utah Repertoire Dance Theater, London School of Dance, Elliot Field's Ballet, and Royal Winnipeg Ballet).

Other comparable schools that have developed over the years for the visual and performing arts include the EDUCATION CENTER FOR THE ARTS in New Haven, Connecticut; WESTERN HIGH SCHOOL FOR THE PERFORMING ARTS, located in Washington, D.C.; THE ARTS CENTER developed by the Rhode Island State Council for the Arts; the NEW YORK HIGH SCHOOL FOR MUSIC AND ART in New York City; FORT HAYES CAREER CENTER in Columbus, Ohio; the SCHOOL FOR CREATIVE AND PERFORMING ARTS in Cincinnati, Ohio; and the CHULA VISTA ACADEMY OF THE FINE ARTS located in Corpus Christi. These are exemplary programs specifically designed for children gifted and talented in the performing and visual arts area.

Other examples of what has been done to develop programs in the arts are illustrated below:

SUPER SATURDAY. This is an enrichment program that takes place at Purdue University. The program is offered outside the regular school setting for gifted students from grades 2 through 9. The children come on campus and experience different activities and learning experiences. This is an illustration of what can be done by any school or school system located close to a metropolitan center, university, or college, using these as good resources vital to stimulating good development in gifted and talented children.

THE ADVANCED PLACEMENT PROGRAM IN STUDIO ART (Hurwitz, 1978) provides an opportunity for students with above-average abilities in art to work on a college level while still in high school and to receive credit for their work in the art school of their choice. The potential student provides a portfolio of original work, which is assembled and mailed to the Advanced Placement division at the Educational Testing Services in Princeton, New Jersey. Here the portfolio is judged by a team composed of high school teachers with a record of involvement in this program, as well as teachers from universities and art schools. Once graded, the work, if creditable, is sent to the college or art school of the student's choice for the purpose of receiving credit. Hurwitz (1978) indicates that some institutions such as Harvard equate "three or more advanced placement courses as an equivalent of a full year's work" (p. 24). To organize an advanced placement program, art teachers work with a few students of high ability and interests, absorbing them into their regular classes and then providing an opportunity to expand the resources within the classroom (art materials, books, slides, productions, and so on).

THE ART PARTNERSHIP NETWORK is a program outlined by Szekely (1981). He suggests the utilization of college students who "adopt" a gifted school child to work with in order to improve and stimulate his or her individual art talent. The Art Partnership Network has five major goals.

1. *Developing an understanding of art and art making.* The college student mentor helps the child become aware of the kinds of decisions that artists must make concerning their work. The preliminary investigations, plans, and exercises are discussed and related to the artist's work. Here the child is helped to develop an attitude toward art and the underlying development of an artistic work.

2. *Developing the child's independence.* In meeting this goal, the child, with the mentor's help, learns to document ideas, record, make observations and notes of ideas, formulate plans for uses of new materials or familiar materials, and envisions how objects can be incorporated or transformed into an artistic work.

3. *Challenging the child.* Szekely emphasizes that the experience of children gifted in art should be as close to that of the adult artist as possible. They should work with the artist's tools and materials, should have the opportunity to search for tools and materials that are suitable for the expression of their ideas, and should also visit and work in an artist's studio.

4. *Providing support.* The college art student mentor serves an important function for the gifted child by letting the child know that he or she is not alone, that others understand the child's special concerns and are ready to share with them similar feelings and attitudes. Szekely (1981) feels that this situation makes it possible for the gifted child to strike a balance between the seclusion needed for creative thought and the ability to work in harmonious relationships with one's peers. Also, the mentor becomes a means by which the child may find a wider, more knowledgeable audience for his or her work. In other words, the mentor broadens horizons for the child by extending the audience viewing the child's work.

5. *Encouraging confidence and risk taking.* The college student mentor attempts to increase the child's interest by opening new vistas through exploration of different mediums, materials, styles of working, and so on. It is not unusual for the child to encounter a limited environment for developing individual art talents within the regular school curriculum. With the help of a college student interested in the same area, a talented child may reach greater development within an area as well as expand interest and knowledge within that area. The mentor can also provide situations in which

the child's self-confidence may be reinforced, as well as ensure that the child does not overstep the boundaries of uncertainty and experience failure with the unfamiliar. In the same regard, a mentor can help the child to become a self-disciplined individual who is confident in making choices and decisions relative to his or her own creative talents and abilities.

Suggested Bibliography for Teachers of the Visual and Performing Arts

Baker, L.: *The Art Teacher's Resource Book*. Reston, Virginia, Reston, 1979.

Balkin, Alfred: *Involvement with Music: Essential Skills and Concepts*. Boston, Houghton Mifflin Co., 1975.

Barnett, E.B.: *Montessori and Music: Rhythmic Activities for Young Children*. New York, Schocken, 1974.

Bayless, K., and Ramsey, M.: *Music: A Way of Life for the Young Child*. St. Louis, Mosby, 1978.

Blond, A., and Janusz, L.: *Spectrum of Visual Arts of Young Children*. Sepulveda, California, Double M, 1976.

Bordon, S. D.: *Plays as Teaching Tools in the Elementary Schools*. New York, Parker Publishing Co., Inc., 1970.

Burger, I. B.: *Creative Play Acting: Learning Through Drama*. New York, Ronald Press, 1966.

Cherry, C.: *Creative Movement for the Developing Child: A Nursery School Handbook for Nonmusicians*. Belmont, California, Fearon, 1971.

D'Amico, V.: *Creative Teaching in Art*, rev. ed. Pennsylvania, International Textbook Co., 1953.

Enthoven, J.: *Stitchery for Children*. New York, Van Nostrand Reinhold, 1968.

Fiarotta, P.: *Sticks and Stones and Ice Cream Cones*. New York, Workman, 1973.

Frank, M.: *I Can Make a Rainbow*. Nashville, Incentive, 1976.

Gelineau, R. P.: *Experiences in Music*, 2nd ed. New York, McGraw-Hill, 1976.

Hart, L.: *Music in Motion*. Mill Valley, California, Music in Motion, 1973.

Haskell, L.: *Art in the Early Childhood Years*. Columbus, Ohio, Merrill, 1979.

Hoeton, O. I: *Introduction to Theater: A Mirror to Nature*. Englewood Cliffs, New Jersey, Prentice-Hall, 1976.

Land, Lois Rhea: *Music in Today's Classroom: Creating, Listening, Performing*. New York, Harcourt, Brace, Jovanovich, 1973.

McCaslin, Nellie: *Creative Dramatics in the Classroom*. 2nd ed. New York, D. McKay Co., 1974.

Pierini, M. P. F.: *Creative Dramatics: A Guide for Educators*. New York, Herder and Herder, 1971.

Raebeck, L.: *New Approaches to Music in Elementary School*. Dubuque, Iowa, Wm. C. Brown, 1974.

Romberg, J.: *Let's Discover* series. New York, Center for Applied Research in Education, 1974.

Schattner, Regina: *Creative Dramatics for Handicapped Children*. New York, John Day Co., 1967.

Wardian, J. I.: *New Century World of Song: Theory and Practice*. New York, Appleton-Century Crofts, 1972.

Winslow, R., and Dalling, L.: *Music Skills for Classroom Teachers*. Dubuque, Iowa, Wm. C. Brown, 1970.

APPENDIX A

ADDITIONAL RESOURCES FOR PROGRAMMING

WITHIN this appendix can be found information, additional to that presented in each of the chapters, on books, journals, programs, and associations that have as their focus improving the education of the gifted and talented child. The contents of this appendix is not an exhaustive list of all the potential sources of information but is only a brief look at primary resource materials. This appendix is organized into sections on books, journals, programs, and associations.

Books for Programming

Alexander and Muia: *Gifted Education*. Rockville, Maryland, Aspen Systems Corporation, 1982.

    This book provides a balance between theory and practice of gifted education.

Callahan, Carolyn M.: *Developing Creativity in the Gifted and Talented*. Reston, Virginia, The Council for Exceptional Children, 1978 (80 pages).

    Strategies that teachers can use to enhance creative thinking abilities are highlighted. Creativity exercises are presented that use techniques such as modeling, operant conditioning, and brainstorming, and many divergent creativity measures are also included.

Clark, Barbara: *Growing up Gifted*. Columbus, Ohio, Merrill, 1979.

    This book is divided into three major sections, with several chapters under each heading. The first section deals with understanding the gifted individual. The first chapter consists of an assessment instrument that allows the reader to look at his or her own beliefs and understandings regarding gifted children. Another chapter deals with a definition of giftedness including specific characteristics such as creative or productive thinking, leadership ability, and a high performance level in visual and performing arts. One chapter has suggestions and activities for developing a nurturing environment for optimal learning.

    In Section II, "The School and the Gifted Individual," information on the need for identifying gifted individuals, including the culturally different and handicapped, by screening for identification is given. This section explains what has been done for the gifted (such as the establishment of continuum models for ability grouping) and what has not been done (no gifted children are served at all in twenty-one states; most programs for the gifted are isolated, experimental, or temporary).

    Section III includes activities to develop basic reading skills in two to four year olds, list of standardized tests, and brain games.

Jackson, David M.: *Curriculum Development*. Guilford, Connecticut, Special Learning Corporation, 1980.

This is an excellent resource reference for gifted program planning. This book is a compilation of articles devoted to curriculum planning and evaluation, screening and identifying for gifted program membership, program examples (i.e. the Counseling Laboratory for the Gifted at Wisconsin, Catskill Saturday seminars, and Children Have to Learn Tonic, teacher preparation, and community involvement.

Nazzaro, Jean: *Computer Connections for Gifted Children and Youth*. Reston, Virginia, The Council for Exceptional Children, 1981.

This book is divided into six sections, each dealing with one aspect of computer programs. The first, "Why Computer Experiences Are Needed Now," describes the computer as an object to think with, which eventually helps the student shift to adult thinking at an earlier age. Section 2, "Perspectives of Gifted Children and Youth," explains how young people get started with computers and what impact computers have on their lives. Section 3 discusses computers at home, including a how-to section to help parents with computer program curriculum. Section 4 talks about successful programs at the preschool, elementary, and secondary levels. Section 5 discusses how some school districts have gone about selecting the right computer system for them. Section 6 explains what computers are not (for example, they are not to replace teachers) and gives addresses to which the reader can write for information about materials and computers in education.

Perrone, Phillip A., and Male, Robert A.: *The Developmental Education and Guidance of Talented Learners*. Rockville, Maryland, Aspen Systems Corporation, 1981 (240 pages).

This book is divided into four sections: "Issues and Problems Related to the Unique Developmental Needs of Persons with Talent Potential," "The Fulfillment of Developmental Potential in Talented Persons," "How to Plan and Implement Programs to Foster Development of Talent Potential," and "Resources." It is aimed at providing a basis for meeting the needs of the talented. The fifth chapter is extremely interesting in that it provides a description of various eminent persons' lives and development.

Perspectives on Gifted and Talented Education. New York, Teacher's College Press, 1980.

This is a series that consists of five different books *Somewhere to Turn: Strategies for Parents of Gifted and Talented Children*, *Elementary and Secondary Level Programs for the Gifted and Talented*, *Training Teachers of the Gifted and Talented*, *Gifted Young Children*, and *Reaching Out: Advocacy for the Gifted and Talented*.

Renzulli, Reis, and Smith: *Revolving Door Identification Model*. Mansfield Center, Connecticut, Creative Learning Press, 1981.

This description of a total programming plan for the gifted and talented is written primarily for teachers of the gifted and talented and is recommended as a college text for undergraduate and graduate courses in gifted education. It could be used as a reference book.

Sanderlin and Cranbury: *Gifted Children: How to Identify and Teach Them*. Mansfield Center, Connecticut, Creative Learning Press, 1981.

This primer for parents addresses the questions of whether education for the gifted is undemocratic, what the IQ is and how valid it is, whether intelligence is hereditary or environmental, whether children should be grouped or accelerated, and what parents can do to assist gifted children.

Torrance, Paul E.: *Discovery and Nurturance of Giftedness in the Culturally Different*. Reston, Virginia, The Council for Exceptional Children, 1982 (96 pages).

This book provides insights and alternatives for recognizing gifted and talented youngsters who are culturally different. A sample checklist of behaviors that may indicate leadership or creative talent is included.

Whalen, Sheila: *Special Gifts*. Phoenix, Arizona, Resources for the Gifted, 1979.

This book is a series of short stories about various types of gifted children (intellectually gifted, musically gifted, learning disabled gifted, leadership gifted) and the challenges they must overcome. Areas discussed in the book are expectations of being the best, giving up goals to please others, misunderstandings, and unrecognized disabilities of the gifted.

Whitmore, Joanne: *Giftedness, Conflict, and Under-Achievement*. Boston, Allyn and Bacon, 1980 (462 pages, hardcover).

The first several chapters provide a history of gifted education; many studies such as Terman's are discussed at great length. The main focus of this book, however, is on the gifted underachiever, the child who expresses "conflict between internal needs for acceptance, success and meaningful learning and the external conditions of the classroom."

The author explains how the classroom teacher should capitalize on the student's strengths rather than devise a curriculum based on remediation of deficient skill areas. She uses her own classroom experiences to show how many activities used with the gifted students were successful. Techniques used to address specific problems of the gifted (supersensitivity, perfectionism, deficient social skills, and unrealistic self-expectations) are discussed in some detail.

Journals for Educating the Gifted

Exceptional Children. The Council for Exceptional Children, 1920 Association Drive, Reston, VA 22091. Published six times per year (September, October, November, January, February, and April).

The main theme of the October, 1981 issue was "Education of the Gifted: A Challenge and a Promise." This included the challenge of having educational institutions shifting from preparation for an industrial society to preparation for a technological society. Another article, entitled "Gifted Children With Handicapping Conditions: A New Frontier," dealt with the new definition of the gifted, a historical perspective, identification of the gifted, opportunities and challenges of the gifted, characteristics (both impeding and revealing) of gifted children, research, teacher education, and professional practice changes (such as early identification and use of information given by community agencies). The "National Survey of Identification Practices in Gifted and Talented Education," which described methods of data collection and grouping, data analysis and trends, instruments used, and data on subpopulations, was another article of importance in this publication.

G/C/T (gifted/creative/talented). G/C/T Publishing Co., Box 66654, Mobile, Alabama 36606. Published five times per year.

This journal contains many articles and activities for and about gifted students. These have included articles on Project GREAT (Gifted Resources Education Action Team), a contractual service of the National State Leadership Training Institute on Gifted and Talented, which offers technical assistance for gifted programs.

"Things to Consider when Establishing Gifted and Talented Programs" included a proper definition of giftedness and information on identification of population, program decisions, establishment of a climate for success (community awareness, available expertise, the extent of commitment by key leaders to the new program), program objectives and activities, evaluation, and dissemination of efforts to others' areas.

Also included in the journal are resources of the private sector, listing ideas and programs that can be beneficial to both the students' education and the private sector, and references to different texts, books, bulletins, journals, and programs available in helping gifted children.

Gifted Child Quarterly. National Association for Gifted Children, 217 Gregory Drive, Hot
   Springs, Arkansas 71901. Published quarterly (January, April, July, and October).

Each issue of this journal includes an average of twelve articles on topics such as results of
specific gifted program evaluations from around the United States; reference lists of textbooks, authors, agencies, articles, models, persons, surveys, and curriculums that would
benefit those who teach and work with the gifted and talented; and reviews of books that have
potential for significant impact on gifted education.

In special issues there is a focus on one main theme; for example, the Winter, 1982, issue
dealt with the myth quotient. It included a fifteen-question, true/false test dealing with issues
confronting gifted education today; A three- to seven-page article gave an in-depth explanation of each question.

Gifted Children Newsletter. Gifted and Talented Publications Inc., 1255 Portland Place, Boulder,
   Colorado 80323.

This is a publication devoted to gifted education that can help the reader identify, understand, and teach gifted students more efficiently. This publication is written for the parents of
children with great promise, but it can also be used as a teaching aid for the professional edu-
cator.

Articles in this publication have included "Six Types of Giftedness" (general intellectual
ability, creative or productive thinking, specific academic aptitude, leadership ability, visual
and performing arts ability, and psychomotor ability), "When Does Support Turn to Push?"
and "Why Are So Many Gifted Students Hyperactive?" A section filled with independent
study projects, critical thinking puzzles and word games, all flexible enough to be used at
home or school, is also a feature.

The Journal of Creative Behavior. Creative Education Foundation, Inc. Buffalo, New York 14203.
   Published quarterly.

One example of the articles found in this journal is "The Progress and Peril of Identifying
Creative Talent Among Gifted and Talented Students," which focused on creative talent, a
concept generally included in the identification of the gifted and talented within the specific
areas of giftedness. The identification of creative talent must be done on a multidimensional
approach because of the complex nature of human abilities as well as the concern for compre-
hensiveness and fairness in identification. This article describes the directions in which
creativity assessment is going. It also explains the continuing problems (including the over-
looking or overemphasizing of creativity procedures) and need for research in this area.

Journal of Education for the Gifted.

This is an excellent source of information on programming for gifted children. Examples
of the articles in this journal include "Instruction for the Gifted; Some Promising Practices,"
and "The Extended Classroom Is a Gold Mine for Gifted Students."

Programs for Gifted Children

Project GREAT (Gifted Resources Education Action Team), initiated in Prince
George's County, Maryland, is a contractual service of the National State
Leadership Training Institute on Gifted and Talented. This program includes
mini-contracts of telephone consultations, materials on gifted education, and
other services including five on-site workshops. Many summer institutes are
planned each year for school administrators, teachers, counselors, and advo-
cates of gifted education interested in development of curriculum and program
planning. There are many branches of Project GREAT throughout the United

States. Project GREAT publishes two monthly bulletins, the BULLETIN and GROUPS FOR GIFTED, which reports on research, new books, programs, funding, calendars of events, and resource lists.

The program for the gifted child in the *Philadelphia Public Schools* includes a search for talent, a point of view regarding the human potential, an understanding of the problems that the school faces in its quest for ability and talent, a sense of pride from having developed intelligent leadership, and a grasp of the confidence the school district would gain because of the ability of the next generation to do a somewhat better job than the previous generation.

The *Houston Independent School District*, Houston, Texas has developed a program for the gifted in the Houston senior high schools. Guidelines established for this program and approved by the Houston Board of Education include identification of students of unusual ability early in their education programs, counseling of students with unusual ability to select courses that will be challenging in their learning careers, after-school opportunities in a variety of fields, and additional educational opportunities in every classroom for students of superior abilities so that they are able to extend and intensify their study.

The *Connecticut State Department of Education Programs for the Gifted and Youth* has programs designed to help teachers and administrators become more sensitive to students with unusual ability, outline identification procedures for the gifted, provide resource lists of school activities that may contribute to the bright student, and outline the role of various groups and resources within the educational community.

The *Dade County Public School System's* general program for talented pupils in elementary school is such that the talented students are kept in the regular classroom and the curriculum is enriched to meet each individual's needs. There are various curriculum activities suggested for each area of the talented student program, including publishing a news sheet in a foreign language, having speed reading classes in language arts, and developing shortened methods of computation in the mathematics courses.

The *Ventura, California School System* program for gifted elementary school children emphasizes the gifted child's special adjustment problems. These might include classmates' resentment of the gifted child's scholastic ability and the adult approval it brings, overcultivation of intellectual interests, neglect of the child's physical and social development, teachers' and parents' reactions to the gifted child's exceptional abilities, and the teacher's jealousy of the gifted child's abilities (which often surpass the teacher's).

The school system distributes a publication that explains its provisions for educating the gifted child in the regular classroom. These include modifying the gifted students' program with more challenging subject matter, helping gifted students to work on school or community projects, and giving students the opportunity to learn how to use human and physical resources in the community in which they live.

The *Panhandle Child Development Association* is an independent nonprofit program in Coeur d'Alene, Idaho. This program does not look for the handicap in being gifted but rather looks at the total needs of the gifted student and then designs a curriculum to meet these needs. This program has been set up for preschool education of the gifted and talented. The focus of the program is two areas of preschool curricula — problem-solving activities and exploration activities that help to identify each child's areas of interest. Parental involvement in this program is crucial. Parents are given an inventory to complete on their child's behavior; if this inventory but not the test scores indicate giftedness, the child is given a trial placement for two weeks. Parents transport their children to and from classes, have formal and informal meetings with the teachers, and participate in actual class activities and educational sessions. This program does not function separately from the public school system. When a child is ready to enter school, a special conference is set up, at which the child's educational plan and appropriate placement are decided. The biggest problem with the preschool gifted programs is that there is little or no follow-up.

Waterford School in Provo, Utah is experimenting with a new concept in computer usage in the school. Even though not specifically designed for gifted children, this innovative private school is attempting to adapt the standard curriculum (reading, writing, and arithemtic) for use with advances in computer technology. Teaching the arts with computer technology is also being explored; for example, children learn the values of notes, musical history, and music appreciation from interaction with the computers. Waterford is truly a school for now and the future that provides a challenging environment for accelerated learners.

The *Governor's School of North Carolina* is a residential school begun in 1963 for high school students. The program focuses on academics and the arts.

Associations for Gifted Children

American Association for Gifted Children
15 Gramercy Park
New York, NY 10003

The Association for the Gifted (TAG)
The Council for Exceptional Children
1920 Association Drive
Reston, VA 22091

ERIC Clearinghouse on Handicapped and Gifted Children
1920 Association Drive
Reston, VA 22091

Foundation for Gifted and Creative Children
395 Diamond Hill Road

Warwick, RI 02886

Parents and individuals interested in the proper education of gifted and creative children. Provides counseling for children and parents; testing of children; and sponsors workshops in the arts, sciences, and creative writing. Also works for the inclusion of special programs for gifted children in public school curriculums.

Publications: Newsletter, monthly.

Office of Gifted and Talented, USOE
Room 2100
7th and "D" Streets, S.W.
Washington, D.C. 20202

National Association for Creative Children and Adults
8080 Springvalley Drive
Cincinnati, OH 45236

A helping organization dedicated to bringing out the best in all, for everyone's happiness, through fostering creativity. Aims are to provide individual and group benefits from new research on creativity; to stimulate constructive means for use of increased leisure time and longer life span; to foster appreciation of the arts as a means of nurturing creativity in human beings. Offers Inservice Teacher Training Program; sponsors annual visitation to participating schools for evaluation; sponsors workshops on creativity and international conferences.

Publications: *The Creative Child and Adult*, quarterly.

National/State Leadership Training Institute on the Gifted and Talented
316 West Second Street PH-C
Los Angeles, CA 90012

National Association for Gifted Children (this association is for parents and teachers)
217 Gregory Drive
Hot Springs, AK 71901
Publications: *The Gifted Child Quarterly*

Gifted Children Research Institute
300 West 55th Street, Suite 4-W
New York, NY 10019

National Commission on Resources for Youth
36 West 44th Street
New York, NY 10036

Gifted Education Resource Institute
Purdue University
West Lafayette, IN 47907

Institute on Gifted Minorities (TAG)
University of Arizona
Tucson, AR 85721

APPENDIX B

CHAPTER QUESTIONS AND ANSWERS

Chapter One

1. Who proposed the first special provision for gifted children in America?
   Thomas Jefferson in 1779.
2. What are the most widely implemented curriculum provisions for gifted and talented children in the public school?
   Special classes, acceleration, and enrichment.
3. What has been the contribution of Terman to the development of programs for gifted children?
   His study helped change the attitude of the general public toward these children and generated a great deal of interest in gifted education.
4. The Intelligence Quotient (IQ) has historically been used as one of the determiners of gifted students. What are some other criteria that are presently being considered in defining this population?
   Creativity and special talents such as superior ability in the performing arts, sports, language arts, sciences, and leadership.
5. Can you outline characteristics of gifted children in the following areas: physical, cognitive, academic, social, and performing arts?
   Physical — Walks and talks early; somewhat above average in physical attributes such as muscular strength and physique; exhibits a high degree of originality in work and play situations.
   Cognitive — Early interest in time; able to interpret events early; interests are varied and spontaneous; curious; longer than average attention span; easily generalizes learning experiences to other situations.
   Academic — Early drive and ability to read; learns easily; higher mastery of academics; advanced vocabulary; demonstrates verbal curiosity through asking a lot of questions; unprodded desire to learn; prefers difficult subjects in school.
   Social — Reacts to comments in a manner that shows understanding; responds quickly; may appear impatient and rebellious; prefers older

peers; displays a keen sense of humor; more inclined to be trustworthy under temptation; less inclined to have emotional disorders.

Performing Arts — Demonstrates unusual poise and a mature ability to express himself/herself; may show unusual skill or creativity in art or music.

6. How useful are teacher nominations in the identification of giftedness? Parent nominations? Peer nominations?

   All three procedures are considered useful although parent nominations are generally considered to be the most reliable of the three.

7. If you were going to develop a program for the identification of gifted children, what would it include?

   Tests of creativity, academic skills, and intelligence; parent, teacher, and peer nominations; auditions or portfolios to demonstrate psychomotor or performing arts ability; and self-nominations based on autobiographical data.

8. How valuable do you feel the reservoir model would be in the identification of giftedness?

   It could prove very valuable since it involves many persons in the process and can be used in practically any cultural or academic setting.

9. What standardized tests are available to assess a child's intellectual, social/emotional, and academic potential?

   Cognitive tests include the following: Author Adaptation of the Leiter International Performance Scale; California Mental Maturity Scale; McCarthy Scales of Children's Abilities; SRA Primary Mental Abilities; Slosson Intelligence Test for Children and Adults; Stanford-Binet Intelligence Scales; Wechsler Adult Intelligence Scale — Revised; Wechsler Intelligence Scale for Children — Revised; Wechsler Preschool and Primary Scale of Intelligence; Woodcock-Johnson Psycho-Educational Battery — Part I, Cognitive.

   Social/emotional tests include: Vineland Social Maturity Scale; Walker Problem Behavior Identification Checklist; Sentence Completion; Magic Circle, Sociogram; The Preschool Attainment Record; "showing" or "show and tell" periods; role playing; creative play; stories; discussion.

   Academic tests include: California Achievement Tests; Metropolitan Achievement Test; Peabody Individual Achievement Test; Stanford Diagnostic Mathematics Test; Keymath; Stanford Achievement Test; Wide Range Achievement Test; Iowa Test of Basic Skills; Woodcock-Johnson Psycho-Educational Battery — Part II, Achievement.

10. What standardized tests are available to assess a child's aptitude in the performing arts area?

    Tests which can be used to assess a child's aptitude in the performing arts include: Creativity Tests for Children; Torrance Test of Creative Thinking; Horn Art Aptitude Inventory; Knauber Art Ability Test; Advanced Placement Program in Studio Art; Musical Aptitude Profile; Measures of Musical Ability; Drake Musical Aptitude Tests; Seashore Measures of Musical Talents; Standardized Tests of Musical Intelligence; Aliferis Music Achievement Test.

Chapter Two

1. What is the meaning of stewardship?

   It is the administration or management of those things in one's life for which one is legitimately responsible.

2. Can you explain the Five Principles of Supervision? How do these principles teach personal stewardship?

   The five principles involve teaching correct principles, allowing the student to set goals in harmony with the principles taught, being thought of as a source of help and being available to provide such help to the student, the student asking for help and receiving it, and finally, the student giving an account of his/her stewardship. These principles teach personal stewardship by placing the responsibility for learning upon the student and allowing him/her to set goals and go about achieving these goals his/her own way with the help of the teacher when solicited. The student must then account for his/her own actions.

3. Why is balance a crucial factor in the happiness and well-being of the gifted or talented? How can balance be emphasized in the programs developed by and for the gifted child?

   Balance is important since overall progress and well-being cannot occur if an area of development is neglected or too much emphasis is placed on one area at the expense of the others. Balance can be emphasized in gifted programs by providing instruction or special activities in all four areas of development and/or by encouraging the student to pursue activities in all four areas on his/her own.

4. What should be the main goals in managing behaviors of the gifted or talented?

   The child's wise management of his/her own behavior, or (in other words) stewardship, should be the primary goal.

5. What are the five *R*s of remediation?

   Recognition, remorse, restitution, resolve, and refrain.

6. What is an Individual Educational Plan (IEP)? How does this relate to goal setting? To stewardship? To the gifted or talented child?

   An IEP is a contract between the child and the teacher in which the child agrees to accomplish certain tasks or master certain skills in a specific way, by a specific time, and with a predetermined reporting or accountability system. Both short-term and long-term goals are set and the student takes on the responsibility and commitment of working on these goals. This process relates to gifted and talented children in that they are freed to establish their own goals in line with their own special gifts and/or talents in a setting that fosters self-discipline, purposeful learning, and stewardship.

Chapter Three

1. What is the perceptual system?
   It is the process of organizing raw data obtained through the senses into the vestibular proprioceptive area of the brain, which then interprets its meaning.
2. What are six of the human sensory receptors?
   Eyes, ears, nose, mouth, skin, and thermalsensitive neurons in the hypothalamus.
3. Can you give an example of selective perception?
   When someone is extremely tired, objects, language, and circumstances are readily perceived in relationship to sleep.
4. Why is comprehending figure-ground relationships important in learning?
   It gives sense and purpose to that which is seen.
5. How can understanding Piaget's stages of intellectual development be helpful to a teacher of gifted children?
   Such an understanding can help the teacher be realistic and fair in his/her expectations of the child's thought processes and abilities.
6. How do thought processes and attitudes affect interpersonal relationships and vice versa?
   Only when the student feels accepted as an individual and is comfortable in the presence of the teacher can the school environment be perceived as a place of freedom and productivity.
7. What are some key principles facilitating memory?
   Recognition, attention, rehearsal, imagery, encoding, decoding, and organizing.
8. How does Erikson's Eight Stages of Social Development relate to thought processes?
   A child's self-concept sets the limits on his/her behavior, which in turn influences his/her thought processes. The self-concept is developed through these eight signs.
9. What is the difference between spontaneous and reflective thinking? What is the difference between convergent and divergent thinking?
   A spontaneous thinker processes information rapidly and is quick to respond, whereas a reflective thinker requires more time to ponder and

consider the alternatives or meanings of a question. The convergent thinker tends to bring things into order and seeks relationships. His/her questions appear relevant and insightful to the topic at hand. The divergent thinker, however, tends to be the brainstormer whose questions may appear alien to the topic at hand due to the individual's creative and innovative thinking.

10. How does language relate to thought processes?
It is through language that thought is conveyed.

Chapter Four

1. What is meant by acceleration?
Grade or curriculum skipping that allows a student to complete his formal education in a reduced amount of time.

2. Can you outline an acceleration program?
Early entrance into kindergarten, junior high, high school, and/or college.

3. What are four different educational programs used for gifted and talented children?
Acceleration, ability grouping, enrichment, independent study, cluster grouping, mentorships, and pull-out time programs.

4. What is the Enrichment Triad Model?
This is a model proposed by Renzulli that provides for three types of enrichment activities: general exploratory activities, group training activities, and individual investigation of real problems.

5. How practical is a mentorship program in the public school?
Due to the typical one-on-one nature of such a program, mentorships are generally too expensive and time-consuming for the public schools.

6. How effective are pull-out programs?
The effectiveness of such programs rests solely upon the capabilities, interests, and training of the teacher.

7. Can you outline the ecosystem of program development?
Such a program centers around the learner. The learner's cognitive capabilities, emotional/social attributes, physical capabilities, and psychic or spiritual orientation are considered, after which an analysis of the learner's external environment is conducted. This analysis entails answering the following question: What are the expectations, the goals, the circumstances, and the criteria that have external influence upon the learner? The information obtained concerning the individual learner and his/her external environment is then utilized to provide the most appropriate learning program.

8. What are the planning steps to follow in developing an educational program for the gifted and talented?

First, state and federal laws, regulations, and guidelines relative to serving gifted/talented children must be investigated. Second, policies and position statements related to this population must be studied and understood. Third, it is necessary to find out the various attitudes of the community towards serving gifted/talented children. Fourth, information from various state and federal resources relating to all aspects of gifted/talented programs must be obtained.

9. What are some "dos" and "don'ts" for working with gifted children?

Dos include instructing in an informal manner; gearing your conversation to the young person's age, interests, and emotional level; expecting a degree of egocentricity; trying to help in any appropriate ways; remembering that you are dealing with an advanced child, not an underage adult. Don'ts include calling the child "genius" or asking him if he is one; expecting infallibility or unlimited versatility; expecting a performance; comparing your prodigy with the "amazing, phenomenal, unbelievable whiz" you read about in the *National Enquirer*; asking the child his IQ unless you have a legitimate reason for doing so.

10. Can you outline the role of the parents in the development of educational programs?

They should support school efforts to plan for gifted children; investigate scholarship programs in their community; work to provide better community understanding and appreciation of the gifted; support community action for gifted children; establish open communication with teachers and administrators about educating the gifed and talented; provide anecdotes illustrating the child's exceptional abilities and interests outside of school when discussing the gifted child with teachers; seek out other parents of gifted children and share concerns and ideas.

Chapter Five

1. What are the procedures for identifying gifted children within handicapped populations?

Direct observation, parent reports, and self-evaluation methods are possibilities for identifying the gifted with handicapping conditions. Also, in identifying this population you should focus on the student's potential rather than only his/her demonstrated abilities, compare the student with other handicapped students rather than with the general population, and observe the student's skills in compensating for the disability.

2. What are four criteria commonly used in identifying giftedness within handicapped populations?

Four criteria commonly used in identifying giftedness among the handicapped yet inappropriate for this population are teacher nomination, group achievement scores, intelligence scores, and previously demonstrated accomplishments.

3. Can you list two educational programs that are specifically designed for teaching gifted handicapped children?

   Two educational programs specifically designed for teaching gifted handicapped childen are RAPYHT (the Retrieval and Acceleration of Promising Young Handicapped and Talented) and the Chapel Hill Training Outreach Project.

4. Can you differentiate between culturally different and disadvantaged gifted children?

   The culturally different child is one who has been raised within a particular culture and then placed within a new culture that has a different set of values and attitudes. The disadvantaged child, on the other hand, is a child who because of economic reasons is precluded from participating in the normal mainstream of educational development at home and in the public school.

5. What are the limitations of standardized IQ tests and achievement tests in identifying culturally different and disadvantaged gifted children?

   Inasmuch as culturally different and disadvantaged gifted children are unlikely to perform in the average range due to negative factors impinging upon them, the use of standardized tests is inappropriate for identifying this population. Also, talents do not necessarily show themselves very well on standardized achievement tests.

6. What are some procedures that should be followed in developing educational programs for the culturally disadvantaged gifted child?

   In developing educational programs for the culturally disadvantaged gifted child, the child's strengths, characteristics, and learning and living styles should be considered. Also, teaching free of limiting expectations, counseling programs, and parental and community support services are necessary.

7. Can you identify three programs specifically designed to serve culturally disadvantaged gifted children?

   Three programs specifically designed to serve culturally disadvantaged gifted children are a model summer program for gifted children, PCEP (Professional Career Exploration Program for Minority and/or Low Income Gifted and Talented 10th grade students), and Patterson and Starcher's language arts program.

8. What are the characteristics commonly associated with preschool gifted children?

   Characteristics commonly associated with preschool gifted children may include an earlier loss of innocence, a desire to explore the world, a preference of communicating with adults rather than with peers, perfectionistic tendencies, and an extremely good memory.

9. What are the most common characteristics of gifted underachievers?
   Common characteristics of gifted underachievers may include a low self-concept, hostility and distrust toward adult authority figures, a lack of academic skills as well as motivation for academic achievement, poor study habits, less popularity with peers, lower aspirations, and a preference for manual activities.
10. Can you list three program-planning strategies to help gifted underachievers perform more adequately in school?
    Three program-planning strategies that can help gifted underachievers are a comfortable and accepting environment, a supportive social milieu, and well-trained teachers who can provide stimulating and positive experiences.

Chapter Six

1. What is creativity?
   Any definition of creativity depends upon the definer's perception of it, and it is therefore different things to different people. Generally, however, creativity is considered to be the process of organizing something from existing elements for some useful purpose.
2. How would you identify a creative child? What are some characteristics?
   Characteristics that can be useful in identifying a creative child include a desire to excel, determination, dominance, strong affection, persistence, constructive criticism, courage, deep conscientious convictions, discontentment, and a sense of destiny, to name a few.
3. What is the Five-Step Creative Process? How does it function in problem solving?
   The Five-Step Creative process consists of defining the problem — providing a basis for an approach to the problem; brainstorming — pursuing alternatives; prioritizing — obtaining commitment and dedication to the plan; experimenting — developing a product; and evaluating — judging the product in terms of time, money, materials, and energy expended and whether the problem and intent of the product were achieved.
4. How might you enrich the life and experiential base for a gifted or talented child?
   This can be achieved through field trips, books, films, mini-class, home experiences, and associations with interesting people of different cultures, vocations, or talents.
5. What is divergent thinking and how can you facilitate this process for the gifted and talented child?
   Divergent thinking is the ability to study a problem and to develop a number of solutions or alternatives. This process can be facilitated by encouraging the child to create new games, plays, songs, dances, jokes, etc;

by asking questions; and by various paper and pencil games.

6. Can you define convergent thinking? How is this implemented for the gifted in the classroom and in the home?

   Convergent thinking involves bringing ideas together in an orderly manner and seeking the best solution. Convergent thinking can be implemented through assignments, games, or activities that stress logic, such as research tasks, exams, puzzles, word games and logo sets.

7. What are some commercial resources (games) on the market today that are founded on divergent or creative thinking?

   Scrabble, The Ungame, Make Your Own Puzzles, Printing sets, and Spill and Spell.

Chapter Seven

1. Can you list seven characteristics of potentially gifted children in the area of math?

   Ability to work independently, self-direction, interest in the "whys" and "hows" of math, long concentration span, willingness to entertain complexity, stimulation by problem solving situations, and good short-term and long-term memory.

2. What is a procedure to follow in identifying children talented in the math area?

   The student's computational skill should be considered along with such factors as the student's attitude and interest in participating in a math problem, his/her ability to work independently, and whether or not he/she is stimulated by the curriculum and/or environment in which the math program is conducted.

3. In setting up a math program for gifted children, what should the goals be?

   The goal of mathematics instruction is to produce students who can solve problems.

4. What should be the components of a math curriculum for gifted children?

   Development of basic computational skills; understanding of fractions, decimals, basic geometry, probability, and statistics; skill in estimation; enrichment activities; and computer literacy should all be included.

5. Which teaching approach is considered essential to working with gifted and talented youngsters in math?

   The problem-solving approach is most favored.

6. What traits are necessary for the teacher of math?

   He or she must be competent, confident, encouraging, open, and willing.

7. Can you list six to eight resources for teaching computer and calculator skills to gifted children?

   See the list of math resources at the end of Chapter Seven.

8. What are five publications that could be helpful in developing a math curriculum for gifted children?

    Arithmetic Teacher, Especially for Teachers: ERIC Documents on the Teaching of Mathematics, Sourcebook of Applications of School Mathematics, Mathematical History: Activities, Puzzles, Stories, and Games, and *Boxes, Squares, and Other Things: A Teacher's Guide for a Unit in Informal Geometry.*

Chapter Eight

1. What are some goals of a reading and language arts program?

    Early identification of student abilities, development of the child's creative potential, and mastery of basic skills.

2. How could you identify children talented in reading and language arts?

    First, standardized tests should be utilized to identify potential candidates. This should be followed by an astute observation of each candidate in the classroom, looking for such characteristics as expressed interest in reading, high level of language development, and flexibility in processing ideas.

3. Can you list some curriculum components of a reading and language arts program?

    Developing of basic skills, creative abilities, and critical thinking skills, as well as making reading and writing enjoyable. Also, a model should be followed in setting up the program.

4. What are some good teaching approaches for reading and language arts?

    The initial step should be to assess the present skill levels of the child. This should be followed by teaching vocabulary development, comprehension skills, critical reading skills, and creative reading and encouraging reading for enjoyment.

5. How can you develop critical reading skills?

    Critical reading skills can be developed by utilizing Directive-Reading-Thinking activities, comparative reading activities, and Hilda-Tabitha discussion strategies and by suggesting ways in which something can be done with what is read.

6. What are some good teaching activities for language arts development?

    Have children describe objects, discuss their observations about an activity and organize the thoughts into categories, create collages, identify facts and solutions to a problem, publish a class newspaper or literary journal, write their reactions to pictures, and conduct interviews.

Chapter Nine

1. What are five charcteristics of children with potential in science?

    Children gifted in science are generally strongly motivated toward learning and achieving in science; able to work well independently in the laboratory, library, and classrooms; curious, asking questions about phenomenon they encounter; stimulated by problem-solving approaches to learning; and readily able to induce, deduce, and make connections between related ideas.

2. What is RETAL and its purpose?

   RETAL (Research Team Approach to Learning) is a method of helping students develop critical and divergent thinking skills in science by having them work through the research or scientific process. It includes the roles of researcher, technician, and recorder.

3. What should be some components of a science curriculum for accelerated children?

   Components of a gifted science program should include general exploratory activities, instructional techniques necessary to learn problem solving, and enrichment activities in which the child becomes the actual investigator, researcher, and scientist.

4. How would you enrich the science program?

   Ways to enrich the science program may include films, visits by professionals involved in science areas, field trips, and games.

5. What are some good resources for materials for the science program?

   Resources useful in providing materials for a gifted science program are books such as *Science Experiences for Young Children, The Whole Cosmos: Catalog of Science Activities, Creative Sciencing: A Practical Approach,* and *The New Field Book of Nature Activities and Hobbies.*

Chapter Ten

1. What is the importance of a visual and performing arts program?

   It provides an outlet for the individual's esthetic nature as well as for the enjoyment of life in general, and support and enrichment for the gifted prodigy in music, art, and the performing arts.

2. Can you list some of the curriculum components recommended for a visual and performing arts program?

   Help the child develop a more complete understanding of art, develop the child's independence, challenge the gifted, provide companionship and support to the child during his or her artistic endeavors, and develop a balance between self-confidence in the skills already manifest and a willingness to risk the unfamiliar.

3. What are some activities appropriate for gifted programs in the following areas: visual arts, music (vocal or instrumental), dance, and drama?

   Visual Arts — Activities may include stimulating art appreciation by exposing the child to great paintings and adding a brief narrative that explains the picture and its artist. Also, activities in which the child learns various art methods from professional artists may be used, along with field trips to museums, art institutes, etc. and having the child illustrate one of the scenes in a story.

Music — Activities may include playing records and having the child identify the various instruments, building rhythm and musical instruments, having the child listen to different types of music each day, taking field trips to concerts, teaching the child about time signatures and methods of conducting, encouraging the child to write original songs, and forming a classroom orchestra.

Dance — Activities may include developing a dance routine for a handicapped person, researching how dance has evolved and changed through the years, designing a disco for the 1800s, creating a totally new dance style, planning a dance marathon for the whole school, and choreographing a favorite song.

Drama — Activities may include performing puppet shows, telling stories and extemporaneous speeches, role playing, miming, playing charades, debating, performing readers' theatre or one-act or full-length plays, and being an announcer or participant in school assemblies.

4. On a national level, what are some programs available for stimulating and developing gifts and talents of children in the visual and performing arts?

The North Carolina School for the Arts; The Pennsylvania Governor's School of the Arts; the High School of the Performing and Visual Arts in Houston, Texas; the Educational Center for the Arts; Western High School for the Performing Arts; the Art Center; the New York High School for Music and Art; Fort Hayes Career Center; the School for Creative and Performing Arts; and the Chula Vista Academy of the Fine Arts are all school programs. Super Saturday; the Advanced Placement Program in Studio Art; and the Art Partnership Network are different types of programs.

REFERENCES

Abeles, S.: Science Education for the Gifted and Talented. *Gifted Child Quarterly, 11*(1): 75-84, 1977.

Abroms, K.I., and Gollin, J.G.: Developmental Study of Gifted Preschool Children and Measures of Psychosocial Giftedness. *Exceptional Children, 46*(5): 334-341, 1980.

Adams, A.: *Creativity and Children.* (Bulletin A-59). Tucson, Arizona, University of Arizona, Cooperative Extension Service and School of Home Economics, 1970.

Aliferis, J.: *Aliferis Music Achievement Test (Audio-Visual Discrimination Test of Musical Elements and Idioms) — College Entrance Level.* Minneapolis, University of Minnesota Press, 1969.

Anderson, H.: *Creativity and its Cultivation.* New York, Harper and Row, 1959.

Anderson, J.E.: The Nature of Abilities. In Torrance, E.P. (Ed.): *Talent and Education,* Minneapolis, University of Minnesota Press, 1960.

Angelino, H.: The Low Achiever: A Closer Look. *The Oklahoma Teacher,* Oct. 1960, p. 12.

Ashbrook, A.: Teaching Mathematics to Gifted Children. *Trends In·Education, 2:* 9-13, 1977.

Atamia, G.C., and Danielson, E.W.: Programs for the Gifted at Talcott Mountain Science Center. *The Gifted Child Quarterly, 21*(1): 69-75, 1977.

Author, G.: *The Author Adaptation of the Lieter International Performance Scale.* Chicago, C.H. Stoelting, 1950.

Bahner, J.M.: Individually Guided Education. In Ingas, E., and Corsini, R.J. (Eds.): *Alternative Educational Systems.* Itasca, Illinois, F.E. Peacock, 1979.

Bailey, D.B. and Leonard, J.A.: Model for Adapting Bloom's Taxonomy to a Preschool Curriculum for the Gifted. *Gifted Child Quarterly, 21*(1): 97-103, 1977.

Baller, W.R., and Charles D.D.: *The Psychology of Human Growth and Development* 2nd ed. New York, Holt, Rinehart, and Winston, 1968.

Bartley, S.H.: *Introduction to Perception.* New York, Harper and Row, 1980.

Beatty, L.S., Madden, R., Gardner, E.F., and Karlsen, J.: *Stanford Diagnostic Mathematics Tests.* New York, Harcourt Brace Jovanovich, 1976.

Beery, K., and Buktenica, N.: *Developmental Test of Visual-Motor Integration.* Chicago, Fallet Publishing Co., 1967.

Bender, L.: *A Visual Motor Gestalt Test and Its Clinical Use.* New York, American Orthopsychiatric Association Monograph No. 3, 1938.

Bender, L.: *The Visual-Motor Gestalt Test for Children.* New York, American Orthopsychiatric Association, 1938.

Bentley, A.: *Measures of Musical Ability.* New York, October House, 1966.

Bernal, E.M., Jr.: The Identification of Gifted Chicano Children. *Educational Planning for the Gifted,* Reston, Virginia, Council for Exceptional Children, 1978.

Bessell, H., and Palomares, U.: *Methods in Human Development: Theory Manual.* San Diego, Human Development Training Institute, 1971.

bility system. Both short-term and long-term goals are set and the student takes on the responsibility and commitment of working on these goals. This process relates to gifted and talented children in that they are freed to establish their own goals in line with their own special gifts and/or talents in a setting that fosters self-discipline, purposeful learning, and stewardship.

Chapter Three

1. What is the perceptual system?

   It is the process of organizing raw data obtained through the senses into the vestibular proprioceptive area of the brain, which then interprets its meaning.

2. What are six of the human sensory receptors?

   Eyes, ears, nose, mouth, skin, and thermalsensitive neurons in the hypothalamus.

3. Can you give an example of selective perception?

   When someone is extremely tired, objects, language, and circumstances are readily perceived in relationship to sleep.

4. Why is comprehending figure-ground relationships important in learning?

   It gives sense and purpose to that which is seen.

5. How can understanding Piaget's stages of intellectual development be helpful to a teacher of gifted children?

   Such an understanding can help the teacher be realistic and fair in his/her expectations of the child's thought processes and abilities.

6. How do thought processes and attitudes affect interpersonal relationships and vice versa?

   Only when the student feels accepted as an individual and is comfortable in the presence of the teacher can the school environment be perceived as a place of freedom and productivity.

7. What are some key principles facilitating memory?

   Recognition, attention, rehearsal, imagery, encoding, decoding, and organizing.

8. How does Erikson's Eight Stages of Social Development relate to thought processes?

   A child's self-concept sets the limits on his/her behavior, which in turn influences his/her thought processes. The self-concept is developed through these eight signs.

9. What is the difference between spontaneous and reflective thinking? What is the difference between convergent and divergent thinking?

   A spontaneous thinker processes information rapidly and is quick to respond, whereas a reflective thinker requires more time to ponder and

and Winston, 1979.

Deutsch, B.: *Poetry Handbook.* New York, Grossett and Dunlap, 1962.

DiNunno, L., and Callahan, C.M.: Tips for Parents: The Gifted Preschooler. *Teaching Gifted Children,* Nov. 1981, p. 6.

Doll, E.: *Vineland Social Maturity Scale.* Circle Pines, Minnesota, American Guidance Service, 1965.

Dorhout, A.: Identifying Musically Gifted Children. *Journal For the Education of the Gifted,* 5(1): 57-66, 1981.

Dorn, C.M.: The Advanced Placement Program in Studio Art. *Gifted Child Quarterly,* 20(4): 450-458, 1976.

Do You Have to be Gifted to Teach the Gifted? *Instructor,* 86(9): 20, 1977.

Drake, R.M.: *Drake Musical Aptitude Tests.* Chicago, Science Research Association, 1954.

Duchek, K.: *Science Curriculum for Gifted Elementary Students.* Unpublished research project, Department of Educational Psychology, Brigham Young University, 1982.

Dunn, L.M., and Markwardt, F.C.: *Peabody Individual Achievement Test.* Circle Pines, Minnesota, American Guidance Service, 1970.

Durst, W., Bixler, H., Wrightstone, J., Prescott, G., and Barlow, I.: *Metropolitan Achievement Tests.* New York, Harcourt Brace Jovanovich.

Education of the Gifted: A Challenge and a Promise. *Exceptional Children.* Reston, Virginia, Council for Exceptional Children, 1981, vol. 48(2).

Erikson, E.H.: *Childhood and Society.* New York, Norton, 1950.

Evans, L.: *Three-Dimensional Mazes, 2.* San Francisco, Troubador Press, 1977.

Evler, M.: *Language Arts for the Gifted and Talented: Questions and Answers from Teachers of English.* Indiana Department of Public Instruction, 1977.

Fairport Central School District.: *Task Force on Gifted and Talented,* 1980.

Fearn, L.: Underachievement and Rate of Acceleration. *Gifted Child Quarterly,* 26(3): 121-125, 1982.

Feldhusen, H.: Teaching Gifted, Creative, and Talented Students in an Individualized Classroom. *Gifted Child Quarterly,* 25:81-82, 1981.

Feldman, D.H., and Bratton, J.C.: Relativity and Giftedness: Implications for Equality of Educational Opportunity. *Exceptional Children, 38:* 491-492, 1972.

Fine, B.: *Underachievers — How They Can Be Helped.* New York, E.P. Dutton, 1967.

Fisher, R.B.: *Musical Prodigies: Masters at an Early Age.* New York, Association Press, 1973.

Fitzpatrick, J.L.: Academic Underachievement, Other Direction, and Attitudes Toward Women's Roles in Bright Adolescent Females. *Journal of Educational Psychology,* 70(4): 645-650, 1978.

Fixx, J.F.: *Games for the Super-Intelligent.* New York, Fawcett Popular Library, 1972.

Fliegler, L.A. (Ed.): *Curriculum Planning for the Gifted.* Englewood Cliffs, New Jersey, Prentice-Hall, 1961.

Flinders, N.J.: *Creativity as Mysticism: A Barrier to Effective Education.* Unpublished manuscript, Brigham Young University, 1982.

Forman, S.G.: Effects of Socioeconomic Status on Creativity in Elementary School Children. *Creative Child and Adult Quarterly,* 4(2): 87-92, 1979.

Frasier, M.M.: Rethinking the Issues Regarding the Culturally Disadvantaged Gifted. *Exceptional Children,* 45(7): 538-542, 1979.

Fuchigami, R.Y.: Summary Analysis and Future Directions. In Baldwin, A.Y., Gear, G.H., and Lucito, L.J. (Eds.): *Educational Planning for the Gifted.* Reston, Virginia, Council for Exceptional Children, 1978.

Gallagher, J.J.: *Analysis of Research of the Education of Gifted Children.* Illinois, State Department of Education, 1960.

Gallagher, J.J.: *Teaching the Gifted Child*. Boston, Allyn and Bacon, 1964.

Gallagher, J.J.: *Teaching the Gifted Child*, 2nd ed. Boston, Allyn and Bacon, 1975.

Gallagher, J.J.: Research Needs for Education of the Gifted. In *Issues in Gifted Education*. Los Angeles, National/State Leadership Training Institute on the Gifted and Talented, 1979.

Gallagher, J.J., and Kinney, L. (Eds.): *Talent Delayed — Talent Denied the Culturally Different Gifted Child*. A conference report. Reston, Virginia, Foundation for Exceptional Children, 1974.

Games Magazine. New York, Globe, 1982.

Gay, J.E.: A Proposed Plan for Identifying Black Gifted Children. *Gifted Child Quarterly, 22*(3): 253-360, 1978.

Getzels, J.W., and Jackson, P.W.: *Creativity and Intelligence: Explorations with Gifted Students*. New York, John Wiley and Sons, 1962.

Gifted and Talented Education: An Overview. *Curriculum Review, 20*(2): 120-138, 140, 1981.

Gifted Education. *Elementary School Journal, 82*(3), 1981.

Ginsberg, G., and Harrison, C.H.: *How to Help Your Gifted Child*. New York, Monarch Press, Simon and Schuster, 1977.

Glasser, W.: *Reality Therapy: A New Approach to Psychiatry*. New York, Harper and Row, 1965.

Gleitman, H.: *Psychology*. New York, Norton, 1981.

Goldman, R., Fristoe, M., and Woodcock, R.: *The Goldman-Fristoe-Woodcock Auditory Skills Test Battery*. Circle Pines, Minnesota, American Guidance Service, 1976.

Gordon, E.: *Musical Aptitude Profile*. Boston, Massachusetts, Houghton Mifflin, 1965.

Gowan, J.C.: Recent Research on the Education of Gifted Children. *Psychological Newsletter, 9*, 1958.

Grant, J., and Renzulli, J.: Identifying Achievement Potential in Minority Group Students. *Exceptional Children, 41*: 255-259, 1975.

Greenes, C.: Identifying the Gifted Student in Mathematics. *Arithmetic Teacher*, Feb. 1981, pp. 14-17.

Greenfield, P.M., and Bruner, J.S.: Learning and Language: Work With the Wolof. *Psychology Today*, 5 (July): 40-43.

Guilford, J.P.: Creativity. *American Psychologist, 5*: 444-454, 1950.

Guilford, J.P.: The Structure of the Intellect. *Psychological Bulletin, 53*: 267-293, 1956.

Guilford, J.P.: Three Faces of Intellect. *The American Psychologist, 14*: 469-479, 1959.

Guilford, J.P.: *The Nature of Human Intelligence*. New York, McGraw-Hill, 1967.

Guilford, J.P.: *Intelligence, Creativity, and Their Implications*. San Diego, Knapp, 1968.

Guilford, J.P.: Creativity: Retrospect and Prospect. *Journal of Creative Behavior, 4*: 149-161, 1970.

Guilford, J.P.: Varieties of Creative Giftedness: Their Measurement and Development. *Gifted Child Quarterly, 19*(2): 107-121, 1975.

Guilford, J.P.: *Way Beyond the IQ*. Buffalo, New York, Creative Education Foundation, 1977.

Guilford, J.P., and Christensen, P.R.: The One-Way Relationship Between Creative Potential and I.Q. *Journal of Creative Behavior, 7*: 247-252, 1973.

Hallahan, D.R., and Kauffman, J.M.: *Exceptional Children, Introduction to Special Education*, 2nd ed. Englewood Cliffs, New Jersey, Prentice-Hall, 1982.

Hanninen, Gail: Developing a Preschool Gifted/Talented Program. *G/C/T, 9*: 18-19, 21, 1979.

Haring, N.G.: *An Introduction to Special Education*, 3rd ed. Columbus, Ohio, Merrill, 1982.

Harris, D.: *Children's Drawings as Measures of Intellectual Maturity*. New York, Harcourt Brace Jovanovich, 1963.

Henshaw, J.: *Visual and Performing Arts for Gifted Children*. Unpublished manuscript, Brigham Young University, 1982.

Hersberger, J., and Wheatley, G.: A Proposed Model on a Gifted Elementary School Mathematics Program. *Gifted Child Quarterly, 24*(1): 37-40, 1980.

Hieronymous, C., and Lindquist, A.P.: *Iowa Test of Basic Skills*. Boston, Houghton Mifflin, 1974.

Hildreth, G.H.: *Introduction to the Gifted*. New York, McGraw-Hill, 1967.

Hildreth, G.H., Griffiths, M., and McGauvran, M.E.: *The Metropolitan Readiness Test*. New York, Harcourt Brace Jovanovich, 1969.

Hollingsworth, L.: *Gifted Children*. New York, Macmillan, 1976.

House, P.A.: One Small Step for the Mathematically Gifted. *School Science and Mathematics, 81*(3): 195-199, 1981.

Hudson, L.: *Contrary Imaginations*. New York, Schocken Books, 1966.

Humphries, C.: Classroom Activities for Able Students: Seventh and Eighth Grades. *Arithmetic Teacher*, Feb. 1981, pp. 51-54.

Hunsicker, P., and Reiff, B.: *Youth Fitness Test Manual*. Washington, D.C., American Alliance for Health, Physical Education, and Recreation, 1976.

Hurwitz, A.: Arts: New Recognition of the Gifted in Art. *School Arts, 81*(1): 32-33, 1981.

Hymes, D.: Discussion following Bullowa, Margaret, Jones, Lawrence G., and Bever, Thomas G.: The Development from Vocal to Verbal Behavior in Children. In Bellugi, Ursula, and Brown, Roger W.: *The Acquisition of Learning*. Monographs of the Society for Research in Child Development, 29(1), No. 92: 107-14, 1964.

Ingram, C.F.: *Fundamentals of Educational Assessment*. New York, D. Van Nostrand Company, 1980.

Irmscher, W.F.: *Teaching Expository Writing*. New York, Holt, Rinehart, and Winston, 1979.

Jastak, J.F., and Jastak, S.R.: *Wide Range Achievement Test*. Wilmington, Delaware, Guidance Associates, 1965.

J.E.G. Journal for the Education of the Gifted. Reston, Virginia, Association for the Gifted, 1981.

Johnson, C.: Smart Kids Have Problems Too. *Today's Education, 70*(1): 26-27, 29, 1981.

Johnson, R.A., and Turock, I.: The Creatively Gifted Preschool Child: Training Teachers to More Accurately Identify Them. *Creative Child and Adult Quarterly, 5*(1): 35-39, 1980.

Jones, T.P.: *Creative Learning in Perspective*. New York, John Wiley and Sons, 1972.

Kanoy, R.C., Johnson, B.W., and Kanoy, K.W.: Locus of Control and Self-Concept in Achieving and Underachieving Bright Elementary Students. *Psychology in the Schools, 17*: 395-399, 1980.

Karnes, M.B., and Bertschi, J.D.: Identifying and Educating Gifted/Talented Nonhandicapped and Handicapped Preschoolers. *Teaching Exceptional Children, 10*(4): 114-119, 1978.

Karnes, M.B.: *Preschool Talent Checklists Manual*. Urbana, Illinois, Publications Office, Institute for Child Behavior and Development, University of Illinois, 1978.

Karnes, F.A., and Collins, E.C.: *Handbook of Instructional Resources and References for Teaching the Gifted*. Rockleigh, New Jersey, Allyn and Bacon, 1980.

Keller, J.D.: Aleron's Exploratory School Program: A Program for Gifted and Talented in Mathematics and Science. *School Science and Mathematics, 80*(7): 577-582, 1980.

Kephart, N.C.: *The Slow Learner in the Classroom*. Columbus, Ohio, Merrill, 1960.

Khatena, J.: *Educational Psychology of the Gifted*. New York, John Wiley and Sons, 1982.

Kirk, S., McCarthy, J., and Kirk, W.: *Illinois Test of Psycholinguistic Abilities*. Urbana, Illinois, University of Illinois Press, 1968.

Kitano, Margie: Young Gifted Children: Strategies for Preschool Teachers. *Young Children, 37*(4): 14-24, 1982.

Klein, P.S.: Right and Left Hemispheres Represent Two Modes of Learning: The Overlooked or Misused Talents of Learning Disabled Children. *Creative Child and Adult Quarterly, 5*(1):

30-34, 1980.

Knutsen, L.: Teaching Fifty Gifted Science Units in Two Easy Steps. *Science and Children, 16*(6): 51-53, 1979.

Kohler, K.: Art and Music Appreciation for the Elementary Grades. Unpublished manuscript, Brigham Young University, 1982.

Kopelman, M., Galasso, V.G., and Strom, P.: A Model Program for the Development of Creativity in Science. *Gifted Child Quarterly, 21*(1): 80-84, 1977.

Koppits, E.M.: *The Bender-Gestalt Test for Young Children.* New York, Grune and Stratton, 1964.

Koppits, E.M.: *The Bender-Gestalt Test for Young Children. Vol. II: Research and Application. 1963-1973.* New York, Grune and Stratton, 1975.

Kramer, V.L.: *Children's Literature for the Gifted Elementary School Child.* Paper presented at the Twenty Third Annual Meeting of the International Reading Association, Houston, Texas, May 1-5, 1978.

Kruger, R.: *Guidelines for the Education of the Scientifically Creative Student: Preschool — 5th Grade.* Indiana State Department of Public Instruction, Indianapolis, Division of Curriculum, 1977.

Larkin, B.: Programs for Gifted and Talented Students in Utah Elementary Schools. Unpublished Honors Thesis, Brigham Young University, 1982.

Laycock, F.: *Gifted Children.* Illinois, Scott Foresman and Company, 1979.

Leonard, J.E., and Cansler, D.P.: Serving Gifted/Handicapped Preschoolers and Their Families: A Demonstration Project. *Roeper Review, 2*(3): 39-41, 1980.

Loomis, A.: "Mazes Amaze." In Clark, B. (Ed.): *Growing up Gifted.* Columbus, Ohio, Merrill, 1979.

Lowerfeld, V.: *Creative and Mental Growth.* New York, Macmillan, 1979.

Lundsteen, S.W., and Tarrow, W.B.: *Guiding Children's Learning.* New York, McGraw-Hill, 1981.

MacDougal, Robert: The Child's Speech for Word and Meaning. *Journal of Educational Psychology,* 4: 29-38, 1913.

MacKinnon, D.W.: The Nature and Nurture of Creative Talent. *American Psychologist, 17*(7): 484-495, 1962.

Madden, R., Gardner, E.R., Rudman, H.C., Karlsen, B., and Merwin, J.C.: *Stanford Achievement Test.* New York, Harcourt Brace Jovanovich, 1973.

Maker, J.C.: *Training Teachers for the Gifted and Talented: A Comparison of Models.* Reston, Virginia, Council for Exceptional Children, 1976.

Maker, J.C.: *Providing Programs for the Gifted Handicapped.* Reston, Virginia, Council for Exceptional Children, 1977.

Malone, C.: Early Childhood Education of the Gifted Child. *Gifted Child Quarterly, 18*(4): 26-28, 1974.

Malone, C.: Gifted Children in Early Childhood Education. *Viewpoints in Teaching and Learning, 55*(3): 25-28, 1979.

Marbach, E.S.: *Creative Curriculum — Kindergarten Through Grade Three.* Provo, Brigham Young University Press, 1977.

Marion, R.L.: Communicating with Parents of Culturally Diverse Exceptional Children. *Exceptional Children, 46*(8): 616-623, 1980.

Marland, S.: *Education of the Gifted and Talented.* Report to the Congress of the United States by the U.S. Commissioner of Education. Washington, D.C., U.S. Government Printing Office, 1972.

Martinson, R.: *Curriculum Enrichment for the Gifted in the Primary Grades.* Englewood Cliffs, New Jersey, Prentice-Hall, 1968.

Martinson, R.: Research on the Gifted and Talented: Its Implication for Education. In

Marland, S.: *Education of the Gifted and Talented*. Report to the Congress of the United States by the U.S. Commissioner of Education. Washington, D.C., U.S. Government Printing Office, 1972.

Mauser, A.J.: Programming Strategies for Pupils with Disabilities Who Are Gifted. *Rehabilitation Literature, 42*(9-10): 270-275, 1981.

Maxwell, S.: Museums are Learning Laboratories for Gifted Students. *Teaching Exceptional Children, 12*(4): 154-159, 1980.

McCarthy, P.: *Manual for the McCarthy Scales of Children's Abilities*. New York, Psychological Corporation, 1972.

McIntyre, M. (Ed.): Preschool Early Childhood. *Science and Children, 16*(6): 62-63, 1979.

Meeker, M.: *The Structure of Intellect: Its Use and Interpretation*. Columbus, Ohio, Merrill, 1969.

Meeker, M.: The Prophecy of Giftedness. *Gifted Child Quarterly, 20*: 100-104, 1976.

Meisgeier, C., Meisgeier, C., and Werblo, D.: Factors Compounding the Handicapping of Some Gifted Children. *Gifted Child Quarterly, 22*(3): 325-331, 1978.

Menuhin, Y.: Foreword. In Fisher, R.B.: *Musical Prodigies. Masters at an Early Age*. New York, Association Press, 1973.

Mindell, P., and Stracher, D.: Assessing Reading and Writing of the Gifted: The Warp and Woof of the Language Program. *Gifted Child Quarterly, 24*(2): 72-80, 1980.

Monson, J.A.: *S.O.I. The Structure of Intellect Model*. Unpublished manuscript, Utah State University, 1981.

Montgomery County Public School System: *Above and Beyond: A Teacher Selected Bibliography of Instructional Materials for Use With Gifted and Talented Students*. Rockville, Maryland, 1978.

Moore, B.A.: Career Education for Disadvantaged, Gifted High School Students. *Gifted Child Quarterly, 22*(3): 332-337, 1978.

Moore, B.A.: A Model Career Education Program for Gifted Disadvantaged Students. *Roeper Review, 2*(2): 20-22, 1978.

Morgan, H.W.: Primary Gifted Programs. *G/C/T*, March/April 1982, pp. 8-9.

Nathan, C.N.: Parental Involvement. In Passow, A.H. (Ed.): *The Gifted and the Talented: Their Education and Development*. Chicago, University of Chicago Press, 1979.

National School Public Relations Association: *The Gifted and Talented: Programs that Work*. Arlington, Virginia, 1979.

Noyce, R.: Resources for Teaching the Gifted Reader. *Gifted Child Quarterly, 21*(2): 239-245, 1977.

Nuffield Foundation. *Beginnings*. London, Naugate Press Ltd., 1967.

Passow, A.H.: Enrichment of Education for the Gifted. In Henry, N.B. (Ed.): *Education for the Gifted* (57th Yearbook, National Society for the Study of Education). Chicago, University of Chicago Press, 1958.

Patterson, P., and Starcher, S.: Characteristics of Culturally Diverse Gifted Students. *G/C/T*, Jan.-Feb. 1982, pp. 7-8.

Payne, J.: The Mathematics Curriculum for Talented Students. *Arithmetic Teacher, 28*(6): 18-21, 1981.

Pendarvis, E.D.: Gifted and Talented Children. In Blackhurst, E., and Berdine, W. (Eds.): *An Introduction to Special Education*. Boston, Little, Brown, and Company, 1981.

Perez, G.S.: Leadership Giftedness in Preschool Children. *Roeper Review, 4*(3): 26-28, 1982.

Piaget, J.: *Psychology of Intelligence*. London, Routledge and Kegan Paul, 1950.

Piaget, J.: How Children Form Mathematical Concepts. *Scientific American*, November 1953.

Platt, K.: *Hey, Dummy*. Chilton, Pennsylvania, Radnor Press, 1971.

Plowman, P.D.: Programming for the Gifted Child. *Exceptional Children*, March 1969.

Porter, R.M.: The Gifted Handicapped: A Status Report. *Roeper Review, 4*(3): 24-25, 1982.

Rathmell, E., and Leutzinger, L.: Classroom Activities for Able Students: In Kindergarten,

First and Second Grades. *Arithmetic Teacher, 28*(6): 48, 53, 1981.

Renzulli, J.S.: Identifying Key Features in Programs for the Gifted. *Exceptional Children*, November, 1968.

Renzulli, J.S.: Talent Potential in Minority Group Students. *Exceptional Children, 39*: 437-444, 1973.

Renzulli, J.S.: The Enrichment Triad Model. Mansfield Center, Connecticut, Creative Learning Press, 1977.

Renzulli, J.S.: What Makes Giftedness: A Reexamination of the Definition. *Science and Children, 16*(6): 14-15, 1979.

Renzulli, J.S., and Smith, L.H.: Two Approaches to Identification of Gifted Students. *Exceptional Children, 43*(8): 512-518, 1977.

Renzulli, J.S., and Stoddard, E.P.: *Gifted and Talented Education in Perspective*. Reston, Virginia, Council for Exceptional Children, 1980.

Reynolds, M.C.: Acceleration. In Torrance, E.P. (Ed.): *Talent in Education*. Minneapolis, University of Minnesota Press, 1960.

Roach, E.G., and Kephart, N.C.: *The Purdue Perceptual-Motor Survey*. Columbus, Ohio, Merrill, 1966.

Roeper, A.: The Young Gifted Child. *Gifted Child Quarterly, 21*(3): 388-396, 1977.

Rogers, C.R.: *On Becoming a Person: A Therapist's View of Psychotherapy*. Boston, Houghton Mifflin, 1961.

Rose, S.E.: The Gifted Student and Social Studies Teaching. *Social Studies, 69*(2): 43-49, 1978.

Rosenthal, R., and Jacobson, L.: *Pygmalion in the Classroom: Teacher Expectation and Pupils' Intellectual Development*. New York, Holt, Rinehart, and Winston, 1968.

Royer, R.: Creating Writing Assignments for the Gifted. *G/C/T*, Jan.-Feb. 1982, pp. 29-30.

Sakiey, E.: Reading for the Gifted: Instructional Strategies Based on Research. Paper presented at a symposium of the Third Eastern Regional Conference International Reading Assoc., Niagara Falls, New York, March 27-29, 1980.

Samuda, R.J.: *Psychological Testing of American Minorities: Issues and Consequences*. New York, Dodd, Mead, 1975.

Sanderson, M.: *Music for Elementary Grades at Home or at School*. Unpublished manuscript, Brigham Young University, 1982.

Sattler, J.M.: Analysis of Function of the 1960 Stanford-Binet Intelligence Scales, From L-M. *Journal of Clinical Psychology*, 21: 173-179, 1965.

Schiff, W.: *Perception: An Applied Approach*. Boston, Houghton Mifflin, 1980.

Schulman, L.: Classroom Activities for Able Students: In Third and Fourth Grades. *Arithmetic Teacher, 28*(6): 49, 56, 1981.

Schwartz, S.: The Young Gifted Child. In McKee, J.S. (Ed.): *Early Childhood Education*. Guilford, Connecticut, Dushkin, 1980.

Searle, J.G.: *Helping Your Child Get the "Most" From the Environment*. Unpublished manuscript, Brigham Young University, 1982.

Seashore, C.E., Lewis, D., and Saetveit, J.G.: *Seashore Measures of Musical Talents*. New York, Psychological Corporation, 1960.

Segal, D., and Raskin, E.: *Multiple Aptitude Tests*. Monterey, California Test Bureau, 1959.

Shanahan, D.: Project Cal — Take 1. *Arithmetic Teacher*, Dec. 1981, pp. 34-36.

Shane, H.G.: Grouping in the Elementary School. *Phi Delta Kappan, 41*: 313-318, 1960.

Sharan, S., and Lazarowitz, R.H.: A Group-investigation Method of Cooperative Learning in the Classroom. In Sharan, S., Hare, P., Webb, D., and Lazarowitz, R.H., (Eds.): *Cooperation in Education*. Provo, Brigham Young University Press, 1980.

Shlesinger, B.E., Jr.: An Untapped Resource of Inventors: Gifted and Talented Children. *The Elementary School Journal, 82*(3): 215-220, 1982.

Shorr, D.H., Jackson, N.E., and Robinson, H.B.: Achievement Test Performance of Intellectually Advanced Preschool Children. *Exceptional Children, 46*(8): 646-648, 1980.

Simpkins, K.: Two-Dimensional Master Mind. Unpublished paper, 1981.

Sisk, D.A.: What if Your Child is Gifted? *American Education, 13*(8), 1977.

"Sixty-seven Ways in One." *Teaching Gifted Children*, 1981, p. 8.

Slosson, R.: *Slosson Intelligence Test for Children and Adults*. East Aurora, New York, Slosson Educational Pub., 1971.

Smith, J.: *Millenial Star,* 13:339, 1851.

Stallings, C.: *Gifted Disadvantaged Children*. Storrs, University of Connecticut, 1972.

Stanley, J.C.: The Case for Extreme Educational Acceleration of Intellectually Brilliant Youths. *Gifted Child Quarterly, 20*(1): 66-75, 1976.

Stanley, J.C.: Rationale of the Study of Mathematically Precocious Youth (SMPY) During the First Five Years of Promoting Educational Deceleration. In Stanley, D., George, W., and Solemo, C. (Eds.): *The Gifted and the Creative: A Fifty Year Perspective*. Baltimore, Johns Hopkins University Press, 1977.

Stanley, J.C., George, W.C., and Solame, C.H. (Eds.): *The Gifted and the Creative: A Fifty Year Perspective*. Baltimore, Johns Hopkins University Press, 1977.

Stanley, J.C., Keating, D.P., and Fox, L.H. (Eds.): *Mathematical Talent: Discovery, Description, and Development*. Baltimore, Johns Hopkins University Press, 1974.

Stefanich, G., and Schnur, J.O.: Identifying the Handicapped-Gifted Child. *Science and Children, 17*(3): 18-19, 1979.

Stephenson, W.: *Testing School Children*. London, Longmans, Greene, and Co., 1949.

Stephens, T.M., Blackhurst, A.E., and Magliocca, L.T.: *Teaching Mainstreamed Students*. New York, John Wiley and Sons, 1982.

Strang, R. (Ed.): A Symposium on the Gifted Child. *Journal of Teacher Education*, Sept. 1954, p. 210.

Street, R.F.: A Gestalt Completion Test. New York, Columbia University, 1931.

Sucher, F.: Girls in Math and Science. *Daily Herald*, Nov. 14, 1982, p. 23.

Suchman, J.R.: Inquiry Training: Building Skills for Autonomous Discovery. *Merrill Palmer. Quarterly of Behavior and Development, 7*: 147-169, 1961.

Suchman, J.R.: *The Elementary School Training Program in Scientific Inquiry*. Urbana, Illinois, University of Illinois Press, 1962.

Swenson, E.V.: Teacher-Assessment of Creative Behavior in Disadvantaged Children. *Gifted Child Quarterly, 22*(3): 338-343, 1978.

Switzer, C., and Nourse, M.L.: Reading Instruction for the Gifted Child in First Grade. *Gifted Child Quarterly, 28*: 323-331, 1979.

Szekely, G.: The Artist and the Child: A Model Program for the Artistically Gifted. *Gifted Child Quarterly, 2*(2): 67-72, 1981.

Talent Development — An Investment in the Nation's Future. White House Task Force on the Education of Gifted Persons. Washington, D.C., U.S. Government Printing Office, 1968.

Tarrow, N.B., and Lundsteen, S.W.: *Activities and Resources for Guiding Young Children's Learning*. New York, McGraw-Hill, 1981.

Tatarumis, A.M.: Exceptional Programs for Talented Students. *Music Educators Journal, 68*(3): 55-60, 1981.

Taylor, C.W.: Who Are the Exceptionally Creative? *Exceptional Children, 28*, 1962.

Taylor, C.W.: Be Talent Developers as Well as Knowledge Dispensers. *Today's Education, 58*: 67-68, 1968.

Taylor, C.W.: *Climate for Creativity*. New York, Pergamon, 1972.

Taylor, C.W.: *Teaching for Talents and Gifts, 1978 Status*. Utah State Board of Education, 1978.

Terman, L.: *Genetic Studies of Genius*, (Vol. 1). Stanford University, Stanford University Press,

1925.

Terman, L., and Oden, M.: The Gifted Child Grows Up. In Terman, L. (Ed.): *Genetic Studies of Genius*. Stanford University, Stanford University Press, 1947.

Terman, L., and Oden, M.: The Gifted Group at Mid-Life: Thirty Five Year Follow-up of the Superior Child. In Terman, L. (Ed.): *Genetic Studies of Genius*, (Vol. 5). Stanford University, Stanford University Press, 1959.

Terman, L., and Merrill, M.: *Stanford-Binet Intelligence Scale*, 1972 Norms Edition. Boston, Houghton Mifflin, 1973.

Thurstone, L.L.: Creative Talent. In *Applications of Psychology*. New York, Harper Bros., 1952.

Thurstone, L., and Thurstone, T.: *Primary Mental Abilities Test*. Chicago, Science Research Associates, 1965.

Tidwell, R.: A Psycho-Educational Profile of Gifted Minority Group Students Identified Without Reliance on Aptitude Tests. *Journal of Non-White Concerns in Personnel and Guidance, 9*(2): 77-86, 1981.

Tiegs, E.W., and Clark, W.W.: *California Achievement Tests*. New York, CTB/McGraw-Hill, 1970.

Torrance, E.P. (Ed.): *Talent and Education*. Minneapolis, University of Minnesota Press, 1960.

Torrance, E.P.: *Guiding Creative Talent*. Englewood Cliffs, New Jersey, Prentice-Hall, 1962.

Torrance, E.P.: *Education and the Creative Potential*. Minneapolis, University of Minnesota Press, 1963.

Torrance, E.P.: *Gifted Children in the Classroom*. New York, Macmillan, 1965.

Torrance, E.P.: *Torrance Tests of Creative Thinking*. Princeton, New Jersey, Personnel Press, 1966.

Torrance, E.P.: Creative Positives of Disadvantaged Children and Youth. *Gifted Child Quarterly, 13*: 71-78, 1969.

Torrance, E.P.: *Creative Learning and Teaching*. New York, Harper and Row, 1970.

Trezise, R.L.: Teaching Reading to the Gifted. *Language Arts, 54*(8): 920-924, 1977.

Turnbull, A.P., and Schulz, J.B.: *Mainstreaming Handicapped Students*. Boston, Allyn and Bacon, 1979.

Tuttle, F.B.: *Gifted and Talented Students: What Research Says to the Teacher*. Washington, D.C., National Education Association, 1978.

U.S. Department of Health, Education, and Welfare: *Education of the Gifted and Talented: Report to the Congress of the United States by the U.S. Commissioner of Education*, 2 Vols. Washington, D.C., U.S. Government Printing Office, 1971.

Van Osdol, W.R., and Shane, D.G.: *An Introduction to Exceptional Children*, 3rd ed. Dubuque, Iowa, Wm. C. Brown, 1972.

Vantassel-Baska, J., Schuler, A., and Lipschutz, J.: An Experimental Program for Gifted Four Year Olds. *Journal for the Education of the Gifted, 5*(1): 45-55, 1982.

Walker, H.M.: *Problem Behavior Identification Checklist*, rev. ed. Los Angeles, Western Psychological Services, 1976.

Wallach, M.A., and Kogan, N.: *Modes of Thinking in Young Children: A Study of the Creativity Intelligence Distinction*. New York, Holt, Rinehart, and Winston, 1965.

Wallas, G.: *The Art of Thought*. New York, Harcourt Brace Jovanovich, 1926.

Ward, V.S.: *The Gifted Student: A Manual for Program Improvement*. Atlanta, Southern Regional Education Board, 1962.

Wavrik, J.J.: Mathematics Education for the Gifted Elementary School Student. *Gifted Child Quarterly, 24*(1): 169-173, 1980.

Wechsler, D.: *The Measurement of Adult Intelligence*. Baltimore, Williams and Wilkins, 1944.

Wechsler, D.: *Manual for the Wechsler Adult Intelligence Scale*. New York, Psychological Corporation, 1955.

Wechsler, D.: *Manual for the Wechsler Preschool and Primary Scale of Intelligence*. New York, Psychological Corporation, 1967.

Wechsler, D.: *Manual for the Wechsler Intelligence Scale for Children — Revised*. New York, Psychological Corporation, 1974.

Wepman, J.M.: *The Auditory Discrimination Test*. Chicago, Language Research Associates, 1973.

Whiting, S., Anderson, L., and Ward, J.: Identification of the Mentally Gifted Minor Deaf Child in the Public School System. *American Annals of the Deaf, 125*(1): 27-34, 1980.

Whitman, J.: Social Studies: The Lifeblood of Education for the Gifted. *Social Education, 43*(2): 159-162, 1979.

Whitmore, J.R.: The Etiology of Underchievement in Highly Gifted Young Children. *Journal for the Education of the Gifted, 3*(1): 38-51, 1979.

Whitmore, J.R.: *Giftedness, Conflict, and Underachievement*. Boston, Allyn and Bacon, 1980.

Whitmore, J.R.: Gifted Children With Handicapping Conditions: A New Frontier. *Exceptional Children, 48*(2): 106-114, 1981.

Williams, J.C.: The Federal Role in Education of the Gifted and Talented. In *Conn-Cept, Connecticut's Program for the Gifted and Talented*. Connecticut, State Department of Education, 1976.

Wing, H.D.: *Standardized Tests of Musical Intelligence*, rev. ed. Slough, England, National Foundation for Education Research, 1961.

Witty, E.P.: Equal Educational Opportunity for Gifted Minority Group Children: Promise or Possibility. *Gifted Child Quarterly, 22*(3): 344-352, 1978.

Witty, P.: *The Gifted Child*. Boston, D.C. Heath and Co., 1951.

Witty, P. (Ed.): *Reading for the Gifted and Creative Student*, Newark, Delaware, International Reading Association, 1971.

Wolf, J., Gygi, J.: Learning Disabled and Gifted: Success or Failure. *Journal for the Education of the Gifted, 4*(3): 199-206, 1981.

Woodcock, R.W., and Johnson, M.: *Woodcock-Johnson Psycho-Educational Battery*. (Parts I, II, III). Hingham, Massachusetts, Teaching Resources Corporation, 1979.

Yeatts, E.H.: The Professional Artist: A Teacher for the Gifted. *Gifted Child Quarterly, 24*(3): 133-137, 1980.

Yunghans, M.: A Pull-out Art Program for Gifted Elementary Students. *School Arts, 80*(8): 50-51, 1981.

NAME INDEX

SUBJECT INDEX